NAVIGATING THE FEDS

NAVIGATING THE FEDS

Navigating the Process of Prosecution and Imprisonment

by Justice Matters

Augusta Publishing Company, LLC
Colorado Springs, Colorado

Portions of this book were written by an experienced trial attorney. Other sections were written by federal inmates and family members of inmates.

Printed in the United States of America
First Printing, 2014

ISBN: 978-0-9905382-0-2

Library of Congress Control Number:
2014946116

Augusta Publishing Company, LLC
2316 North Wahsatch Ave
Colorado Springs, CO 80907
www.AugustaPublishingCompany.com

Cover illustration by Beth Genz.
Cover and interior design by Michelle M. White.
www.mmwgraphicdesign.com

DEDICATION

For the two of you:
Wherever you go, our hearts go with you.

CONTENTS

Introduction

Why We Wrote This Book

We wrote this book to help Americans under prosecution and/or imprisonment to receive fair, humane treatment. It is our hope that all Americans are treated fairly, respectfully, lawfully, and safely while going through the justice system.

Fear

We all have fears. You are reading this book in part because of what the government, its people, or the entire process will do to you or your loved one. You fear many things, including the allegations the government has made. You fear being arrested and locked in a cell. You are concerned about what the press will say about you. Even more so, you are afraid about what your own family will think. You worry over how vicious the prosecutors will be. Federal prosecutors win ninety to ninety-nine percent of their cases. You loathe the prospect of a sentencing hearing. You fear imprisonment with people you don't know who have been accused of a myriad of crimes, including violent offenses.

Your safety is important. There are no guarantees of freedom or safety, just advice from those who have gone through it.

The Warden's Commission

No one envies the responsibilities of wardens. Their efforts are tireless and often unnoticed. One day, the Warden called one of us to the side. He was making small talk. He asked several harmless questions. The conversation ended with him saying. "You should write a book." He never said exactly what should be in the book. Nevertheless, the assignment was taken seriously.

Types of Advice

This book offers information and advice on:

1. How to survive an initial allegation, arrest, and appearance before a federal magistrate judge.

2. How to prepare for trial or decide if you want to take a plea bargain.

3. How to go through trial.

4. How to prepare for and survive a sentencing hearing.

5. How to enter the Federal Bureau of Prisons (BOP).

6. Your safety.

7. Special circumstances, like divorce, bankruptcy, closing your business, and surrendering special licenses.

FOOD FOR THOUGHT

"Success is to be measured not so much by the position that one has reached in life as by the obstacles which he has overcome."

Booker T. Washington

Misinformation

There is so much false information that defendants often walk away from a conversation more confused than when the discussion started. We have been told hundreds of times that the Good Time Bill was already passed because "President Obama ordered it." If you believe that, then there is an inmate that has a bridge to sell you. The U.S. Congress passes some laws and refuses to pass most bills, despite what our president "orders". We've been told hundreds of times that "You always take a plea bargain to get a better deal," though most plea bargains were not that great of deals. Some are; many are not. Many just save attorneys time, effort, and money.

False rumors we've heard include that your judge knows all the federal law. We heard all sentences are fair. They said your family can mail you food into prison in a care package. We were told you can buy personal TV's in the federal system. They said you can earn two thousand dollars per month in UNICOR (Federal Prison Industries, Inc.). We wish all of these things were true but they are not. The inmate rumor mill is referred to as Inmate Dot Com. It is a figure of speech. Half of the information from Inmate Dot Com is false. Be careful. True or false, however, "news" spreads rapidly along the information super highway of Federal Detention Centers (FDC's) and prisons – often with consequences.

Significantly, even the staff from the United States Department of Justice (DOJ) does not know their own policies in some instances. Inmates have been told, "You can never go to a Federal Work Camp (FWC) if you have a verbal public safety factor on your file." (You can in some instances; you just need to know how to apply for it.) Many DOJ staff members lie to defendants. They feel so insecure that the only way they can feel good about themselves is to mistreat defendants.

In writing this book, we have tried to dispel as many false rumors as we can. We have asked multiple sources about topics to increase accuracy. We've read legal documents, when able. We've gone back and read actual official prison policies in what are formally known as Program Statements. Portions of this book were written with the advice and editorial benefit of a highly successful trial attorney. Nevertheless, even we get duped now and then.

FOOD FOR THOUGHT

"Extraordinary people survive under the most terrible circumstances, and they become more extraordinary because of it."

Robertson Davies

The List of Fictitious Characters

In writing this book, we decided to lighten up the reading by including some fictitious characters to demonstrate characteristics of people you may encounter along the way. While some of these people may sound very familiar to you, they are by no means actual representations of any particular person.

Lefty, Greedson, and Slickman, Attorneys at Law:: This law firm is more interested in collecting your money than doing the right thing for your case.

Officer Good Cop: This is an excellent police officer, correctional officer (CO), or federal agent that is honest, obeys the law, follows policies, is hard-working, and does so in a respectful manner. He or she is an asset to society and deserves our appreciation and respect. Unfortunately, only half the officers fall into this category. If you are a good cop, CO, federal agent, or BOP staff member and you are reading this book, thank you for your service. Help lead the way teaching other officers how to do their jobs more professionally and respectfully.

Officer Bad Cop: This police officer, CO, or federal agent is the opposite of Officer Good Cop. He or she lies, is abusive, lazy, steals, violates the law and prison policies, and is downright mean.

Officer Maxaft Cop: This police officer, CO, or federal agent was Officer Good Cop at one time but has now got such a large bottom that they cannot get out of their chair to help you in any way. They know what the DOJ's policies are but they are too lazy to follow the policies. Their pay checks and job benefits are more important than your well-being or any policy or law.

Officer Corrupt O. Cop: This police officer, CO, or federal agent is more concerned about what he or she can steal than your safety. They are willing to lie to build their case. They incorrectly try to justify their lies as "serving the greater cause of justice." Such perverted justice is actually evil.

Officer Drill Sergeant Cop: This police officer, CO, or federal agent usually knows the law and policies but he/she cannot get anything done without yelling and cursing, like a drill sergeant. They need a Happy Pill from their doctor.

Officer Creepy Cop: This police officer, CO, or federal agent is deviant. My hope is you will never encounter him or her. Most defendants don't experience actual assaults. However, many defendants do encounter a creepy officer who stares just one or two seconds too long in compromising situations.

Lazy Inmate: An inmate so lazy that no other inmate wants to live or work with him or her. You don't want to be a Lazy Inmate; no one wants to be your friend, work with you, or live with you.

Freaky Inmate: An inmate that is so bizarre that he or she stands out in a crowd in a really bad way. Freaky Inmate's safety is jeopardized because of his or her appearance and/or behavior.

Grievance Hungry Inmate: An inmate that files numerous grievances, lawsuits, or multiple appeals on every possible issue in the system, no matter how insignificant the issue. The staff hates him or her because he or she causes them a lot of extra work. Other inmates despise him or her because the staff spends all their time answering his or her requests instead of helping other inmates with real issues. This one inmate makes other inmates look bad.

Repeat Inmate: An inmate that has been locked up in the system over and over again. He or she has their name on ten different prison beds in ten different states, for multiple offenses; they are severely institutionalized. Such is their choice.

Now that you know the intent of the book and the cast of characters, let's get started.

CHAPTER 1:

The Initial Allegation

The Search

You are minding your own business when you hear a knock at the door. You open it only to find a series of law enforcement personnel: Officers Good Cop, Bad Cop, Maxaft Cop, Corrupt O. Cop, Drill Sergeant Cop, and Creepy Cop. One of them flashes a badge and a search warrant. Your life has changed forever.

Now is not the time to fight or run. Step back. Let them do what they are going to do. They will do it anyway. Officer Bad Cop wants you to reach for a weapon. It would give him the excuse to joyfully pump six rounds into your chest.

Officer Bad Cop forces you to sit down. He then proceeds to take a family portrait off the wall, looking to see if you have hidden something behind it. He tosses the portrait to the floor and steps on it, leaving a boot print across your family photo and says, "I want to make sure I leave the right impression on your family."

Officer Maxaft Cop is looking through your mail with his right hand while eating the donut he holds in his left hand.

Officer Corrupt O. Cop starts taking one drawer after another out of your kitchen cabinets. He dumps each drawer's contents onto the floor.

In theory, you have a right to know what they are searching for. The officers may or may not tell you. The search warrant is a legal document that allows them to search your property without your permission. The search warrant was ordered by a judge. It is based on statements and an affidavit made by one of the investigating officers. While you cannot see the affidavit at this time, your defense attorney may be able to see it at a later date and question its legality.

Even if the officers don't have a search warrant, realize they can enter your property in two other circumstances:

1. Probable cause exists. Probable cause means an officer has enough information to believe a crime has probably occurred and evidence of the crime is in your home or place of business.

2. Officers can conduct a security sweep while they are waiting on a judge to approve a search warrant. During a security sweep, officers remove any obvious weapons while asking everyone to exit the building so no one tampers with or destroys potential evidence. Once the search warrant is approved, they can come back in and continue searching for and seizing evidence.

FOOD FOR THOUGHT

"A good listener is not only popular everywhere, but after a while he gets to know something."

Wilson Mizner

Miranda Rights

Officer Corrupt O. Cop comes forward and says, "I have some questions for you. Let's talk."

A U.S. Supreme Court case known as *U.S. v. Miranda* established some basic rights all citizens should be aware of. You have probably heard of these on TV:

1. "You have the right to remain silent. Anything you say can and will be used against you in a court of law."

2. "You have a right to an attorney. If you cannot afford one, one will be appointed for you."

Law enforcement officers may read you these rights before or after they arrest you or they may be printed on a sheet of paper they ask you to sign. If the sheet of paper asks you to waive your rights, do not sign it. You need to protect your rights by not answering their questions. You need to get an attorney.

The most you should tell a law enforcement officer is your name, home address, and date of birth. That's it. Even though the other questions seem very basic, they can be used against you in a court of law. Do not try to explain anything to the officers, no matter how basic it seems or how helpful to your defense you think it will be.

Officers are trained to ask you hundreds of questions, hoping you will answer at least a few of them in their favor. Let's suppose you give answers to 200 questions in your favor and one answer that is in a grey area. The officer will record the grey answer. On the witness stand, Officer Corrupt O. Cop will say he doesn't remember any of the 200 nice things you said in your defense.

Suppose officers get you to admit you drive a white Toyota pickup truck, you were at a mall on March 4th at 4:00 P.M., and you knew the murder victim. You tell law enforcement you were at a restaurant on the other side of town at 9:00 P.M. when the murder occurred on March 4th. It turns out the real criminal was spotted driving a white Ford pickup truck after he left the murder scene at 9:00 P.M. If this case goes to trial, the officers will testify you admitted the following:

1. You were at the scene of the crime on the date of the murder.

2. You knew the victim.

3. You drove a white pickup truck away from the crime scene.

On the witness stand, Officer Corrupt O. Cop will conveniently "forget" that you said you were at the crime scene at 4:00 P.M. and that at 9:00 P.M, you were at a restaurant across town. They will tell the jury they "don't recall" you saying anything about a "white Toyota pickup truck." They will magically recall that you said you drove a "white pickup truck."

Do you see how selectively they can build a case against you? They selectively forget about your alibi and the fact that your pickup truck has a different manufacturer than the murderer's truck.

The U.S. Supreme Court decided that any request you make to law enforcement for an attorney to represent you cannot be told to a jury if your case goes to trial. In other words, the police cannot tell the jury you requested an attorney.

Do the following:

1. Don't answer any questions other than your name, home address, and date of birth. Show them your photo ID if they ask for it. (Note: Failure to identify yourself to a law enforcement officer when questioned is a crime in some cities. You must identify yourself.)

2. Tell them, "I'm new at this. I would like an attorney to represent me before this goes any further. Can I have an attorney?"

If you do the above, it turns the tables on law enforcement. Anytime you ask for an attorney, several things happen:

1. The interrogation must legally stop except for asking for your name, address, and date of birth.

2. They have to start the process of getting you an attorney. (It may take a week or two.)

3. Anything you say after that point is subject to being thrown out of court because you requested an attorney and they continued interrogating you without an attorney present. Don't rely on this issue. To be safe, don't talk about your case.

Officer Bad Cop may try to keep questioning you, even after you asked for an attorney. They will testify in court they "never heard you ask for an attorney." To protect yourself from this possibility, request an attorney several times from different officers and other clerical staff. While Office Bad Cop and Officer Corrupt O. Cop will lie on the witness stand saying they don't recall you asking for an attorney, Officer Good Cop will tell the truth. He heard you ask for an attorney. This may help you down the road.

If they keep questioning you after you asked for an attorney, just say, "Stop harassing me. Why are you breaking the law? Where is my attorney?"

Note: If your case involves an immediate threat to national security, they don't have to read your Miranda Rights to you before they question you. (This is a part of the Patriot Act of 2001.)

Tip: Your place will look like a tornado went through it when the officers are done with the search. Tell your family or co-workers to take photos and document what was broken during the search. Your attorney may need this documentation if Officer Bad Cop went too far. You may want to try to recover damages. Also, you may want to show the photos to the jury if you go to trial. Officers are supposed to be reasonable professionals. If you show photos of your place totally trashed by law enforcement agents, it hurts their professional appearance.

FOOD FOR THOUGHT

"Setting an example is not the main means of influencing another; it is the only means."

Albert Einstein

Getting Arrested

If you are arrested by federal agents, you will most likely be taken to a Federal Detention Center (FDC), which is the federal equivalent of a jail. FDC's are either operated by or overseen by U.S. Marshals.

If you are arrested, they should tell you why you are being arrested. If they didn't arrest you, you are not out of the woods yet. You will still be under investigation for several months, and can be arrested at a later date. No matter what, your life has changed forever. The government is after you. The rest of this book is devoted to helping you navigate through the vast sea of federal bureaucracy. We want to help you "Navigate the Feds."

Please understand us: We have no predisposition for evil. We are not trying to promote illegal activity in any way. We simply want you to understand the law and your rights. The feds will use your lack of knowledge of the law to hurt you. In many instances, the feds will misuse their power to overstep the law. They will take actions against you out of convenience or anger. Many officers truly believe they are "judge, jury, and executioner." We've heard many officers say, "I am the law." They are not. No matter what you are accused of, you have a right to know the law, a right to be treated fairly, and you are entitled to certain basic human rights. Some law enforcement officers and prosecutors are intellectually mature enough to understand and respect these principles. Others lack such integrity.

Tales from the Street

You are supposed to have your Miranda Rights read to you when you are arrested. These rights may be read to you both before and after you are arrested. You will quickly realize not every officer is an Officer Good Cop. One inmate described it like this: "After they handcuffed me, they sat me on my bed. I was like, 'What's going on?' I just sat there watching the federal agents look at all of the shoes in my closet. They took them out and tried them on. They each found a pair of my shoes they liked. They took me out to their car and put my shoes in their trunk. I could see they had a collection of clothes and jewelry already in the trunk. Could these be stolen, too? The agents robbed me while they arrested me. It was all messed up."

CHAPTER 2:

Courtroom Etiquette

Introduction

You need to know a few rules about courtroom etiquette. The last thing you want to do is make a bad impression on the judge and jury.

Dress Code

Men should wear a black, blue, gray, or brown suit and a conservative tie in court. This is not a time for bold colors. Women should ask their attorney what the standard is; pant suits, skirts, or dresses. Some judges require dresses or skirts for all women that testify. That is their prerogative. If you wear a dress or skirt, the hemline should be below the knee. This is not a time for men to show off their chest hair or for women to display their cleavage. Everyone should wear dark-colored dress shoes. Avoid all jewelry except a simple watch, wedding band, and very simple earrings. Avoid bling. Keep it simple.

Please Rise

Each and every time the judge and/or jury enter or leave the courtroom, you need to stand. The bailiff usually announces the entrance by stating, "Please rise." Remain standing until the judge tells you that you can be seated. (The exception to this rule is if you are confined to a wheel chair or are otherwise unable to stand.)

Pay Attention

You are the main character in your trial, and the jury will be watching you throughout – not just when you testify. Pay close attention to the proceedings: the jury needs to know that you are *interested* and that you *care*. If a door in the courtroom opens, ignore it. Your attention should be on the person speaking –the judge, lawyer, or witness.

Speaking to the Judge

Do not speak unless you are spoken to by the judge. Your lawyer is legally supposed to speak on your behalf.

If you speak to the judge, include "Your Honor" in every answer. For example, "Yes, Your Honor," "No, Your Honor," or "I don't know, Your Honor." Speak plainly and deliberately, and maintain steady, respectful eye contact. Be sincere and truthful. Relax; the judge is a human being too.

Objections

Your attorney may object to certain things the prosecutor says or tries to say. An objection is when one side calls "foul" on the other. The judge then has to decide if the objection will be sustained (validated) or denied (invalidated). In an ideal world, you would like to win all of your objections. In reality, you will win some and lose some. It is important that you allow your lawyer to concentrate on the proceedings without frequent interruption. Do not presume to tell him when to object unless you strongly suspect that some important point has been overlooked. In that case, tap your lawyer on the forearm, and lean forward to calmly and quietly explain the point.

The Bench

The desk the judge sits behind is referred to as "the bench." The witness stand is right next to the bench. This entire area is the judge's personal space. No one should approach the bench without first getting permission from the judge: "May I approach the bench, Your Honor?" Anyone who fails to get such permission may be handcuffed and charged with contempt of court.

Where You Sit

For the most part, you should talk to your attorney when you first enter the courtroom. Your attorney will tell you where to sit. The prosecutor's table is always closest to the jury. The docket (appointment calendar) may have several defendants scheduled at the same time. You may have to wait an hour or two until your name is called.

FOOD FOR THOUGHT

"If you believe in yourself and have dedication and pride – and never quit – you'll be a winner. The price of victory is high, but so are the rewards."

Bear Bryant

Testifying on the Witness Stand

If you testify, you need to follow a few simple rules:

1. Look at the jury when you speak, not at the attorneys.

2. Answer questions fully, not just "yes" or "no." Prosecutors like to lead you into a "yes" or "no" trap. You can fight this by answering in complete sentences that give a full explanation to the jury, not just a simple "yes or no" answer.

3. In a similar fashion, take control of your testimony by speaking in whole sentences. It throws the prosecutor off guard. Prosecutors will often work from a script. When you speak in long sentences, you mess up their script. You sound calmer. It requires the prosecutors to think on their feet. Give an answer that paraphrases the question. For example the prosecutor asks, "Were you at the beach last night?" You can answer, "I was not at the beach last night."

4. You and your attorney should practice your testimony in private before you take the witness stand. Your attorney should play the role of the prosecutor while questioning you. Using what you learned during your practice sessions, think ahead three questions while on the witness stand.

5. If you are especially anxious, ask your doctor if a low dose anti-anxiety medicine can help you. This medicine will help calm the "butterflies" which often attend being a witness in court. If you use medication, be aware that it may cause side effects. Always take your first dose several days before your trial starts so you do not experience a severe side effect during the middle of your trial.

Leaving the Courtroom

You are not allowed to leave the courtroom until the judge is finished with all of the defendants in the room, or the judge specifically excuses you. You may have to sit in the audience and wait until the judge adjourns (finishes) the hearing.

Tales from the Courtroom

There is an amazing video of a sentencing hearing that involved a violent and mentally unstable defendant. The defendant previously had made several angry and violent gestures in the courtroom. One of the bailiffs took the extreme measure of keeping an electric taser aimed at the defendant throughout the hearing. When the judge read out the sentence, the defendant stood up, screamed, and started running toward the judge. He was only able to take two steps before the bailiff shot him in the back with the taser.

The scene was captured with two different video cameras. The second camera's footage was more interesting: It showed the judge as she read the sentence. She never stopped reading the sentence during the ordeal. In fact, she never even blinked as the defendant convulsed on the floor.

CHAPTER 3:

Appearing Before a Federal Magistrate Judge

FOOD FOR THOUGHT

"A dog has many friends because he wags his tail, not his tongue."

Unknown

Judges

There are generally four types of U.S. federal judges:

1. Magistrate judges

2. District court judges

3. Circuit appeals court judges

4. U.S. Supreme Court judges

A federal magistrate judge is a type of judge that does the following:

1. Hears evidence from federal law enforcement personnel in secrecy to determine if it is sufficient to issue search warrants and/or arrest warrants.

2. Hears initial criminal complaints from federal law enforcement personnel to determine if there is enough evidence to detain you.

3. Upon determining that the criminal complaint is valid, they can hear evidence to determine if you can get out on bail and bond or not.

4. Oversees Preliminary Hearings.

5. Oversees Grand Jury Hearings to determine if you should be criminally indicted.

6. If both parties consent in writing, a magistrate judge may preside over any other proceedings in your case, including the trial.

7. Makes initial recommendations on certain types of initial appeals after a conviction (i.e. petitions for a writ of *habeas corpus*).

8. If you receive a federal criminal indictment, the federal magistrate judge turns your case over to a federal district court judge.

A federal district court judge oversees the following:

1. Plea bargain hearings

2. Pretrial legal motions

3. Trials

4. Sentencing hearings

5. Supervised release/probation violation hearings

6. Appeals from certain rulings made by magistrate judges (i.e. detention orders)

7. Certain types of initial appeals after a conviction (i.e. petitions for a writ of *habeas corpus*)

Circuit court judges are a group of federal judges that hear appeals stemming from the rulings made by federal district court judges. They do not oversee trials.

U.S. Supreme Court judges are a group of nine judges that hear appeals stemming from the rulings made by circuit appeals court judges. The U.S. Supreme Court is extremely selective about which cases it hears. Like the circuit appeals court judges, the U.S. Supreme Court does not oversee trials.

Legal Definitions

Before proceeding, you should understand the meaning of important legal terms that may be used during your trial proceedings:

Probable Cause – A term that means there is enough evidence to cause a judge to believe something. For example, a credible witness states she saw you buy some dope and take it into your apartment. There is now probable cause to believe you possess dope in your apartment.

Search Warrant – A legal document in which a judge authorizes law enforcement personnel to search you or your property for the purpose of looking for specific evidence related to a crime.

Arrest Warrant – A legal document in which a judge directs law enforcement personnel to arrest you for violating the law.

Criminal Complaint – A legal document written by law enforcement personnel in which they allege a specific crime was committed.

Criminal Indictment – A legal document formally accusing you of committing a crime. Criminal indictments can only be issued by a grand jury.

Criminal Information – A legal instrument prepared by the prosecuting authority (i.e., U.S. Attorney (USA) or District Attorney (DA)) which formally charges you with a crime. Some states utilize the criminal information as an alternative to a grand jury indictment, and some states use both. Occasionally, the United States court system uses an instrument such as this as an initial alternative to a grand jury indictment. In federal criminal procedures, it is called a criminal complaint, but it is prepared by the USA, not the "police".

Grand Jury – A group of law abiding citizens randomly selected. They meet with prosecutors and federal magistrate judges in private several times each month to determine if there is enough evidence to warrant criminal indictments against suspects.

Federal Detention Center (FDC) – A jail for people accused of committing a federal crime. If you are accused of breaking a city, county, or state law, you will generally be locked up in a county jail. If you are accused of breaking a federal law, you will be locked up in a FDC. Exceptions exist. Sometimes the federal government contracts with local county sheriffs' offices for use of a specific part of a county jail as a FDC.

Bail or Bond (B & B) – A sum of money you give in trust to the government to allow you to get out of jail while your case is investigated before a trial or plea bargain takes place. The judge is trusting you to attend all of your court appearances while you are trusting the government to return your money if you follow all of the rules. It is fully refunded when (if) you return for trial or other proceedings. A bail bond company will usually post the bail bond for you if you are willing or able to pay the exorbitant fee (normally 10%). Although the U.S. Constitution guarantees the right to *reasonable bail*, Congress and the Supreme Court have decided that bail can be denied in some cases.

FOOD FOR THOUGHT

"When life's problems seem overwhelming, look around and see what other people are coping with. You may consider yourself fortunate."

Ann Landers

Sequence of Events in Federal Criminal Cases

The general sequence of events for federal criminal cases is as follows:

1. Evidence of possible criminal misconduct causes suspicion by federal law enforcement personnel and prosecutors.

2. The level of evidence may or may not be strong enough to support probable cause for a search warrant and/or arrest warrant.

3. A hearing before a federal magistrate judge takes place in secrecy. A search warrant and/or arrest warrant may or may not be issued by the judge.

4. Your property is searched and/or you are arrested.

5. You are taken to a FDC if you are arrested by a federal agent. You are taken to a jail if you are arrested by a local or state law enforcement officer.

6. You will have a hearing before a federal magistrate judge during which a criminal complaint is submitted by law enforcement.

7. You may get out on "bail and bond," or you may have to stay in detention until your circumstance is decided.

8. A preliminary hearing may or may not take place.

9. You may or may not receive a criminal indictment from a grand jury.

10. If you are indicted, you may or may not have a hearing where you enter a plea of "guilty" or "not guilty." In many instances, you can file your plea electronically, saving you from having to appear in court.

11. You may have a series of pretrial hearings, including evidentiary hearings and pretrial motions.

The above sequence of events will result in one of the following:

1. You plead guilty and accept a plea bargain.

2. You plead not guilty and go to trial.

3. You flee (hopefully not).

4. You die in the process (hopefully not).

5. The prosecutor leaves you locked up or out on bail and bond indefinitely while he performs an unusually long investigation (hopefully not).

6. The federal prosecutor drops the charges against you. (This is the best outcome.)

FOOD FOR THOUGHT

"Don't bunt. Aim out of the ballpark. Aim for the company of immortals."

David Ogilvy

Appearing Before a Federal Magistrate Judge

You were arrested because federal agents allegedly saw you commit a crime, a search warrant of your property revealed evidence of illegal conduct, or a warrant was issued for your arrest.

You are now locked up in a FDC or a jail. According to federal law, you have a right to know what the charges are against you. The federal government must bring you before a federal magistrate judge in a hearing to inform you of these charges. An Assistant United States Attorney (AUSA) represents the federal government. United States Attorneys (USA's) and federal judges all work for the DOJ. Your appearance before the judge generally happens on the first business day after you are arrested. It may be delayed up to three calendar days if a weekend or holiday is involved.

You generally will be woken up at 4:00 A.M. or 5:00 A.M. in your cell. A CO will tell you to start getting ready. Around 6:00 A.M., the CO's will take you to a holding tank (area), where you will wait with other inmates going to court that day. You will get breakfast. You will be searched. Around 7:00 A.M., there will be a headcount and you will be hand-cuffed and shackled. You will be loaded on a bus or van and taken to the federal courthouse. Be patient and follow directions.

At the federal courthouse, another headcount will be conducted. You will be placed in the custody of the U.S. Marshals. You will get out of your vehicle and enter the back of the building. Any time you stop, you will have to turn and face the wall. This is a security protocol to protect the officers and other inmates. When you ride in an elevator, you must also face the back of the elevator.

Once you are inside, the leg shackles will be removed from your legs and the handcuffs removed from one arm. This allows you to eat. You will be searched and patted down. Another headcount will be taken. Use the restroom when you can because you don't know when you may have another opportunity.

Fights in a courthouse are rare because inmates are almost always under direct observation of the U.S. Marshals. To be safe, be polite and don't discuss your case with anyone. For more detailed information on safety concerns, refer to "Chapter 18: Inmate Safety Issues."

FOOD FOR THOUGHT

"The worst bankruptcy in the world is the person who loses his enthusiasm."

H. W. Arnold

While you wait to appear before the federal magistrate judge a U.S. Pretrial Services Officer (PTSO) or U.S. Probation Officer (PO) may visit you in a separate cell. A PO will visit you if you are currently out of prison on supervised release. If you are *not* currently serving time on federal supervised release (probation), you will be interviewed by a PTSO. You will be asked about your job, income, living situation, foreign travel, and family ties. This information is used to help make a recommendation on bail and bond.

Two to five inmate names will be called at a time. You will be fully handcuffed and shackled again. The U.S. Marshals will escort you to a courtroom in front of a federal magistrate judge. You need to stand out of respect when the judge enters and leaves. You must be still, quiet, and attentive. You should only speak when you are asked a question. When you give your answer, you should stand. Then be seated.

You will meet the federal case agent who is filing the criminal complaint against you. The case agent is the lead investigator that is investigating you on behalf of a federal agency. The agent will swear to the criminal complaint's accuracy. You will also meet the AUSA that will prosecute you. The judge will hear a brief presentation by the AUSA and federal agent about your alleged criminal misconduct. They will tell you what the minimum and maximum sentences are if you are found guilty and discuss any potential fines.

The judge will then turn to the subject of bail and bond. Some people get approved to be released during the investigation while others are not. In some instances, you will have a separate B & B hearing at a later date. Many factors are included when the judge determines if you will get out on B & B:

1. If you are accused of a serious crime, the cost of your B & B will be higher. For example, someone accused of first degree murder across state lines will have a higher B & B than someone accused of tax evasion.

2. The more money you earn, the higher your B & B will be.

3. The more crimes you have committed in the past, the more dangerous the judge will consider you to be to society and the less likely will get out on B & B. If you do get B & B, you will pay more for B & B because you are a greater risk to society.

4. If you previously evaded law enforcement while you were on B & B, or if you have ever escaped from prison/jail, you will not get out on B & B.

5. If you have frequent international travel or you own property outside the U.S., you are less likely to get out on B & B, and you will probably be required to surrender your passport, if you are released. In any circumstance, a judge can order you to surrender your passport to make it more difficult for you to flee the country.

6. The greater your risk of danger to society as determined by the judge, the less your chances are that you will get out on B & B.

7. If you have a job and numerous close family ties in the area, your chance of getting out on B & B is more likely.

Based on the above factors, your federal magistrate judge will decide if you can get released on B & B. If you have a job, a place to live, have no previous criminal history, and a good credit history, the judge may release you on a Personal Recognizance Bond (PR bond) (sometimes called an Own Recognizance Bond (OR bond)). This is the best type of B & B as you pay absolutely nothing for either bail or bond unless you don't show up for your court appearances (hearings). If the judge gives you a $25,000 PR bond, you pay nothing to be released on B & B. If you miss one court hearing, your bond will be revoked, you will owe the U.S. government $25,000, and the judge will issue a warrant for your arrest.

Instead of an "OR" or "PR" bond, the judge may simply order a cash bond in a particular amount. You will be required to pay the cash amount, in trust, to the Court *before* you are released. When (and if) you appear for trial or other proceedings, the money will be refunded to you, as promised. If you don't appear, it will be forever forfeited. For a large fee – usually 10%, a bail bond company will post the bond for you, unless you are considered to be too big of a risk.

The federal magistrate judge expects that all defendants may say anything in order to be released and they may not believe you. The judge will get a better understanding of your risk by challenging your spouse, parents, or a sibling to co-sign a bond. If you don't show up for an appearance in court, the co-signer has to pay some of their own money. If your family refuses to co-sign a bond, the judge will take that as a sign that you are too risky to release on B & B. If your family agrees to co-sign it, the judge will take that as an indication you are a low risk out on B & B.

FOOD FOR THOUGHT

"No problem of human destiny is beyond human beings."

U.S. President John F. Kennedy

One more hitch: Before you can be released, you must clear up any and all other detainers. A detainer is a formal request from some prosecuting authority (city, county, state, or United States) asking the jail or detention center where you are confined not to release you. For example, if you are accused of burglary in the state of Mississippi, a Mississippi county judge will issue a warrant for your arrest. They then will issue a detainer request across the entire U.S., asking any law enforcement personnel or judges to detain you on their behalf.

You then leave Mississippi before you are arrested and two years later, you are arrested in New Orleans by Federal Drug Enforcement Agency (DEA) agents for smuggling dope across state lines. Before you can be released, you have to get B & B from both the federal magistrate judge in Louisiana and the county judge in Mississippi. This is very unlikely because you are considered more dangerous by the judge and you are more likely to flee the authorities because you are facing a longer prison term due to multiple charges.

Additional Comments:

1. You should ask as many questions about your release on B & B as you can. You are expected to abide by all of the rules. If you don't, you will immediately be locked up again.

2. You do not have to plead guilty or not guilty at this time.

3. Although it is not necessary to have an attorney present at this time, one is allowed. It is suggested that you get an attorney as soon as possible. You can hire an attorney while you are detained or after you are released. If you cannot afford an attorney, one will be appointed to you.

4. If you do get out on B & B, you will not be released in the court room. You will have to ride back to the FDC or jail and will be released from there. This may take several hours.

5. Sometimes you are "released" on the condition that you wear an electronic tracking device and/or live in a halfway house facility.

CHAPTER 4:

Your Family, Friends, and the Media

FOOD FOR THOUGHT

"That's one man's opinion."

Walter Cronkite

Family

Unless you have been prosecuted before, your family will be shocked by the allegation against you. Many of them will run and hide; some will stand by your side no matter what happens. This is a test of your relationships.

You need to be honest with your family about what the actual accusations are that are being made against you. Be open about the criminal allegation. State what the charges are, your dates in court, your prosecutors, and your defense attorneys. Do not discuss evidence, witnesses, alibis, or possible plea bargains. Even after you and your attorney have discussed the facts of the case, only talk to those in whom you have complete trust.

If you are locked up in a Federal Detention Center or jail, tell your kids you will be out some day and will be with them again. (Unless you are facing a life sentence or the death penalty.) Tell your kids not all jails are like the ones portrayed on T.V. Tell your kids you love them and not to worry. Tell them you will call them and write them often. Then do so.

For more information on how to take care of your significant other and your children while you are in prison, please see "Chapter 22: Your Significant Other" and "Chapter 24: Your Children."

Friends

You will find out who your friends really are after you are accused of a crime. Some of your spouse's friends may also break off their friendships. Don't talk about the details of your case except the alleged accusation made against you, your court dates, and the names of your prosecutors and defense attorneys.

FOOD FOR THOUGHT

"Glass, china, and reputation are easily cracked and never mended well."

Benjamin Franklin

The Media

The media loves juicy stories; the more outrageous, the better for their business. Don't watch the TV news or read the newspaper. The media can be infuriating; you cannot change what they say. They will always say the worst about you, and any efforts to clarify your story will often be futile. Reporters want spicy sound bites. Don't talk. Protect your case. Your story will blow over.

If you do speak to the media, don't answer their questions. Make a very brief, truthful statement. If you lie, it will come back to hurt you at trial or during sentencing. If you were wrongfully convicted, just say "I'm appealing my case." Don't name other suspects as someone else may end up wrongfully prosecuted. Let your attorney handle this.

If the media shows up and sets up cameras in your driveway or they look in your windows videotaping your living room, call 911. Have the police remove them from your property and charge them with trespassing.

For More Information

For more information, see:

• Chapter 22: Your Significant Other

• Chapter 24: Your Children

CHAPTER 5:

Hiring a Criminal Defense Attorney

FOOD FOR THOUGHT

"Anyone who has never made a mistake has never tried anything new."

Albert Einstein

Introduction

You now find yourself facing federal criminal charges. Your world may soon change for the worse. In fact, the U.S. DOJ has a greater than ninety percent conviction rate. You need to hire a good, experienced, professional criminal defense attorney. This chapter will give you good ideas to consider.

Locating an Attorney

You may not know any criminal defense attorneys or anyone that has used one. Start by looking in the phone book, newspaper, and on the Internet. Realize that some of the largest ads you see are there because the attorney really needs your business. That's true in some, but not all instances.

Other great attorneys don't take out any ads because their business is generated by their good reputation. Many great civil attorneys, plumbers, doctors, and mechanics operate this way. They never advertise yet their businesses are so full that they do not take on new clients. If you find this type of criminal defense attorney, cherish him or her.

Legal Fees

Most attorneys will meet with you for an hour to discuss your case. In some instances, that meeting will be free. In other cases, the attorney charges a fee of a couple of hundred to a couple thousand dollars for that first meeting. They do this to weed out people that are looking for completely free legal advice.

Most attorneys will require a down payment for their services. It's at least one-third to one-half of the cost. Some attorneys require one-hundred percent of the payment up front.

Many attorneys will divide their work into two different phases. The first phase consists of the initial arrest/investigation through the indictment and hearing for bail and bond. They may charge one fee for these services and then charge a separate set of fees for a more thorough investigation, plea bargain versus trial, and sentencing hearing. If you go through a plea bargain or trial with an attorney, it is customary for them to be your lawyer at the sentencing hearing. If you are filing an appeal, you must generally file a motion for intent to file an appeal in *ten days* from the date of your sentencing hearing. Your original defense attorney should help you file this. (You will pay the filing fee, which is $450.00.)

Some criminal defense attorneys charge different rates for services to different clients, depending on their client's income. If you are a wealthy diamond manufacturer, you will pay the "A list" price. If you are a librarian, you will pay the "B list" price. If you are unemployed, nice, and groom yourself appropriately, you may get the "C list" price, which is free or almost free. If you are not appropriately groomed or you have a rude demeanor, they may turn your case down or charge you the "A list" price.

Copies

In most states, you are supposed to be given a copy of the contract between you and your attorney at the time you sign it. Please read it carefully before you sign it.

Ask your attorney to give you a copy of the following:

1. Your indictment(s)
2. The U.S. Criminal Statutes you are charged with under Title 18 U.S. Code
3. Any search warrants
4. Criminal complaints/initial police reports

Carefully read all of the above documents, build a timeline of events, and make a list of any relevant mistakes in the documents to discuss with your lawyer. Also, make a list of questions for your attorney as well as a to-do list for yourself.

FOOD FOR THOUGHT

"Luck is a dividend of sweat. The more you sweat, the luckier you get."

Ray Kroc

Communicating with Your Attorney

1. Make a list of questions or comments before you call, write, or meet with your attorney.

2. Always be respectful, even if you disagree with your attorney. Remember; don't bite the hand that is trying to help you.

3. Be succinct. A one page memo is superior, if you are able. The more requests you make in a large memo, the less likely any single request will get done.

4. Write: "Confidential: Attorney-Client Privilege" on every page of every memo you send to your attorney. This protects the contents of the memo from being used against you in court. You should also write the confidentiality notice on both sides of envelopes containing your legal mail.

5. Use memos, not letters. The memo format makes it easier for your attorney to keep up with what each document is about. Use the memo:
   To: Lefty, Greedson, and Slickman, Attorneys at Law
   From: John Doe
   Date: 5/12/13
   Subject: Search Warrant from 1/12/13

6. Keep a copy of all your letters/memos for your file.

7. Be patient. Realize you are not the only client your attorney has. It takes most attorneys two or three days to return phone calls. It may take a few weeks for most attorneys to answer letters.

Cynical Attorney Agendas

After dealing with attorneys for awhile, you realize the following and may become cynical:

1. Most attorneys protect themselves and their agendas. Federal congress generally consists of people who are currently attorneys or have been an attorney in the past. You will notice many laws and prosecutors protect congress, lawyers, and law enforcement in ways the general public is not protected. Recognize this hypocrisy.

2. Most attorneys are highly paid. For example, a civil attorney charged $300 to create a two-page document. Preparing this document took less than 30 minutes; all that was required was to complete a pre-existing form with appropriate name, date and address, and print it out.

3. Attorneys often get paid for half or all of their work up front. Mechanics, plumbers, and doctors usually don't require this.

4. Most attorneys take off most nights, weekends, and holidays. They will re-schedule your court appearances and attorney meetings over and over again.

5. If something goes wrong, they usually blame someone else.

Firing an Attorney

Realize your attorney-client relationship may be in trouble if:

1. Your attorney lies to you.

2. Your attorney fails to communicate with you after several reasonable attempts and you have been waiting patiently. (Don't keep calling over and over again unless it is an emergency. Give them a chance.)

3. Your attorney's agenda hurts you if:

   a. Politics are more important than your case.

   b. Your attorney's health prohibits them from adamantly fighting your case.

   c. Your attorney is related to, or dating, or has dated the prosecutors, police officers, or judge in your case.

   d. Your attorney refuses to fight for you in court. They are willing to give you the worst plea bargain/sentence you can get so they can go home early. (I've seen cases where each of the above happened. That's messed up.)

4. Your attorney asks you to falsify documents or commit other crimes.

If you choose to fire your attorney, do so politely. Just say, "I don't think our relationship is working out. I'm going to have to find another attorney." Put the message in writing, even if you are in a face to face meeting. Keep a copy for your records. (You may need this for an appeal later on.) In your letter, include permission to release your records to your new attorney. Include the new attorney's name, address, and phone number. Ask your new attorney, in writing, to file a motion with the court to have your previous attorney officially removed from your case.

CHAPTER 6:

Preliminary Hearings

Introduction

While every defendant gets a bail and bond hearing in front of a federal magistrate judge, every defendant *does not* get a preliminary hearing. Preliminary hearings are conducted to determine if there is sufficient evidence to prosecute an accused person. The burden of proof upon the government is very slight. Although you *may* offer exculpatory evidence at the preliminary hearing, your lawyer usually elects not to do so. Because of the diminished burden of proof, the defendant is normally bound over for trial, and chooses not to "show his hand" at the preliminary hearing. If you get a hearing; take advantage of it. Learn what evidence the government has against you. Have your attorney ask as many questions to the government's witnesses as possible. Try to determine the prosecutor's strategy.

Definitions

An understanding of the following terms is recommended.

Evidence: Evidence is something such as an object or a statement, which is presented in a legal proceeding.

"Relevant evidence" is evidence having any tendency to prove or disprove an issue in the case. Generally, relevant evidence is admissible while "irrelevant evidence" is not admissible. "Irrelevant evidence" is evidence not having any tendency to prove or disprove an issue in the case.

Evidence is either direct or circumstantial. Direct evidence is based upon the personal knowledge of the witness. For example, the witness states: "I saw him pull the trigger." Circumstantial evidence, on the other hand, always contains an element of inference. For example, when you went to bed the road was clear; when you woke up, it was covered in snow. You made the inference that it snowed during the night, based upon that circumstantial evidence. In some instances, federal law allows a defendant to be convicted based on circumstantial evidence. In other instances, prosecutors must prove their case using direct evidence. It depends on the federal law and the case law in the jurisdiction where the hearing is being held.

Hearsay: Hearsay is testimony which relates *not* to what the witness knows by way of personal knowledge or observation, but, instead to what he or she has heard *someone else* say. Because that "someone else" is not subject to cross-examination, the hearsay about what he or she said is usually not admissible. For example, a witness states, "Joe said that the light was green." This is hearsay and is inadmissible. (Note: There are twenty-eight specific exceptions to the hearsay rule; all of them apply in federal court, and almost all of them apply in most state courts.)

Hearing: A hearing is a meeting with the judge, prosecutors, defense attorneys, and you, the defendant. A court reporter is also present. Court reporters are transcriptionists. A hearing is almost always public.

Legal Motion: A legal motion is a formal request for a judge to take an action or make a decision on some point of law relevant to the case.

Brief: A brief is a legal document in which a lawyer argues why his or her point of view should be adopted by the judge. Briefs are usually submitted before a hearing. Your judge may delay his or her decision by a short time while both sides submit an additional brief after a hearing.

Case Law: Case law is distinguished from traditional law. The U.S. Congress passes traditional laws, which the U.S. President may or may not sign. Traditional laws often have ambiguous terms or phrases, which appeals courts must later decipher. When an appeals court clarifies an ambiguity in a traditional law, the case being appealed is referred to as case law. Case law has the same legal power as traditional law. In either circumstance, the U.S. Congress can create new laws which override previous case law or previous traditional law.

FOOD FOR THOUGHT

"A battle is lost less through casualties than by discouragement."

Frederick II, Roman Emperor

The Hearing

If you are going to have a preliminary hearing, it will occur before you are indicted. A magistrate judge will preside over the hearing. The evidence as of that date will be discussed. The limits to the knowledge will also be discussed. In other words, your attorney may be able to determine what your prosecutor does not know about your case.

In addition to learning about the limits to the prosecutor's knowledge of your case, you can also learn if they failed to have enough knowledge about your alleged crime before they obtained a search warrant. Your attorney may decide to file a motion to suppress evidence obtained by an illegal search warrant. Likewise, if your attorney learns the prosecutor has prejudicial evidence against you, they may want to file a motion to exclude this information from your trial. Both of these types of motions are referred to as motions *in limine* (motions made "preliminary" or "before trial").

The Conclusion of the Hearing

Both sides can file legal motions at the end of the hearing or within a few days after it. For instance, the prosecutor will want to move the process along so they will file a motion to convene a grand jury. The grand jury will indict you if they find sufficient evidence that you might have committed the crime.

Your defense attorney may decide to file several motions, such as a motion to suppress circumstantial or prejudicial evidence from a grand jury hearing. Your attorney may also file motions to force the government to give your attorney access to more evidence regarding your case.

Realize that the more you learn from the hearing, the better off you will be in preparing for your defense.

CHAPTER 7:

U.S. Pretrial Services

Are You on B & B?

A federal magistrate judge will decide if you are going to get out of jail on B & B prior to your trial. If you fail to get out on B & B, you may want to skip this chapter.

Jurisdiction

If you were previously out of prison on federal supervised release, federal parole, or federal probation, and you were under the U.S. Probation Office's jurisdiction when you were arrested, you will be under their jurisdiction while you are out on B & B. If you were not on federal supervised release, federal parole, or federal probation when you were arrested, you will be under the jurisdiction of U.S. Pretrial Services while you are out on B & B. While discussing U.S. Pretrial Services, the U.S. Probation Office and U.S. Pretrial Service operate the terms of B & B in a similar way. If you were out of state prison on parole or probation when you were arrested, you still have to report to your state parole or probation officer.

Federal Home Confinement and Home Detention

If you are released on B & B, you will usually be detained in your home under federal home detention or federal home confinement. In both cases, you can only leave your home under specific, authorized circumstances and you must return to your home every night. Federal home detention is less restrictive than home confinement.

If you are on home confinement, you will be able to see your attorneys and doctors with prior approval from your PTSO. You may or may not be able to work. You *cannot* go shopping, run errands, go to school, or go to religious services.

If you are on home detention, you can go to work, visit your attorneys and doctors, go to school, and go to religious services. You may or may not be able to run certain errands while you are on home detention depending on your PTSO. You need to talk with your PTSO about where you can and cannot go and whether you need permission just once or each time you go somewhere. Each PTSO handles things a little differently.

Pretrial Service Officers

When you first meet your PTSO, ask lots of questions. It is recommended that you sit in their waiting room when you are done with the initial meeting and read all the instructions again. Make a list of questions and ask to speak to your PTSO again, if necessary. It's better to be very thorough rather than violate your B & B provisions because of a misunderstanding.

Tip: Each time you speak to a PTSO, keep a journal entry of the date, time, questions, answers, and which PTSO you spoke with. If you get accused of violating your B & B terms, your journal may be helpful in your defense.

Curfew

You cannot leave your home during the curfew time.

If you are on home detention and you have a daytime, Monday thru Friday job, your schedule will most likely look like:

Monday Curfew:	7:00 P.M. to 7:00 A.M. Tuesday
Tuesday Curfew:	7:00 P.M. to 7:00 A.M. Wednesday
Wednesday Curfew:	7:00 P.M. to 7:00 A.M. Thursday
Thursday Curfew:	7:00 P.M. to 7:00 A.M. Friday
Friday Curfew:	7:00 P.M. to 8:00 A.M. Saturday
Saturday Curfew:	12:00 Noon to 7:00 A.M. Monday

You cannot leave your home on Saturday afternoon, Saturday night, Sunday, or Sunday night.

You need to get permission from your PTSO in advance if you want to go to a religious service on Saturday night or Sunday.

Because of unexpected traffic and weather conditions, you need to plan on being home 30-45 minutes before your curfew starts each evening.

Inspections

After you meet your PTSO, they will come to inspect your home and your place of employment. In some cases, the PTSO's will look in your closets, cabinets, garage, and attic. In some cases, they will just walk from room to room. They are looking for contraband material and evidence of criminal activity.

Once they leave, they can come back at any time – day or night. You have to let them in even if they don't have a search warrant; it is a provision of your B & B. Expect them to show up randomly although most of the inspections are during routine daylight hours on weekdays. The longer your criminal history is and the more trouble you get into, the more frequently they will come out to inspect everything. (In one case, they only came out three times in twenty-one months.)

You need to let your boss know the PTSO's can theoretically come inspect where you work whenever they want to. If your boss is not okay with the inspections, you have to resign or your B & B is revoked and you go back to jail. The good news is most PTSO's are professional. They show up in dress clothes and show their ID's. They usually come in for five minutes during business hours, walk around politely, and leave. Tell your boss it's no big deal.

FOOD FOR THOUGHT

"The way to get started is to quit talking and begin doing."

Walt Disney

Alcohol, Drugs, Weapons, and Computers

You cannot possess, use, or manufacture weapons of any kind, including, but not limited to, guns, martial arts weapons, hunting knives, explosives, fire crackers, swords, etc.

You cannot possess, use, or manufacture illegal drugs. You may have to submit to urine or blood drug tests. You cannot use any medicines prescribed for someone else. (It's a felony.) You cannot store prescription narcotics outside a properly labeled prescription bottle. (It's illegal.) You cannot store your Ambien, Vicodin, etc. in a pillbox. They must be stored in the original bottles.

You may or may not be able to possess, manufacture, and consume small amounts of alcohol. Your judge will indicate this on your orders. If you violate the above by being charged with public intoxication or driving while intoxicated, you can get your B & B revoked and end up back in jail.

You may have to take alcohol breathalyzers.

You may or may not have a computer restriction, depending on if a computer was used in committing the alleged crime. (For example: identity theft, fraud, child pornography, threats of violence, etc.) In some instances, you can use and possess a computer at work but not at home. A U.S. Pretrial Service Technician will install monitoring software on your computer. It will show a warning message each time the computer is restarted. Everything you do will be recorded and transmitted to a remote monitoring company. The U.S. Pretrial Service Technician will inspect each computer you use and seal it. If you break the seal, you may get locked up.

- You may have additional restrictions, depending on your case:
- No establishing new lines of credit or ID cards (for fraud cases).
- No possessing or viewing pornography (for sex offenses).
- No e-mailing or texting (for electronic harassment cases).
- No establishing new phone accounts without permission.

Contact Restrictions

You will be prohibited from contacting alleged victims and/or alleged co-conspirators. If you are accused of a sexual offense involving a minor, you cannot associate with or contact minors. You also cannot go to places where minors congregate (schools, libraries, playgrounds, day cares, etc.).

Travel Restrictions

You will have to turn in your passport. You cannot leave your federal district without written permission. There are several hundred federal districts in the U.S. Each district encompasses a few hundred to a few thousand square miles. (If you were locked up in a FDC, the last three digits of your federal register number/U.S. Marshals Number on your ID badge is the federal district number.)

If you do travel outside of your federal district, you have to get permission in writing. If you get permission, store one copy in your baggage, one copy in your glove compartment, and one copy in your wallet or purse. Recreational trips are usually prohibited. Your attorney may want to get an order from your judge, which overrides your PTSO's personal opinion. You will have to list your dates of departure and return, your destination, method of travel, vehicle license plate, make, model, and year, where you will stay, who you will travel with, and who you will stay with, etc.

Moving

You cannot move unless you get prior approval from your PTSO.

Electronic Monitoring

Your federal magistrate judge may require you to wear electronic radio frequency (RF) monitoring equipment, a Global Positioning Satellite (GPS) monitor, both, or neither. It depends on your previous criminal history and the nature of your criminal allegation.

How Electronic Radio Frequency Monitoring Works

Typical electronic RF monitoring consists of a pager-size ankle bracelet that detects if you are in your home or not. The ankle bracelet emits a RF signal periodically to the base unit, which is connected to your phone line. The base unit sends a signal to a monitoring company, which sends a report to your PTSO.

Your ankle bracelet transmits a signal to the base unit periodically. If you are in your house, a green light should appear on the unit. If you are not close enough to the base unit, the signal will not be received, and the monitor will send a signal to the monitoring company to let them know you are breaking your curfew. When the ankle bracelet is out of range of the base unit, a red light comes on that lasts a couple of seconds and then flickers.

If you can afford it, you will have to pay for your electronic monitoring. A simple ankle bracelet costs a few dollars per day. If you cannot afford it, you will have to make a partial payment every month. They only accept cashier's checks and money orders; no cash, credit cards, or personal checks.

Problems with Electronic Radio Frequency Monitoring

The monitoring company tracks where you are at specific points in time. Since your personal clocks may not match the clock the monitoring company uses, you need to stay in your home five to ten extra minutes past the end of your curfew each morning. Likewise, you need to get in your home at least ten minutes before your curfew starts. Plan on being home 30-45 minutes early, just to be safe.

If the electronic RF monitoring equipment has a malfunction or the electricity to your house goes out, call your PTSO *immediately*. Leave a message stating your name, phone number, date, time, and what is going on, if he is not there. If your electricity comes back on, call and let them know. One person was locked up because he waited a day or two to notify his PTSO's when the power went out in his home. The PTSO's cited security concerns and had him arrested.

The electronic RF monitoring equipment uses your telephone line to communicate with the monitoring company. If you are on the telephone and the base unit by the phone emits a loud beep, it means you should hang up immediately so the electronic RF equipment can transmit information back to the monitoring company.

Do not tamper with any of the equipment. If you tear or cut off the ankle bracelet, you will break an electric circuit. A red light on the base will come on for two seconds followed by flickers. When the circuit is broken, it will transmit the signal back to the monitoring company. You will be arrested and charged with escape.

The ankle bracelet can be worn in the shower. You are not supposed to soak it in liquid because the seal on the case is imperfect.

The ankle bracelet's signal is not perfect. It gets distorted or blocked when you stand next to some appliances or go upstairs or downstairs, depending on the electrical make-up and building materials used in your phone.

FOOD FOR THOUGHT

"A fool is a man who never tried an experiment in his life."

Erasmus Darwin

The electronic RF monitoring equipment has a range of 75 to 100 feet. It may be more or less because of the interference issues mentioned above. When you first get your device, check the range when you are not under your curfew. Have a trusted family member stand by the base unit while you walk to different locations in your yard. Your family should watch the light on the base unit to see when the light turns from green to red, indicating you have gone too far. You and your family can tell where the border exists. For your safety, subtract ten feet from this distance to use as a safety buffer zone. (Make sure you are wearing your GPS unit if you are ordered to do so. While your ankle bracelet will show that you are too far from your base unit, your GPS unit will show that you are still on your property.)

Because the electronic RF monitoring equipment has a limited range, consider placing the base unit in the center of your home. Otherwise, if you place it in the north end of your home, it may erroneously report you as having escaped each time you go to the south end of your home.

At some point, your PTSO will call you and question you about some issues with your electronic RF monitoring equipment. Tell him or her you didn't break your curfew.

Keep a record in your journal. In most cases, if the electronic RF monitoring equipment shows a possible "escape" for only five to ten minutes, you won't get in trouble the first couple of times it happens. If it is longer or more frequent, they will report it to the judge for a possible B & B revocation hearing.

If you have too many problems with your electronic RF monitoring equipment, have a phone conversation or meeting with the U.S. Pretrial Service Technican. Ask if they can check the battery.

How GPS Monitoring Works

The GPS system uses a series of satellites to triangulate the location of the GPS device, allowing the government to track your location. In some instances, you will have to wear a GPS unit any time you leave your home. The unit may be a little larger than a large cell phone and you wear it on your belt. It tracks where you are and sends a signal to the monitoring company which sends a report to your PTSO. This helps the government make sure you are located where you are supposed to be and not in a community safety zone, which is a restricted area for you based on your alleged criminal characteristics.

A cheap GPS system costs $5 per day. An expensive GPS system costs $8 per day. If you cannot afford it, you will have to make a partial payment every month. They only accept cashier's checks and money orders; no cash, credit cards, or personal checks.

Problems with GPS Monitoring

If the GPS equipment has a malfunction or the power goes completely out, call your PTSO *immediately*. Leave a message stating your name, phone number, date, time, and what is going on, if he is not there.

Do not tamper with any of the GPS equipment. You will be arrested and charged with escape.

The U.S. Department of Defense (DOD) uses a very accurate GPS system for military purposes. The system is classified. The DOJ uses a less accurate system. The DOD's device is accurate to within five feet of your location. The DOJ's device only tells your PTSO which address you are at or near. If you are in a large football stadium, the DOJ won't know exactly where. The DOJ will just know you are at or near that address.

One of the technical issues with the DOJ's GPS system involves a satellite triangulation error. The combined use of three or four satellites produces the most accurate location for your GPS device. The satellite's orbits occasionally only allow one or two satellites to determine your location. If one of the satellites is low in its orbit on the horizon, it will accidentally mistake your location. Think of a shadow. When the sun is directly over your head at twelve noon, the head of your shadow is directly at your feet. At sunset, the head of your shadow may be hundreds of feet off from your actual location.

One alleged victim got a restraining order against her ex-husband, who moved a few blocks from his ex-wife. In the evening, the GPS system inaccurately showed he left his home after his curfew started and went to his ex-wife's house, which is a B & B violation. The good news is his ankle bracelet showed he was in his home the entire time. You need to understand the technical issues so your attorney can defend you if you are blamed for being somewhere you are not supposed to be. If you have too many problems with your GPS system, have a phone conversation or meeting with the U.S. Pretrial Service Technician.

FOOD FOR THOUGHT

"The world can change about you, but your dream will not. It will always be the link with the person you are today. If you hold onto it, you may grow old, but you will never be old."

Tom Clancy

Community Safety Zones

Your PTSO may designate certain areas as community safety zones. A community safety zone is an area where you cannot go because it causes a risk to someone. If you are accused of smuggling immigrants across the border and enslaving them in a sweat shop, your PTSO may create community safety zones at the sweat shop and each alleged victim's home. If you are accused of distributing narcotics, your PTSO may create community safety zones at the area where you allegedly sold drugs plus any known drug trafficking locations. If you are accused of possessing child pornography, your PTSO may create community safety zones at schools, libraries, parks, day cares, etc. A GPS monitor will show if you have violated a safety zone. You can be locked up.

Just in case you are wondering, how do you drive from point A to point B without violating a community safety zone? In most instances, you can travel in a safety zone in a vehicle so long as you don't stop there. Your PTSO can tell you drove thru it at 35 MPH while you were on your way to work. If you stop for a minute at a red traffic light, that is okay. If you stop for ten minutes, that is a violation of your B & B.

Tip: If you have car trouble, don't pull over in a safety zone; drive through it and pull over down the road. Then, call your PTSO immediately to let them know what happened.

PTSO Scheduled Meetings

You will have to meet with your PTSO at least once a month. Your PTSO will tell you which week of the month to go in. Consider going in on a Tuesday or Wednesday. Mondays are busy as the PTSO's are playing catch up from the weekend. If you wait until Friday and a conflict occurs, you will miss your meeting without any chance to make it up. You can get locked up for "failing to report" to U.S. Pretrial Services every month.

Plan ahead for your next meeting:

1. You should write the date of your PTSO meeting on your calendar. Call to schedule it a week or two in advance. Talk to your boss about it in advance.

2. Before you head in, memorize the date of your next court appearance (motion hearing, docket call, trial, etc). Your PTSO will quiz you.

3. Make a list of questions for your PTSO.

4. Don't urinate right before the meeting because you may have to provide a urine specimen.

5. Take something to read. (You might have to wait a while.)

When you enter U.S. Pretrial Services, they usually have a computer kiosk. You will place your thumb or index finger on an infrared fingerprint scanner. The software will access your file. You will confirm your identity, address, phone number, and place of employment. It will ask if you had any contact with law enforcement. If you are accused of another crime, your B & B can be revoked and you will be locked up.

You will wait until your PTSO or a substitute PTSO calls you into their office. They will review your answers to the above questions. They will ask you about your next court date. You will have a chance to ask your questions. The actual meeting usually only takes five minutes. However, you may wait anywhere from five minutes to two hours before a PTSO calls you back for your meeting.

CHAPTER 8:

Getting Your Affairs In Order

FOOD FOR THOUGHT

"When you feel the stampede coming, you can either run for cover, or grab the bull by the horns."

D. A. Freeman

Introduction

At this stage in the game, you realize the situation is pretty serious. The Feds win their cases 90-99% of the time. You need to get your proverbial house in order in case you do end up serving time. Hopefully, things will work out for you. If not, you are prepared.

Establishing Contacts

If you do end up in prison, you will need at least two reliable contacts on the outside. One of these may be your significant other. Beware: Half of all relationships don't make it through prison. Those contacts need to be people who you really trust. They must be willing to communicate with you several times per month and visit you now and then.

Power of Attorney

You should consider several different legal documents that give specific legal powers to another person. The person may or may not be an actual attorney. Consider generating the following powers of attorney, if you have not already done so:

1. General Power of Attorney: This document allows someone you designate to pay your bills, conduct some forms of business, etc. This document excludes healthcare decisions.

2. Banking Power of Attorney: This document allows someone you designate to open and close bank accounts. (Note: In Texas and many other states, a routine power of attorney cannot do banking for you. You have to get a special banking power of attorney form. Ask your bank which power of attorney they honor.)

3. Medical Power of Attorney: This document allows someone you designate to make healthcare decisions for you.

4. Living Will: This document allows you to make specific instructions to your doctor that become effective if you become incapacitated. For instance, no CPR, no feeding tubes, etc.

Address List

If you don't already have an address list, you need to make one. Use either an address database or a word processor. List names, addresses, phone numbers, e-mail addresses, etc. Make sure you include your family, friends, business associates, U.S. Social Security Department, State Department of Motor Vehicles, driver's license division, other permits or licensing agencies, insurance agencies, mortgage company/landlord, banks, utility companies, etc. Make sure both of your contacts have this list. If you end up in prison, your contact can mail you a copy of your address list as you move around.

FOOD FOR THOUGHT

"Success is often achieved by those who don't know that failure is inevitable."

Coco Chanel

Debt and Income Lists

Make a list of everyone you owe money to. Make a second list of everyone that owes you money. Make sure your power of attorney gets a copy of this list. If you get locked up, you will need someone to pay certain bills you owe. You will need this information if you get sentenced. A U.S. Probation Officer (PO) will need this information when they generate your Pre-Sentence Report (PSR). You may also need this information if you choose to file bankruptcy.

Passwords and PIN'S

One of your contacts and your power of attorney will need a list of your passwords and PIN's (Personal Identification Numbers). I would make two copies in case one gets lost.

Correspondence/Visits

Whatever happens to you, you want to keep in contact with your two main contacts. Let them know you are okay. Make a list of questions for them. Have them make a list for you.

Licenses and Permits

If you are allowed to, you may want to get your driver's license and any other permits renewed. If you are locked up, it's harder to do this. In some cases, your license won't have to be renewed but once every five or seven years. You will hopefully be released before then.

Healthcare

Get as much routine and preventative care as you can, if it is appropriate for you. If you are supposed to have a colonoscopy or mammogram, get it done. Prisons have horrible healthcare. You will be neglected at times.

Get an eye exam. If your vision needs correction, get eyeglasses. Get two pair in case one breaks. Getting contact lens solution in prison is difficult.

Get your teeth examined and cleaned. Dentists appear rarely in prisons. Many of them will pull your teeth out rather than fill a cavity. Some prisons have a dental hygienist. Many do not. You may go several years without getting your teeth cleaned.

FOOD FOR THOUGHT

"It's better to look ahead and prepare than to look back and regret."

Jackie Joyner-Kersee

Finances

See if you can put enough money aside to pay your mortgage and automobile payments when you are gone.

Kids, Parents, Pets, Plants, Etc.

If you have kids, frail parents, pets, or plants, figure out who will care for them if you get locked up. Talk to your family attorney about these issues.

Reading Materials

If you get locked up, you will end up reading a lot. Go to a used book store and buy one soft-cover book for each week you will be locked up for. Then, make an alphabetical list of the books. Make copies. Have a copy of the list mailed to you once you are in prison. Alternatively, make a list of books you want people to buy you. Plan on reading at least one book per week.

CHAPTER 9:

Sentencing Guidelines

Introduction

Because an allegation of a federal crime has been filed against you, you need to understand what you are potentially facing. Before you decide to take a plea bargain or take your case to trial, you should know a little about how defendants are sentenced in federal court. Unless otherwise indicated, this chapter is derived from Title 18 U.S. Code § 3553: The Sentencing Guidelines.

Refer to the Sentencing Table below to determine your possible sentence duration. Understanding this table can be a daunting task. Don't worry. The rest of this chapter is dedicated to help you understand the Sentencing Table.

Sentencing Table

Effective Nov. 2, 2001 (In Months of Imprisonment)

Key:

A   Probation available

B   Probation with conditions of confinement or home detention available

C   No probation available

D   No probation available

Zone	Offense Level	Criminal History Category (Criminal History Points)					
		I (0 or 1)	II (2 or 3)	III (4,5,6)	IV (7,8,9)	V (10,11,12)	VI (13 +)
A	1	0–6	0–6	0–6	0–6	0–6	0–6
	2	0–6	0–6	0–6	0–6	0–6	1–7
	3	0–6	0–6	0–6	0–6	2–8	3–9
	4	0–6	0–6	0–6	2–8	4–10	6–12
	5	0–6	0–6	1–7	4–10	6–12	9–15
	6	0–6	1–7	2–8	6–12	9–15	12–18
	7	0–6	2–8	4–10	8–14	12–18	15–21
	8	0–6	4–10	6–12	10–16	15–21	18–24
B	9	4–10	6–12	8–14	12–18	18–24	21–27
	10	6–12	8–14	10–16	15–21	21–27	24–30
C	11	8–14	10–16	12–18	18–24	24–30	27–33
	12	10–16	12–18	15–21	21–27	27–33	30–37
D	13	12–18	15–21	18–24	24–30	30–37	33–41
	14	15–21	18–24	21–27	27–33	33–41	37–46
	15	18–24	21–27	24–30	30–37	37–46	41–51
	16	21–27	24–30	27–33	33–41	41–51	46–57
	17	24–30	27–33	30–37	37–46	46–57	51–63
	18	27–33	30–37	33–41	41–51	51–63	57–71
	19	30–37	33–41	37–46	46–57	57–71	63–78
	20	33–41	37–46	41–51	51–63	63–78	70–87
	21	37–46	41–51	46–57	57–71	70–87	77–96
	22	41–51	46–57	51–63	63–78	77–96	84–105
	23	46–57	51–63	57–71	70–87	84–105	92–115
	24	51–63	57–51	63–78	77–96	92–115	100–125
	25	57–71	63–78	70–87	84–105	100–125	110–137
	26	63–78	70–87	78–97	92–115	110–137	120–150
	27	70–87	78–97	87–108	100–125	120–150	130–162
	28	78–97	87–108	97–121	110–137	130–162	142–175
	29	87–108	97–121	108–135	121–151	140–175	151–188
	30	97–121	108–135	121–151	135–168	151–188	168–210
	31	108–135	121–151	135–168	151–188	168–210	188–235
	32	121–151	135–168	151–188	168–210	188–235	210–262
	33	135–168	151–188	168–210	188–235	210–262	235–293
	34	151–188	168–210	188–235	210–262	235–293	262–327

Zone	Offense Level	Criminal History Category (Criminal History Points)					
		I (0 or 1)	II (2 or 3)	III (4,5,6)	IV (7,8,9)	V (10,11,12)	VI (13 +)
D	35	168–210	188–235	210–262	235–293	262–327	292–365
	36	188–235	210–262	235–293	262–327	292–365	324–405
	37	210–262	235–293	262–327	292–365	324–405	360–life
	38	235–293	262–327	292–365	324–405	360–life	360–life
	39	262–327	292–365	324–405	360–life	360–life	360–life
	40	292–365	324–405	360–life	360–life	360–life	360–life
	41	324–405	360–life	360–life	360–life	360–life	360–life
	42	360–life	360–life	360–life	360–life	360–life	360–life
	43	life	life	life	life	life	life

The vertical axis of the Sentencing Table is formed by the Offense Level (1-43). The horizontal axis of the Sentencing Table is formed by the Criminal History Category. (Definitions of your Offense Level and Criminal History Category are discussed later in this chapter.) The federal guidelines will stipulate a range in months in which you can be incarcerated. This range is determined by finding the intersection of the Offense Level and Criminal History Category. For example, the sentencing guideline range for a defendant with an Offense Level of 12 and a Criminal History Category of II is 12-18 months of imprisonment.

There are a few instances in which a total Offense Level is less than one or more than 43. A total Offense Level of less that 1 is to be handled as an Offense Level of 1. An Offense Level of more than 43 is to be handled as an Offense Level of 43.

Offense Levels

There are federal sentencing guidelines for different Offense Levels of prison sentences. The higher the Offense Level, the more time you are sentenced to serve in prison. Judges have to sentence you within the guidelines, unless they have a special reason to go above or below the guidelines. For example, a drug dealer can receive a sentence that is above the original guidelines if a gun was present during the drug transaction. If you have such a reason in your case, your attorney will inform you. Each crime or count of a criminal indictment is assigned an Offense Level. Certain features of the alleged criminal activity may add additional Offense Levels to the sentence. These are called enhancements. For instance, you may be indicted on a fraud case and then get an enhancement because of the huge amount of money that was involved.

Ask your attorney for a copy of the indictment and a list of Offense Levels for each alleged crime and enhancements. Ask your attorney if any past or current criminal allegations will increase the length of your sentence.

Criminal History Category

You must determine your Criminal History Category (Criminal History Points). The Criminal History Category is the level of prior significant crimes you have committed in your life. The more significant the crimes you have committed, the higher your Criminal History Category. Certain criminal convictions will count towards the Criminal History Category while others will not. For example, minor traffic violations don't count. If you have a past Criminal History, ask your attorney how that affects your Criminal History Category. If you have no past criminal convictions, you will have a Criminal History level of I.

The Criminal History Category in the Sentencing Table is determined by calculating the total points from items a through f below. (See Title 18 U.S. Code § 3353 § 4A1.1).

- a. Add **3 points** for each prior sentence of imprisonment exceeding one year and one month.

- b. Add **2 points** for each prior sentence of imprisonment of at least 60 days not counted in (a).

- c. Add **1 point** for each prior sentence not counted in (a) or (b), up to a total of **4 points** for this item.

- d. Add **2 points** if the defendant committed the instant offense (current offense) while under any criminal justice sentence, including probation, parole, supervised release, imprisonment, work release, or escape status.

- e. Add **2 points** if the defendant committed the instant offense less than two years after the release from prison on a sentence counted under (a) or (b) or while in imprisonment or escape status on such a sentence. If **2 points** are added for item (d), add only **1 point** for this item.

- f. Add **1 point** for each prior sentence resulting from a conviction of a crime of violence that did not receive any points under (a), (b), or (c) above because such a sentence was counted as a single sentence, up to a total of **3 points** for this item.

FOOD FOR THOUGHT

"Life is not dated merely by years. Events are sometimes the best calendars."

British Prime Minister Benjamin Disraeli

Sentences Counted and Excluded

Sentences for all felony offenses are counted. Sentences for misdemeanor and petty offenses are counted, except the following as defined by Title 18 U.S. Code § 3353 § 4A1.1:

1. *Sentences for the following prior offenses or similar offenses and offenses similar to them, by whatever name they are known, are counted only if:
   a. The sentence was a term of more than one year or a term of imprisonment of at least thirty days, or
   b. The prior offense was similar to an instant offense:
      Careless or reckless driving
      Contempt of court
      Disorderly conduct or disturbing the peace
      Driving without a license or with a revoked or suspended license
      False information to a police officer
      Gambling
      Hindering or failure to obey a police officer
      Insufficient funds check
      Leaving the scene of an accident
      Non-support
      Prostitution
      Resisting Arrest
      Trespassing

2. Sentences for the following prior offenses (or similar offenses) and offenses similar to them, by whatever name they are known, are never counted:
      Fish and game violations
      Hitchhiking
      Juvenile status offenses and truancy
      Local ordinance violations (except those that are also violations under state criminal law)
      Loitering
      Minor traffic infractions (e.g. speeding)
      Public intoxication
      Vagrancy

*Prior felony conviction means a prior adult federal or state conviction for an offense punishable by death or imprisonment for a term exceeding one year, regardless of whether such offense is specifically designated as a felony and regardless of the actual sentenced imposed." (Title 18 U.S. Code § 3353 § 4A1.1)

Career Offender

A defendant is a career offender if the defendant meets each of the following criteria:

1. The defendant was at least eighteen years old at the time the defendant committed the crime;

2. The current offense is a felony that is a violent crime or a controlled substance offense;

3. The defendant has at least two felony convictions of either a crime of violence or a controlled substance offense.

Probation

- You can get probation only if your sentence is in Zone A of the Sentencing Table.

- You can get probation plus home detention or community confinement if your sentence is in Zone B of the Sentencing Table.

- You cannot get probation if the conviction is a Class A or B felony or the offense expressly excludes probation as a sentence.

- The length of probation must be one day to three years if the Offense Level is 5 or less. It must be one to five years if the Offense Level is 6 or more.

FOOD FOR THOUGHT

"There's always room at the top."

Daniel Webster

Upward and Downward Departures

Most federal crimes carry a minimum mandatory sentence established by federal statutory sentencing guidelines. For instance, carrying a weapon while on supervised release after serving a federal prison sentence carries a minimum mandatory sentence of five years. One advantage to signing a plea bargain is you may receive a sentence that is below the statutory sentencing guidelines. The bad news is you can actually get sentenced above the guidelines in some circumstances. A "downward departure" refers to a sentence below the statutory sentencing guidelines while an "upward departure" refers to a sentence above the statutory guidelines.

"Upward Departures from Category VI: In a case in which the court determines that the extent and nature of the defendant's Criminal History, taken together, are sufficient to warrant an upward departure from Criminal History Category VI, the court should structure the departure by moving incrementally down the Sentencing Table to the next higher Offense Level in Criminal History Category VI until it finds a guideline range appropriate to the case." (Title 18 U.S. Code § 3353 § 4A1.1)

"Downward Departures: If reliable information indicates that the defendant's Criminal History Category substantially over-represents the seriousness of the defendant's Criminal History or the likelihood that the defendant will commit other crimes, a downward departure may be warranted."

Fines

You have to pay a fine unless you can prove that you are unable to pay and are not likely to be able to pay a fine in the future.

The fines listed below are generally accurate. However, in some instances, your alleged crime will have a different specific fine because the criminal statutes can specifically call for a different fine. You may also have a fine for each day of a violation of a criminal statute.

In determining your fine, the judge will consider:

1. "The need for the combined sentence to reflect the seriousness of the offense (including the harm or loss to the victim and the gain to the defendant), to promise respect for the law, to provide just punishment and to afford deterrence." (Title 18 U.S. Code § 3353 § 4A1.1)

2. Any evidence of your ability to pay the fine "in light of your earning capacity and financial resources."

3. The burden that the fine places on you and your dependants.

4. Any restitution or separation you have made or are obligated to make.

5. Any other consequences of your conviction, including civil lawsuits.

6. Whether you were fined for a similar offense during the sentencing hearing.

7. The expected costs of probation, imprisonment, and supervised release.

8. Any other relevant issues such as harm to third parties, interest, etc.

Ofense Level	A Minimum Fine	B Maximum Fine
1–3	$ 100	$ 5,000
4–5	$ 250	$ 5,000
6–7	$ 500	$ 5,000
8–9	$ 1,000	$ 10,000
10–11	$ 2,000	$ 20,000
12–13	$ 3,000	$ 30,000
14–15	$ 4,000	$ 40,000
16–17	$ 5,000	$ 50,000
18–19	$ 6,000	$ 60,000
20–22	$ 7,500	$ 75,000
23–25	$10,000	$100,000
26–28	$12,500	$125,000
29–31	$15,000	$150,000
32–34	$17,500	$175,000
35–37	$20,000	$200,000
38 and above	$25,000	$250,000

Paying Your Fines

Payments can be required in a lump sum or installments.

If you knowingly fail to pay a delinquent fine and you have the ability to make payments, you shall be resentenced under Title 18 U.S. Code § 3614.

FOOD FOR THOUGHT

"Intellectual growth should commence at birth and cease only at death."

Albert Einstein

Concurrent or Consecutive Sentence

If you are indicted on multiple counts of alleged criminal activity, ask your attorney if you will be sentenced consecutively or concurrently on each count. In consecutive prison sentences, you have to finish serving time in prison on one sentence before you can begin serving time on the next sentence. Concurrent prison sentences allow you to serve several prison sentences at the same time. For example, let's say your judge sentences you to three five-year sentences to run concurrently. Since you will serve all three sentences at the same time, the maximum time you will spend in prison is five years. If your judge sentences you to three five-year sentences to run consecutively, the maximum time you will spend in prison is fifteen years (5 years + 5 years + 5 years). You want concurrent sentencing. Federal sentencing guidelines will dictate whether your sentences will run concurrently or consecutively.

Tip: If you take a plea bargain, try to negotiate dropping a charge that will run consecutively in exchange for signing the plea bargain.

For More Information

For more information, see Title 18 U.S. Code § 3553.

CHAPTER 10:

Preparing For Trial

Introduction

This chapter on preparing for trial does not substitute for legal advice nor is it all-inclusive. It includes additional information that was noted during the trial process.

Scheduling Trial

You have a right to a speedy trial, and that right is guaranteed by the U.S. Constitution. The right applies to both state and federal prosecutions.

In federal cases, the term "speedy" has been precisely defined in Title 18 U.S. Code §§ 3161-3175 – "The Speedy Trial Act" – which establishes two separate time limits which are germane to all criminal cases. First, the time between arrest and indictment cannot exceed 30 days. Second, the time between indictment and the commencement of trial cannot exceed 70 days. These deadlines can be extended in limited cases. For example, a key witness cannot be found. Barring such an extension, failure to comply with the specified time limits *requires* the judge to dismiss the case. Whether the dismissal is with or without prejudice is up to the judge.

In state cases, the term "speedy" means exactly 180 days if it is being used in connection with your demand for a speedy trial in order to resolve a detainer under the "Interstate Agreement on Detainers Act."

In all other circumstances, there are no hard-and-fast rules. Rather, pertinent case-law on the subject suggests that most delays of less than five months are acceptable, while delays of more than eight months are not. In between those limits, cases go both ways.

The purpose of having a right to a speedy trial is to force the government to make a decision on whether or not they will prosecute you. They cannot lock you up indefinitely while they research your case for several years (in theory). You have the right to waive a speedy trial while both sides investigate the case more thoroughly. Should you choose to waive your right to a speedy trial, your attorney will file a motion on your behalf.

The judge will issue a trial date for your case. Your attorneys and the prosecutors may decide to schedule the trial for a later date. To do this, they will file a motion for continuance, which postpones the trial. How many motions for continuance the judge will allow depends on the judge and the complexity of your case. Minor tax evasion cases may go to trial in six months while murder trials are often delayed for at least a year. One serious case took five years to go to trial because of a complex investigation and obstruction of justice issues related to witness tampering.

Mark your calendar with the dates of the trial, any meeting dates with your attorneys, and any hearing and due dates for plea bargains and motions.

Discovery

Discovery is another word for investigation. Each side attempts to discover information that they hope will be helpful to their case.

During the discovery process, you have certain obligations:

1. You must be truthful with your attorneys. They cannot help you if you lie to them.

2. Tell your attorneys in detail what happened on the date of the alleged crime(s); where you were, what happened, who was there, etc.

3. To avoid obstruction of justice:

   a. You cannot contact the alleged victim(s) in any way other than through your attorney for specific reasons.

   b. You cannot lie to law enforcement, the prosecutors, experts, your judge, or jury.

   c. You cannot threaten or harm any alleged victims, witnesses, law enforcement, the jury members, the prosecutors, or your judge.

   d. You cannot bribe anyone to falsify evidence or change their testimony.

   e. You cannot falsify or alter any evidence.

   f. You cannot destroy evidence.

g. You cannot hide any evidence.

h. You cannot impede the investigation.

i. You cannot encourage or ask anyone to do any of the above.

If you commit any of the above, you can get separate legal charges and may face additional prison time and fines. Also, the jury will know about it and it will hurt your case.

4. If you gather evidence for your case, your attorney must get the evidence from primary sources, if possible. That is, it must come directly from independently verifiable sources, not you. For instance, if you have records on where you bought your car, your attorney will want to get copies from the previous owner. That way, your evidence is untainted by you. In the same way, your witnesses can only speak of things they saw, heard, or experienced. They cannot report information to a jury that is second or third hand. Rumors are not allowed.

5. Not all evidence which is "discovered" during pretrial proceedings is admissible at the actual trial. In fact, *much* of it is not admissible.

You cannot simply steal information from other people or businesses to help your case. It must be obtained by means of issuing a subpoena. A subpoena is a legal order from your judge that compels a person or business to give the information needed to fight your case. Anyone who fails to obey a subpoena can be found to be in contempt of court and can be fined or locked up. People may try to fight subpoenas by hiring an attorney to state that the subpoena does not apply to them. Federal judges have the power to issue subpoenas which apply to *any* state or U.S. territory, not just their federal district. Some civil attorneys often don't understand this. As a last resort, federal judges have the power to have non-compliant people handcuffed by U.S. Marshals and physically transported across the country to disclose the information requested in the subpoena.

FOOD FOR THOUGHT

"Be strong and follow your own convictions. You can't assume there is a lot of time to do what you like."

Marc Bolan

Brady Motion

If you are going to trial, your attorney needs to file a Brady motion. A Brady motion is a legal tool in which the judge orders the prosecutor to turn over any and all evidence

– good or bad – to the defense lawyers. In a case known as *Brady v. Maryland, (1963)* U.S. Supreme Court justices declared that prosecutors and investigators have to be upstanding enough to disclose any and all evidence they found that might help you in your defense. Unfortunately, prosecutors won't always do this. For example, in one case a man was set up for a crime. Investigators learned before his trial that the alleged victim confessed to setting up the defendant so he could file a large lawsuit after the criminal trial. The prosecutors and investigators never notified the defendant or his defense lawyers. The defense lawyers filed a Brady motion before the trial. The defendant went to trial and was convicted. Because the defense lawyers filed a Brady motion before the trial, and the prosecutors knowingly withheld evidence of the confession, the conviction was thrown out. You must convince your attorney to file a Brady motion.

Some prosecutors purposely withhold some of their best evidence until a week or so before trial. They will sometimes tell the judge in a hearing that all of the evidence was turned over to the defense team. They will "forget" to hand over the critical information. A Brady motion, in theory, helps reduce this withholding of critical evidence until the last minute.

Finally, almost all federal courts hold that a prosecutor's failure to disclose significant exculpatory evidence prior to a guilty plea violates the principal of the *Brady* case. This Brady violation nullifies the plea agreement, allowing the defendant to withdraw the plea agreement if he wishes. Unfortunately, courts in the 5th Circuit Federal Court of Appeals and some other circuits do not follow this rule.

The Ultimate Research Method

All attorneys spend some time researching who each witness is in a trial. All attorneys spend some time researching the characteristics of evidence used in a trial. The reality is, your attorney's time is limited. They will often never learn of important weaknesses in a prosecutor's case because they didn't do enough research.

FOOD FOR THOUGHT

"Life is a struggle – fight it. Life is a goal – achieve it. Life is a puzzle – solve it. Life is eternal – believe it."

Author Unknown

If you have the money, you should utilize the ultimate research method. The ultimate research method is an extremely thorough investigative technique which seeks to discover every detail that will help your side of the case. The ultimate research method is taking investigative research to a whole new level. The idea is to out-research the prosecutors. Instead of hiring one private investigator, you hire eight or ten. The investigators thoroughly investigate every witness for the prosecution. If a cop is expected to take the witness stand, you investigate him or her. You find out he had an affair after promising his marital faithfulness. Then, your defense team attacks his credibility on the witness stand: "If you lied to your spouse in front of your family, friends, and God, why should we trust what you say now to the jury?" If your investigator finds out the cop lied in a previous trial, your lawyer should bring this up in your trial. If the expert against you cheated on a test in high school, your lawyer should bring it up in trial to discredit the expert.

Prosecutors will use this type of information against your experts and witnesses; you can use it against their witnesses. For example, Defense Lawyer Johnny Cochran found out police investigator Mark Furman used a racial slur while investigating O.J. Simpson. Cochran confronted Furman with the racial slur on the witness stand. Rumor has it that Cochran won all or almost all of his trials because he implemented the ultimate research method.

Private Investigators

Your private investigator needs to be professional. Most states require private investigators to be licensed. You should get one that is methodical. A methodical private investigator follows up each lead in the case and creates a detailed written record. You should ask for periodic productivity reports because private investigators will often charge a large sum of money only to turn up few real answers. Furthermore, your private investigator needs to start working quietly on the outside of an investigation. They should talk to people out of town or on the periphery of a case first. Then, they can move on to the main suspects.

FOOD FOR THOUGHT

"My attitude is not one of pitfalls. My attitude is one of challenges."

Dr. Jonas Salk

Motions to Suppress Evidence

You may wish to keep evidence out of a trial. If so, you and your attorney should consider a motion to suppress evidence. Ask for a copy of your search warrants. Consider the following issues for a motion to suppress evidence:

1. Was there enough data known by law enforcement to warrant a search warrant? The evidence about possible criminal activity should be specific, not vague. For example, one law enforcement agency wanted to catch people making meth. So they went to a private electric company and requested the utility bills of all the residents in their jurisdiction. When they found a house with a high utility bill, they obtained a search warrant. A motion to suppress this evidence could be filed because the cops cannot get a search warrant based on a hunch.

2. Is the search warrant for the correct location? This is not about a typo in the document. Normally, law enforcement describes the location to be searched in great detail so even a typo won't matter. However, suppose you are charged with purchasing stolen automobiles from Mexico and shipping them into the U.S. You were accused of using a credit card to make the purchases. Your fourth-story apartment was searched for the stolen automobiles. During the search, they found receipts of the transactions. As you are preparing for trial, you realize the search warrant only mentions trying to find automobiles in your fourth-story apartment, not receipts. It would be incredibly unlikely to assume someone had stored stolen vehicles in a typical fourth-floor apartment. A motion to suppress evidence from your apartment should be filed.

3. Is the search warrant about someone else or you? Search warrants can be hundreds of pages long, encompassing several years of investigations and thousands of suspects. The issue is not about the huge investigation or the thousands of suspects. The issue is about what actually ties you to the investigation. If the actual link to you is trivial, you should ask for a motion to suppress evidence. For example, 1,000 truck drivers are being investigated for transporting marijuana into the state of New York. The search warrant only mentions that you drive a truck in New York. The warrant is too vague and should be challenged.

4. Is your confession or plea bargain coerced? Any confession or plea bargain should not be coerced other than with jail time and a fine. If you were physically threatened, you should file a motion to suppress evidence. If you signed a plea bargain without a lawyer present who thoroughly evaluated the plea bargain, the plea bargain should be thrown out. For example, the U.S. Supreme Court has ruled that any confession that occurs after you have been interrogated for more than five hours without a break is unconstitutional. In this case, a motion to suppress the evidence of the confession should be filed.

FOOD FOR THOUGHT

"The dog that trots about finds a bone."

Israeli Prime Minister Gold Meir

Miranda Rights

A U.S. Supreme Court case known as U.S. v. *Miranda (1966)* forced law enforcement to read the following statement to you: "You have the right to remain silent. Anything you say can and will be used against you. You have the right to an attorney. If you cannot afford one, one will be appointed for you." If you made a confession or damaging statement without those rights being read to you, you may be able to file a motion to suppress the statements. (Note: The "U.S. Patriot Act" of 2001 allows federal agents to interview you without reading you your rights if your case involves national security. The definition of national security varies.)

Witnesses

You and your attorney will have to select witnesses for your defense. Such witnesses should have a good reputation so that they appear to be believable by the jury. Recall that while you are looking for flaws in the prosecution's witnesses, the prosecutors are looking for flaws in your witnesses. You need to be careful when considering who you would like to be called as a witness. Sometimes you have no other choice.

Almost all witnesses become nervous at the prospect of testifying in court. Even those who are not nervous to begin with, often become nervous under the stress of a skillfully conducted cross-examination. Nothing has the potential to ruin the credibility of a witness – or the cogency and utility of his or her testimony – more than excessive nervousness. It is an issue which should be dealt with long before trial. Many lawyers recommend that their clients use an anti-anxiety drug to help attenuate the physiological manifestations of stress and anxiety before testifying. Such drugs are generally safe, predictable, and effective for the purpose suggested. You should take a test dose several days before your trial starts to assess any potential adverse affects.

Many people are like a Rubik's cube: They have different sides. When they are stressed out, they say true or false things they may not otherwise say. They have good days and bad days. So the defense team wants to show your green side while the prosecutors want to show your red side. Realize this potential in each witness. Will they help your lawyer paint your green side or will they help the prosecutors paint your red side? Recognize that you can subpoena a lot of witnesses to appear at your trial, but only a few of them may actually take the witness stand. You should subpoena people you might need just in case the prosecutors make negative comments about you.

Juries typically remember the last witness for each side of the case. Keep in mind who that should be: The primary witness? Your expert witness? You?

FOOD FOR THOUGHT

"If you want to be happy, set a goal that commends your thoughts, liberates your energy and inspires your hopes."

Andrew Carnegie

Experts

1. Your expert witness needs to be very competent, experienced, and reputable in his field.

2. Make sure they are qualified/licensed to testify as an expert in federal court. Many people are experts in the private world, but not in federal court.

3. "Vet" your expert. Investigate everything your expert has done professionally or privately. Be prepared. The prosecutors will attack your expert using any information they have to use against your witness.

4. Many people on the jury will not believe a word that your expert says simply because you paid your expert to appear in court. One ideal tactic is to get an unpaid expert to appear in court on your behalf. This cannot be your relative or your best friend, as the prosecutors will point that out to the jury. Since the government's expert is paid by the government, your volunteer expert may have more respect from the jury.

5. Realize that many government experts have a severe limitation: Many of them are trained to prosecute, not to provide independent thought on tough, technical questions. They answer questions from the prosecutor in a scripted, rote manner. Your defense lawyer and defense experts should ask technical questions the government's expert cannot answer. This is the government's Achilles' heel.

6. Experts have powers:

    a. They are experts and are respected as such.

    b. They are usually exempt from The Rule of Sequestration that bars witnesses from hearing other witnesses' testimony. The Rule prevents witnesses from tainting each other's testimony.

c. They can hear all witnesses testify and summarize their case.

d. Since they can hear all witnesses testify, they can make specific statements to refute what other witnesses say.

e. They can take the witness stand several times to clarify and further build their case.

Mock Jury

If you can afford it, hire a research law firm and a mock jury. The law firm will hire a group of people to come listen to a miniature version of your trial. The people they hire will be similar to people on your jury. It will cost about $100 per day per person to sit and hear your case. Food must also be provided. The people will be split up into two different jury rooms which are equipped with video recorders. Surveys will be given to each member of the jury during each step of the mock trial. The research law firm and your defense lawyers will review the results and determine which parts of your case are the toughest and how juries think. This helps your lawyers develop a strategy. It costs anywhere from $15,000 to $50,000, depending on how many people you want there and how many days it lasts.

Shadow Jury

Additionally, you can hire a shadow jury. This is a group of people that sit in the court room during your actual trial. They give their opinions on each piece of evidence and each witness. They privately ask questions after the day's events. These opinions and questions are relayed back to your attorney, who may use the information to help your case.

FOOD FOR THOUGHT

"Always desire to learn something useful."

Sophocles

Jury Selection Form

There are law firms that help specialize in jury selection. If you have the financial ability, hire a law firm to help create the jury selection form. The members of such a firm study jurors and how and why they vote. They will know which ten questions are the most important to ask on a jury selection form. It costs $1,000 - $2,000 for a simple form. Jury selection forms can be longer. However, most judges will not allow long jury selection forms because they slow down the jury selection process.

A jury selection specialist is also very helpful, if you can afford one. The specialist is a lawyer or team of lawyers that will sit in the court room with your lawyers during jury selection. They will literally draw a map of the potential jurors. They will read all the jury selection forms and rank them from very helpful to very dangerous to your case. They cost anywhere from a few thousand dollars for a one day jury selection to $30,000 for a jury selection process that takes thirty days.

Getting Organized for Trial

Just like any other profession, some trial lawyers are organized while others are not. This is your life. You need to be prepared. While some of the advice in this chapter is expensive to carry out, this advice is cheap.

1. Make a timeline of events. Use a word processor so you can edit it.

2. Make two lists of evidence: one for the defense team's evidence and one for the prosecution's evidence.

3. Make two witness lists: One for the defense and one for the prosecution.

4. Make a folder for each witness.

   a. Make a list of questions you want your defense lawyer to ask the witness.

   b. Make a list of questions you expect the prosecutor to ask. How should your attorney handle these questions?

   c. Make a list of ways to discredit each of the prosecutors' witnesses. The prosecutors will make a series of assumptions about what each witness can testify about. You need your attorney to attack each of these assumptions. (See "Chapter 13: Trial-The Government's Case – Government Witnesses" for more details.)

   d. Make a list of the evidence that should be shown to this witness.

5. Make to-do lists for yourself and your attorney. Review them daily

The Trial Triad

There are three important sets of issues that juries consider:

1. The evidence

2. The law

3. The melodrama

The evidence may include documents, photos, videos, eye witnesses, DNA, or fingerprints. It may include testimony from experts.

The law will be discussed in terms of what it actually requires to achieve a conviction. The prosecutors will describe how the evidence shows the defendant committed the crime. Defense lawyers will argue the witnesses and the evidence show that the crime could not have been committed by the defendant.

One would think that the law and the evidence would be the most important issues a juror pays attention to. Trial lawyers maintain that the melodrama in the courtroom is far more influential to the jury. The melodrama includes everything from the way you react to a question to how your attorney reacts to an answer. It's when they yell or point a finger at you or the evidence. Prosecutors sometimes re-enact a crime in front of the jury to increase the dramatic effect.

Opening and Closing Statements

You and your attorney need to work on opening and closing statements. Consider various themes and strategies that you may introduce in voir dire (jury selection), discuss in the opening statements, pull out evidence to be used in the trial, and then discuss again in the closing arguments.

FOOD FOR THOUGHT

"A good idea will keep you awake during the morning, but a great idea will keep you awake during the night."

Marilyn vos Savant

Rule 29 Motions

You and your attorney should discuss Rule 29 motions. A Rule 29 motion is a legal motion that asks the judge to decide if the prosecution produced enough evidence to satisfy each element of each count in the case. Rule 29 motions are based on a federal law which states that you cannot be convicted of a federal crime unless the government can satisfactorily prove that all of the elements of a crime were committed by you. For instance, they try to prosecute you for stealing $50,000 or more in a fraud case. They can show that you stole the money. They can show when, where, and how. But, the actual records show that the amount was $25,000, not $50,000. If the federal statute the prosecutors use in the indictment is for $50,000 or more, your attorney should ask for a Rule 29 motion after the prosecution rests its case. In other words, your attorney should ask the judge to rule that the specific charge against you should be dropped because the prosecutors failed to prove one or more of the required elements in your case. If you lose the trial, this is also helpful for your appeal. Your appellate attorney can base a future appeal on the fact that you believe the judge ruled incorrectly on the Rule 29 issue.

Change of Venue

If your case was heavily publicized in your geographic area, you should consider having your case tried in a different city. This is referred to as a change of venue. Your attorney should file a motion to request a change of venue. This is only fair as your jurors should not have a prejudiced opinion of you.

Double Jeopardy Charges

You and your attorneys should read through your indictments carefully to see if the prosecutors made any indictments based on the same crime on the same date. For instance, let's say you are being prosecuted for smuggling marijuana from Mexico on January 1, 2009. The prosecutors use this specific shipment on this specific date in both counts two and five. After the prosecutor rests the government's case, your attorney should ask the judge to throw out one of the charges. Another example is if the prosecutor charges you with attempted burglary and burglary at the same house on the same date. You can only be convicted of one crime, not both.

FOOD FOR THOUGHT

"In great straits and when hope it small, the boldest counsels are the safest."

Titus Livius

Innocence by Reputation Defense

If this is the first crime you have been accused of and you have a good reputation in the community, you should discuss with your lawyer the innocence by reputation defense. This type of defense is used when the jury's decision of guilt versus innocence is a very close and debatable call. The jury can essentially rely upon your good reputation to vote in favor of your innocence. What you do in your career and private life may influence whether you can use this defense. If you are a priest, school teacher, nurse, or a police officer, you can try to use it. If you are a used car salesperson, loan shark, repossession specialist, or you play an evil villain in mud wrestling in your spare time while millions of fans watch you, you may not do so well with the innocence by reputation defense. In such a defense, you call the mayor, city council members, deans of schools, CEO's, etc. to testify that they know you very well and don't believe you can commit the crime you are charged with. Your witness's vouching for you can influence the jury to vote in your favor.

CHAPTER 11:

Plea Bargains

Background

To sign a plea bargain or not to sign a plea bargain…that is the question. A plea bargain is a legal agreement in which you agree to plead guilty on one or more of the counts against you. After you are indicted, you may or may not be offered a plea bargain. In an ideal world, your plea bargain will get you a real bargain on your sentence. In an ideal world, your plea agreement will be a well-thought out agreement between you, your prosecutor, and your judge. Unfortunately, many plea bargains are not a bargain at all. Many plea agreements are not agreements by all of the interested parties.

No one can tell you if you should take a plea bargain or not. However, there are hundreds of dissatisfied inmates who took a plea bargain and wished they hadn't or wish they would have negotiated harder and smarter. This chapter is devoted to the issues many defendants wish they would have known before they signed a plea bargain. You need to talk to your attorney about whether a plea bargain is right for you or not. If you sign a plea bargain, use this chapter to help make sure it is done to your advantage.

Your Sentence

Before you can begin to evaluate your plea bargain proposal, make sure you understand the possible sentence you are facing. Make sure you have read "Chapter 9: Sentencing Guidelines." Make sure your attorney has told you what Offense Level you are facing. You need to understand which enhancements will be applied to your case. Get an idea if your attorney thinks you will get sentenced above, within, or below the sentencing guidelines range. Most federal crimes carry a minimum mandatory sentence established by federal guidelines. For instance, possessing a weapon while on supervised release after serving a prison sentence carries a minimum mandatory sentence of five years of imprisonment. One advantage to a plea bargain is you may receive a sentence that is below the sentencing guidelines.

Can I get a reduction in my sentencing Offense Levels by signing a plea bargain?

Yes. You may get a two to three Offense Level reduction on your sentence by accepting responsibility. Make sure this is included in your plea bargain. (You receive a three Offense Level reduction by accepting responsibility very early on, such as within the first month or two after you are indicted. If you wait several months and cause the prosecutor to spend a great deal of time and effort preparing for your trial, you will only receive a two Offense Level reduction.)

Is the plea bargain really a bargain?

Many plea bargains are not that good because defendants are pressured into signing them before they know if the plea bargain is a real bargain or not. Prosecutors may be lazy. They don't want to go to trial. They may scare you by telling you they will give you the maximum sentence.

Now that you know what the sentencing guidelines are and how to read the Sentencing Table, you need to see if the sentence you are agreeing to in a plea bargain is a real bargain. You need to ask your attorney, "How long is the average federal defendant with my Criminal History Category and Offense Level sentenced to for this alleged crime?"

Most plea bargains only give the defendants about 20% off of their sentences. Is 20% off your sentence really worth giving up your right to file a meaningful appeal? Negotiate a plea bargain to get 40% to 50% off your sentence, not 10% or 20%. If you have multiple counts against you, see if you can negotiate to get one or two counts dropped if you take a plea bargain.

Defense attorneys may tell you to "always take a plea bargain because you will get a longer sentence if you go through trial and get convicted." That's not always true, especially if you have a good attorney. Defendants with good attorneys can get convicted at trial but still get sentenced below the national average sentence for their crimes.

Figure out if your attorney is going to fight hard and intelligently for you or is he going to just sit quietly and let the prosecutor run the show. In one case, a U.S. Public Defender was notoriously lazy and actually got his client a plea "bargain" with a sentence for *more* than the national average sentence. The U.S. Public Defender said almost nothing during the sentencing hearing. It was no bargain.

FOOD FOR THOUGHT

"Never be bullied into silence. Never allow yourself to be made a victim. Accept no one's definition of your life, but define yourself."

Harvey Firestone

Is the plea agreement/bargain really a legally binding agreement? Is the plea agreement an agreement with the prosecutor, the judge, or both?

One would think a plea agreement would be legally binding between you, your prosecutor, and your judge. It's not. The agreement is between you and your prosecutor. The judge can sentence you to more time than is stated in your plea agreement. Most, but not all, judges stick to the plea agreement range. Furthermore, your prosecutor can ask for a longer prison sentence than what you agreed to. For instance, a defendant agreed to a 25 year prison sentence in a plea agreement. During his sentencing hearing, his prosecutor asked for a life time prison sentence. The judge granted it. So much for an agreement.

How many cases has your defense attorney represented in plea bargains in federal court for the crime you are accused of? How many plea bargains has your defense attorney worked out with your prosecutor? How many plea bargains has your defense attorney done that resulted in a defendant being sentenced by your judge? Did your prosecutor abide by the agreements? Did your judge adhere to the plea agreement on the sentence or issue a longer sentence?

Before signing a plea agreement, ask your defense attorney each of the above questions. You should gauge their response. If they say that they have done a couple dozen plea agreements with your prosecutor and your judge, and the plea agreements were followed every time, you may want to consider a hard-fought, intelligent plea engagement. If your defense attorney says your prosecutor and/or your judge have a history of failing to abide by plea agreements, you may want to go to trial. If your attorney does not have enough experience with your prosecutor or judge, you need to consider a consultation with another criminal defense attorney or ask your family and friends if they know someone prosecuted by your prosecutor or sentenced by your judge.

Are you truly guilty of the crimes you are accused of? What does the federal law say about pleading guilty to accept a plea bargain?

The law says you are not supposed to plead guilty if you did not commit the crime. It's illegal. You can be convicted of perjury and/or obstruction of justice for lying to the judge. Most defendants will be told the U.S. DOJ has a 90-99% conviction rate at trials. Because of this, I have seen many defendants plead guilty just out of fear of a long sentence.

What are the elements of a federal crime and how may they affect a decision to sign a plea bargain?

The federal criminal laws list a series of elements that are legally necessary to be convicted of a specific crime. Federal law states you must have *each* and *every* element to be convicted of the alleged federal crime. If you don't have one element, then you cannot be convicted of the alleged federal crime. Before you plead guilty, you need to know what each element is for each alleged crime you are accused of. You need to know what the evidence is for each element of the alleged crime. For instance, let's say you are accused of a crime with elements A, B, and C. If the U.S. DOJ can prove A and B but not C, in theory, you cannot be convicted of the crime. (If you are convicted, you can appeal it.)

FOOD FOR THOUGHT

"One of the greatest pains to human nature is the pain of a new idea."

Walter Bagehot

Does your alleged crime require a component of intent or knowledge as a mandatory element of the crime? If so, what is the U.S. DOJ's evidence of knowledge and intent?

Suppose you are accused of knowingly possessing grapefruit from Cuba. Even if they arrested you with grapefruit hidden under your truck in a secret compartment, what is the U.S. DOJ's evidence that you knew it was there? Some of the U.S. DOJ's cases completely fall apart because they cannot prove the knowledge element.

In other cases, the prosecutors cannot prove the criminal intent element. For example, the prosecutor threatens to have you sentenced to lifetime imprisonment if you don't take a plea bargain for first degree murder. First degree murder requires the prosecutor to prove you not only killed someone but the killing was premeditated. That is to say you intended in advance to kill someone and you planned the killing. Then, you executed your plan. If the prosecutor takes you to trial, proves you did the killing but no proof is offered on premeditated intent, their entire case falls apart.

Does your alleged crime have a component of interstate commerce as a mandatory element of the crime? If so, what is the standard for defining interstate commerce and does the evidence support the standard?

Let's go back to the accusation of possessing illegal grapefruit from Cuba. Suppose the law says it is illegal to knowingly possess grapefruit from Cuba that you transported in interstate commerce. The U.S. DOJ proves you knew about the grapefruit hidden under your truck because your neighbor took a photograph of you hiding the grapefruit. Then, you find out that several stores sell the same grapefruit in your state. How does the U.S. DOJ know your grapefruit came from Cuba, which is across state lines and illegal? How do they prove you didn't buy the grapefruit at a local store, which is not illegal under federal law?

Have you and/or your attorney been able to accurately verify the evidence the prosecutor says they have? Has your attorney physically looked at all the evidence?

There was a case that a prosecutor made against a defendant. The prosecutor's evidence was a videotape allegedly showing the defendant committing the crime. The prosecutor wouldn't let the defense attorney see the tape until right before the trial started. When the defense attorney finally saw the video, he realized the video showed nothing illegal. The prosecutor was bluffing, hoping the defendant would quickly sign a plea bargain without ever checking out the evidence.

There have been other cases where the defendants were convicted of crimes but the defense attorneys never looked carefully at all of the evidence. After the convictions, the defendants appealed their cases only to find out the actual evidence never agreed with what the prosecutors alleged in their indictments.

Did you read your plea bargain carefully to make sure it accurately states what you and your attorney discussed?

In one case, a defendant agreed to a prison sentence in a rough draft of a plea bargain. He signed a final draft of the plea bargain not realizing the prosecutor secretly increased the prison sentence on the final draft. He found out about the last minute switch at his sentencing hearing. He got a longer sentence and had to appeal.

If you are innocent but you plead guilty in order to get a plea bargain for a lower sentence, what unusual things can happen after you are sentenced?

There have been defendants who have signed plea bargains who later found out new evidence on their behalf. The defendants wished they never would have signed a plea bargain. Some of them found out the police and/or prosecutors lied in their cases. Some were taking bribes. In some cases, the U.S. DOJ's case was based entirely on one officer's false testimony.

Once the officer's testimony was proven false in one case, hundreds of other cases had to be re-examined to see if they could be appealed. Since this defendant plead guilty, it made it harder to appeal because the defendant "admitted his guilt" in his plea bargain.

There have been several cases where defendants signed plea bargains only to find out after they were sentenced that someone else confessed to the crime. In one case, a defendant was falsely accused of committing armed robbery with hostage taking. He took a plea bargain to avoid a lengthy sentence even though he was innocent. He was sentenced to 25 years. The real burglar and his girlfriend/accomplice confessed to the crime several years later. Since the innocent inmate pleaded guilty to get a plea bargain, it made it very hard for him to win his appeal, even though two other people confessed to the crime.

FOOD FOR THOUGHT

"The expectations of life depend upon diligence; the mechanic that would perfect his work must first sharpen his tools."

Confucius

Can I appeal my case at all if I sign a plea bargain?

1. Yes and no. You can appeal if you take a plea bargain but your appeal is limited and less likely to succeed.

2. Your word is shot if you reverse your plea from guilty in your plea bargain to not guilty in your appeal.

3. You give up certain types of methods and strategies of appealing.

4. You can still appeal for ineffective assistance of counsel. You claim you had a bad defense attorney.

5. You can still appeal if your sentence is greater than your plea bargain stated or it was above the statutory guideline maximum.

6. The reality is, greater than 95% of appeals fail. This is why it is so important to make sure any plea bargain you sign is thought out very well.

Should I sign a plea bargain if the prosecutor wants it to include a waiver of my right to appeal?

Your prosecutor will try to add a waiver of your right to appeal a plea bargain. You do not have to accept this waiver. See if you can get it removed. You may want to agree to a waiver on appealing most issues while retaining your right to appeal certain issues.

I have been offered a plea bargain with a sentence of 10-20 years. How likely is it the judge will sentence me to 10 years?

Your plea bargain may recommend a range of sentences, such as 10-20 years. You will almost always get a sentence near the top of the range in a plea bargain. Don't focus on how low the bottom number is. Try to negotiate to get the maximum sentence reduced since the judge will sentence you near the top of the range. In other words, a plea bargain for 10-15 years is better than a plea bargain for 0-20 years. Again, focus on the top numbers of each range.

My prosecutor offered me a plea bargain with a sentencing range that is below the minimum mandatory sentence. Am I likely to get a sentence below the minimum mandatory sentence?

No. You will most likely get a sentence above the minimum mandatory sentence.

FOOD FOR THOUGHT

"Somewhere, something incredible is waiting to be known."

Carl Sagan

Some defendants do get a sentence that is below the statutory minimum mandatory sentence. How can I?

You can if:

1. You get a 5K1.1 letter of cooperation from your prosecutors after you snitch/debrief. A 5K1.1 letter of cooperation is a letter of recommendation from your prosecutor to your judge. The letter recommends that the judge go leniently on you in sentencing because you have given critical information that helped prosecute other defendants.

2. You qualify for a Safety Valve. A Safety Valve is a legal rule that helps certain defendants receive a smaller sentence.

3. The prosecutor agrees to reduce the charges. For example, a first degree murder is reduced to manslaughter in a plea bargain.

If I decide to snitch/debrief, how do I make sure I get a good plea bargain?

1. Make sure you have something the prosecutors really want.

2. Let your attorney do the arrangements, not you.

3. If you do a debriefing (snitching session), make sure you get a clear deal from the prosecutor before you debrief. Get it in writing, if possible. If you debrief without a clear deal, the prosecutor may say your information isn't that helpful and they won't give you a good plea bargain.

One defendant was trying to debrief with several different law enforcement officers from different agencies in the room. He wanted a plea bargain for 5 years. He had no firm agreement with the prosecutor. He ended up getting a seventeen year sentence even after he debriefed.

What if I committed one crime but they prosecuted me with several different crimes? Can I plead guilty to one charge and not guilty to the others?

Yes. You may want to plead guilty to one and not guilty to the others. If you go to trial, the jury may believe you for accepting responsibility for what you did do. Prosecutors know this and they may drop frivolous charges.

There was a case where a defendant got drunk, took one narcotic, drove while intoxicated, and committed vehicular manslaughter. He was charged with vehicular manslaughter, DWI, and five narcotics possession charges based on contradictory lab tests. He only recalled drinking alcohol and using one drug. He was facing a potentially very long prison sentence if he was convicted on all of it. He and his lawyer realized the evidence was weak on some of the narcotics charges. By pleading guilty on the vehicular manslaughter and DWI charges, he was able to successfully fight the narcotics charges. His sentence was far lower than what the prosecutor wanted.

Can I negotiate a plea bargain to serve time in military service instead of prison?

For the most part, no. Several decades ago, defendants were allowed to serve in the military instead of going to prison for certain offenses. This seldom happens anymore. However, there was a case where the defendant was 16 years old when he was indicted as an adult for possessing and selling marijuana. Because of his young age, he was actually able to get a plea bargain to serve twenty years in the U.S. Army instead of serving ten years in prison. His case was very unique. It doesn't hurt to ask about your case.

FOOD FOR THOUGHT

"Both now and for always, I intend to hold fast to my belief in the hidden strength of the human spirit."

Andrei Sakharov

Before you sign a plea bargain, you need to consider if you might qualify for one of the following defenses in a trial:

1. Impaired mental judgment caused by alcohol, drugs, or a psychiatric episode

2. Insanity

3. Self-defense

What do I lose by signing a plea bargain?

1. Your freedom (usually).

2. Your right to challenge evidence gained unlawfully using a motion to suppress evidence.

3. Your right to challenge the sufficiency of evidence in each charge against you. (You lose the right to make a Rule 29 motion.)

4. Your right to appeal your case using every type of appeal possible.

Can I be sentenced for alleged misconduct I did even though no charges have been filed against me?

Yes. This is where plea bargains and sentencing hearings get complicated. You will not only be sentenced for alleged crimes in your indictment but also alleged crimes your prosecutor and U.S. Probation Officer (PO) find out about.

After you sign a plea bargain or after you are convicted at trial, you will meet with a PO in what is called a Pre-Sentencing Interview (PSI). Your PO will generate a Pre-Sentencing Report (PSR), which is sent to your judge. The judge uses your PSR in determining how long you will be sentenced.

Here is the rough part: Your PO will include any allegations of crimes or strange behavior you have *ever* had, not just your current criminal allegations. These allegations can come from your prosecutors, previous prosecutors, PO's, CO's, law enforcement officers, your family, your friends, your enemies, or anyone else.

The standard of evidence in reviewing these allegations in a sentencing hearing is low. In a trial, your guilt must be proved beyond a reasonable doubt. At a sentencing hearing, the evidence only has to be a preponderance of the evidence. This is awful because a mere allegation of a crime can increase your sentence. Your attorney can try to defend you at the sentencing hearing but it is difficult because of the preponderance of evidence legal standard.

Imagine a defendant who gets indicted on three counts – A, B, and C, which carry a maximum fifteen- year sentence. The defendant signs a plea bargain in which he pleads guilty to crime A in exchange for dropping counts B and C. The defendant believes he will get sentenced to five years.

At the sentencing hearing, the prosecutors bring up the issues surrounding counts B and C. They also pull out of the PSR issues D and E, which are other allegations of criminal misconduct. The defendant gets sentenced to eighteen years, even though he signed a plea bargain. It happens.

FOOD FOR THOUGHT

"Intuition separates the good leader from the great – the feeling of knowing the right thing to do. Learn to trust that feeling."

General Leo Baxter

Since a PSR can include additional criminal allegations I might get sentenced to, how can I fight it using a plea bargain?

Ask your attorney for a pre-plea PSR *before* you sign a plea agreement. You should request a pre-plea PSR before you sign a plea bargain so you know exactly what you are getting into. This forces the prosecutors, your PO, the police, and everyone else to put all of their cards on the table before you sign a plea agreement. There will be no surprises at the sentencing hearing.

Checklist

Before you sign a plea bargain, make sure:

1. You talk over the plea bargain in detail with your attorney.

2. You believe your lawyer has worked hard on your behalf.

3. Your plea bargain spells out your sentence with the lowest top end of a range that is possible.

4. Your plea bargain lists which offenses will be included or excluded.

5. You understand how other alleged criminal misconduct will be handled at the sentencing hearing.

6. You get a 2-3 Offense Level reduction for signing the plea bargain.

7. You have reviewed your pre-plea PSR.

8. You get in writing how much time off you will get for snitching/debriefing.

9. You don't sign a waiver of appeal or that you only sign a limited waiver of appeal after careful discussion with your lawyer.

10. You believe you are getting a true bargain.

11. You know if you can trust your prosecutors and judge to accept the terms of your plea bargain.

12. You understand all of the elements of each count against you and what the U.S. DOJ's evidence is for each element of each count.

13. You consider if intent, knowledge, or interstate commerce is a required element of each charge against you and you understand what the U.S. DOJ's evidence is for intent, knowledge, or interstate commerce.

14. You consider if a defense of insanity, self-defense, or mental impairment could be used.

15. You have read "Chapter 9: Sentencing Guidelines".

16. You have read this chapter at least twice.

CHAPTER 12:

Trial – The Beginning

Introduction

This chapter is dedicated to the beginning of your trial. You need to know what to expect. This summary blends personal experience with input from an actual trial attorney who has been through many trials.

Courtroom Etiquette

If you have not already read the section on courtroom etiquette in "Chapter 6: Preliminary Hearings," now is the time to do so.

Custody

At the beginning of your trial, you will be given instructions as to who has custody of you. If you have been locked up while awaiting trial, the U.S. Marshals and the bailiff will be in charge of you during the trial. Federal bailiffs are usually retired law enforcement officers from non-federal jobs. They are cheaper to pay than U.S. Marshals because U.S. Marshals have so many federal benefits. The bailiffs are there to escort the jury and judge in and out. They will announce the judge's entrance.

You will be assigned at least two U.S. Marshals. One usually stands or sits behind you. The other usually stands or sits between you and the jury or prosecutors. If your offense was very violent or you have a high profile case, expect more U.S. Marshals to be present.

If you are on pretrial release (bail and bond) before your trial, you will meet your attorney each day in the federal court house. There are usually a series of meeting rooms for defense attorneys and their clients. You need to show up early because you and your attorney will need to discuss your trial strategy, evidence, witnesses, and legal motions.

Your U.S. PTSO will give you a set of boundaries to stay within during the trial. It will be a certain number of miles from the court house and your hotel or home. They will give you a map for you to follow. You will get a curfew. The best way to deal with the rules is to get a hotel near several restaurants. It's also best to get a hotel room near your lawyer's hotel room so you can meet as late as you need to each night while still complying with the U.S. PTSO's requirements. In general, during the trial, you are expected to be either in the court room, with your lawyers, or in your hotel room. This is not a time for shopping.

The Beginning

The bailiff will enter the court room and ask you to rise when the judge enters. You will be told when to be seated. The judge will read your name, case number, and charges. The judge will then ask each lawyer to state their name and position: lead prosecutor, assistant prosecutor, lead defense counselor, etc. A discussion of the charges will then take place.

The judge will hear and decide any last minute motions from either side. The judge will ask each side how long they expect their respective cases will take: A day, two weeks, 30 days? Don't be surprised if the prosecutor states his case is more important than yours. They will be arrogant and selfish with time. They will act like you have no defense even though you are legally entitled to all the time that is necessary for your defense. If the judge has not already said so, he will state how long each side has for opening arguments and how long voir dire (jury selection) will take.

The judge will give out some rules on how the media will be handled, as well as his expectations for the audience; who can come or go, when, where to sit, etc.

Note: Since the terrorist attacks of 9/11/2001, there has been a federal court rule that no cameras or recording devices of any kind can enter any federal court room without explicit permission from the judge. This includes cameras built into cell phones and laptop computers. Warn your family and friends so they don't get arrested by the U.S. Marshals.

FOOD FOR THOUGHT

"Innovation distinguishes between a leader and a follower."

Steve Jobs

Voir Dire

Voir dire is the Latin name for jury selection. The potential jurors are notified 1 to 3 months in advance of the trial. They are called to meet in a room where their identities are checked and they are given a brief orientation.

Most judges will allow attorneys for both the prosecution and defense to use a short jury selection form. The jurors will fill out this form while you are in court meeting with the judge and prosecutors. The jury selection form may be 1 or 2 pages long for each side of the case.

Both sets of attorneys will want to identify and weed out jurors that will not be sympathetic to their side. Defense attorneys will want to identify anyone who is or was in law enforcement or anyone who is married to someone in law enforcement. They will also want to identify anyone who was a victim of a crime similar to the one at issue in your case. Additionally, they want to find out if anyone is overly sympathetic to the alleged victims. They want to strike (remove) these people from the pool of potential jurors.

Prosecutors want to remove anyone that has ever been investigated or prosecuted for any significant crime or anyone related to anyone that has. This includes potential jurors related to people who have served time in prison. Prosecutors also want to remove anyone that donated money to the American Civil Liberties Union, the Libertarian Party, the Democratic Party, MoveOn.org, or the Brookings Institute. (You have to stop and wonder: If investigations, prosecutions, and prison sentences were all carried out in a fair, humane, and honest manner, then why would they care if these people are on the jury? What do they have to hide from these American citizens?) In some instances, the prosecutors will not get to ask these questions. The reality is prosecutors have both limited time to interview potential jurors and they can only strike a limited number of potential jurors from the potential jury pool.

The presence of a potential black male juror should be noted. In general, you want this man on your jury if he has no red flags. If you are a well-known member of the KKK or other white supremacist group, you obviously won't want black men on your jury. Both prosecutors and defense lawyers know that black males are likely to vote "not guilty" about 90% of the time. The reason is thought to be that black males have friends or family members that have served time in prisons, and they know about many of the injustices in the justice system. Also, completely innocent black males are five times more likely to be pulled over and searched by the police for no reason as compared to innocent white males. The theory states that these black men are prejudiced against prosecutors and law enforcement officers. In some parts of the country, prosecutors are very successful at selecting all white juries. This increases their conviction rates. Your attorney usually understands these issues and acts accordingly. Notably, The U.S. Constitution prohibits any lawyer from considering race as a basis for excusing a jury through "peremptory challenge" ("strike") (see below).

If you have the financial ability, hire a law firm to help create the jury selection form. These are law firms that specialize in jury selection. They study jurors and how/why they vote. They will know which ten questions are the most important to ask on a jury selection form. It costs $1,000 to $2,000 for a single form. A jury selection specialist is also very helpful, if you can afford one. They cost anywhere from a few thousand dollars for a one day jury selection to $30,000 for a jury selection process that takes thirty days. The specialist is an attorney or team of attorneys and psychologists who will sit in the court room with your attorneys during jury selection. They will literally draw a map of the potential jurors. They will read all the jury selection forms and rank them from very helpful to very dangerous to your case.

The judge will ask if anyone knows you, any of the attorneys or witnesses in your case, or the judge. They will be eliminated if they do. They will ask if anyone is too sick to serve on the jury. The judge will ask if anyone is prejudiced against you. The bad news is the judge may then try to convince these people to stay and serve on the jury. This is unfair. Anyone prejudiced should be automatically excluded.

Once the judge has selected a group of potential jurors, each side will have an opportunity to question the potential jurors. Some judges will only allow 30 seconds to question each potential juror from both sides. Some judges will allow a few hours. More time is usually to your advantage.

You and your defense team should start a particular theme during voir dire. Even though you have not made opening statements, the jury is learning about your defense strategy by the questions your attorney is asking. This is helpful because you want to pick jurors that believe in your strategy so they will vote for you. For example, if your defense is based on insanity, you want jurors who believe insanity is a legitimate defense. If your defense is based on self-defense, you want jurors that believe in the right to self-preservation. The combination of your jury selection form and verbal questions should help both screen out unwanted jurors while planting the seeds of your defense case. If you choose to use the ultimate research method, start hinting at the most important government evidence or expert you plan to attack.

After all questions have been asked, each side gets to issue their strikes ("peremptory challenges"). Each side gets to eliminate some of the potential jurors that are adverse to their side of the case. In all, the Court (Judge) will swear in fourteen or fifteen jurors. Twelve primary jurors will hear the case and vote while two or three alternates will hear the case without voting unless a primary juror is excused for illness, for discussing the case outside of the court room, or for any other reason the judge determines.

Throughout the trial and during each recess, you cannot communicate with the jurors unless you are called to testify on the witness stand. The most you could say to any of them is "Good Morning" or "Good Evening." If you strike up any other conversation, you can be charged with obstruction of justice (jury tampering). In general, you should avoid contact with the jurors.

Opening Statements

Each side will be given an opportunity to make an opening statement. The judge determines the length allowed for the statement. In general, they last ten to sixty minutes each. Bear in mind that the average human only concentrates for fifteen minutes. They might forget everything after that. They may even fall asleep. Less is more.

You and your attorney should have a well-developed strategy. The opening statement should either directly disclose the entire strategy or at least introduce specific circumstances to the jury. Just like the seeds planted in voir dire, your attorney should be planting seeds in the opening statement. This includes placing hints about the results of your ultimate research method. Ask to hear and read your lawyer's opening statement several days before your trial starts. Make polite suggestions, if necessary.

FOOD FOR THOUGHT

"Tackling adversity means moving forward with the knowledge that some questions need action, not answers."

Christopher Novak

Invoking The Rule

After opening statements are given, one of the attorneys will usually ask the judge to invoke "The Rule." The Rule of Sequestration is a federal court policy that forbids witnesses from being in the court room while other witnesses are on the witness stand. This keeps witnesses from influencing each other's testimony. The Rule also forbids lawyers from speaking to witnesses outside the courtroom, and it forbids witnesses from discussing the trial among themselves until the end of the trial.

Once a witness gives testimony, the judge will ask the lawyers for both parties if the witness can remain in the courtroom. The decision is up to the lawyers. (Some witnesses can testify more than once in the same case.)

Also, certain expert witnesses for both sides may be exempt from The Rule when an expert's expertise has a significant role in multiple aspects of the case. For instance, if a defendant is on trial for murdering six people, transporting their bodies across state lines, and burying them in a mass grave, a forensic anthropologist may be able to stay in the courtroom throughout the trial if she was present when each of the bodies was exhumed and she performed each autopsy.

The experts have several advantages compared to regular witnesses:

1. Experts are supposed to be the best at what they do. Hence, juries believe their testimony more than the regular witness's testimony.

2. Since experts can be exempted from The Rule, they can hear all of the witness's testimony. This gives them the power to summarize all testimony for their case. Hence, their testimony can be influenced by other regular witness's testimony.

3. If the expert hears a statement made by another witness that hurts their case, they can try to find a way to contradict that statement.

4. The judge may also allow experts to take the witness stand several times. Regular witnesses may be allowed to only testify once on the witness stand unless the lawyers and judge agree that information is critical. The experts will make lists with their respective attorneys about what they need to say in a second appearance on the witness stand.

Regular witnesses are not considered experts so they are not as believable. Regular witnesses have to follow The Rule so they never know what the other witnesses are saying. They cannot refute statements the other witnesses make.

It is to your advantage to have several experts testify on your behalf.

CHAPTER 13:

Trial –
The Government's Case

Government Witnesses

Recall the three dynamics of trials: the law, the evidence, and, most importantly, the courtroom melodrama. The prosecutors will usually have a very well-planned sequence of witnesses to testify against you. To simplify the issues, most prosecutors will call witnesses to the witness stand in the chronological order that makes most sense to their case against you. For instance, the first witness may be someone who sees something suspicious and calls the police. The second witness may be the police officer that responded first to the crime scene. Then the investigator, then the lab technician who conducted forensic tests on the evidence will be called. This natural sequence of events is easiest for the jury to keep up with.

The exception to the rule of the sequence of witnesses is the last witness. Jurors tend to recall the testimony of the last witness the most.

Recall the concept of the Rubik's cube in relationship to the melodrama of the courtroom. Most people are like a Rubik's cube; they have many faces; some good, some not so good. The government will try to spin every piece of evidence and every witness to create an evil image of you. The defense team will spin all the evidence and witness testimony to create a wholesome image of you.

As each witness for the prosecution takes the stand, you need to make sure your attorney can:

1. Get the witness to admit on the witness stand the nicest things about you that the witness knows. Example: "Isn't the defendant the man who saved your brother from that house fire?" Everything positive about you needs to be heard by the jury, unless the judge orders the jury to exclude such evidence as a result of a prosecutor's objection to it on the basis of a lack of relevance.

2. Attack the credibility of the witness. Example: "Didn't you also claim to have been abducted by aliens in their spaceship last year?" Example: "Didn't you serve time in prison for fraud?"

3. Attack the assumptions made by the witness or the prosecutors. For instance, the prosecutors want the jury to use circumstantial evidence to make the assumption that since you were at a crime scene, you must be guilty. Example: The witness testifies they saw you at a crime scene. Your attorney points out that the witness actually saw several people at the crime scene. The defense attorney gets the witness to state they never actually saw who committed the crime. Example: Your fingerprint is on a door knob. The defense attorney gets the lab technician that identified the fingerprint to admit that she never witnessed the murder and that many innocent people could have touched the door knob. All of the problems with circumstantial evidence must be addressed by your attorneys. Not just once, but over and over again.

4. Prepare an opposing witness on each issue to be used during the defense's phase of the trial. Example: The prosecution gets a government witness to say you said something incriminating. Later in the trial, your defense witness states he was present for the entire conversation and he refutes the incriminating statement.

Evidence for Prosecutors

Each piece of evidence will be introduced into official evidence by the witness who discovered it. This is often a cop or federal agent. You need to watch closely. Several defendants witnessed evidence show up in the courtroom that they never saw or heard of before. Apparently, cops, prosecutors, and defense attorneys all have a problem in that any of them can haphazardly throw a bunch of evidence in a box. Evidence from different cases can get mixed up.

You and your attorney need to keep up with the essential elements of each crime as they are listed in federal law. The evidence introduced must support each and every required element.

FOOD FOR THOUGHT

"Treat a man as he is, he will remain so. Treat a man the way he can be and ought to be, and he will become as he can be and should be."

Johann Wolfgang Von Goethe

The Government Finishes

After the prosecutors finish questioning their last witness, the judge will ask them if there are any more witnesses. The prosecutors will announce, "The government rests its case." For the most part, that's it for the government. However, keep in mind that expert witnesses for the government can be called back to the witness stand during the defense phase of the trial. Also, the government will get to make closing arguments at the end of the trial.

At this point, your attorney can ask for a series of Rule 29 motions. A Rule 29 motion is a legal motion that asks the judge to decide if the prosecution produced enough evidence to satisfy each element of each count in the case. For instance, if you are charged in one count of selling 100 to 200 kilograms of a drug but the only evidence produced in court was one kilogram of dope and a witness who saw one kilogram of dope, then the judge can throw out that count because the evidence was insufficient. A Rule 29 motion is ultimately a sufficiency of evidence ruling.

Note: Your attorney needs to make a Rule 29 motion for *each element of each alleged crime*. You will need this for an appeal if you get convicted. You can appeal without Rule 29 motions, but it is more costly and time-consuming. It is far simpler to get your attorney to make Rule 29 motions on each element of each alleged crime.

CHAPTER 14:

Trial – The Defense's Case

FOOD FOR THOUGHT

"Carry the battle to them. Don't let them bring it to you. Put them on the defensive."

U.S. President Harry Truman

You Have No Obligation to Present a Defense

When prosecutors are finally finished with their side of the case, they will announce, "The government rests its case." From a legal stand point, you are not obligated to present a defense. You legally don't have to call a single witness to the witness stand nor do you have to present any evidence on your behalf. You don't have to have an expert. Your attorney doesn't have to even make any closing statements. Your attorney is required to be present but he or she doesn't have to help you much. The minimum professional standard for defense attorneys in federal cases is lower than one might expect. Your prosecutors would prefer that you make no defense at all. Their chances of winning a conviction increase and they get to go home early.

All of the attorneys in the courtroom and the judge realize the above facts. Many attorneys and judges hope you will go quietly to prison without challenging any part of your case at all. It is in your best interest to make sure your defense is solid, easy to understand, and very believable.

Defense Witnesses

Recall the three critical aspects of the courtroom: the law, the evidence, and the melodrama. In an ideal world, the evidence and the law would have far more impact on the jury than the melodrama in the courtroom. In reality, the jury will base its decision in large part on the dramatic presentations put on by the attorneys and witnesses. You need to take advantage of this. The jury's emotions often influence their decisions more than the law and the evidence. The law and the evidence become more important if you lose your trial and have to appeal the conviction.

For every witness your attorney calls to the witness stand, your attorney must:

1. Use the concept of the Rubik's Cube. Your side of the case must put forth every possible good feature about you. Every time the prosecutors try to paint you as a red cube, you must turn the cube around to a green face. You need to work with your attorney on every potential witness to show your best green attributes.

2. Use the witness to attack statements or observations made by the prosecutor's witnesses. For example, the government's witness states you were at the same crime scene. Your witness states they were at the crime scene and you were never there.

3. Use your expert witness to discuss how tests run by the government's experts can have errors or that they are based on assumptions. Your expert needs to find the errors and attack the assumptions.

4. Build the credibility of your witnesses. If the witness does not know you personally, that fact should be pointed out to the jury. If the witness is a leader, point out the difficult decisions the leader makes in their profession, such as a CEO that hires and fires people. The jury needs to respect your witnesses. For instance, Sunday school teachers, nurses, and priests should be credible. If they are leaders, the jury needs to know it. For example, CEO's, military officers, city council members, etc. How long each witness has known you should be emphasized. The objectivity of each witness should be proven to the jury.

5. Assess the vulnerability of each witness. Realize the prosecutors will attack your witnesses. Which issues about your witnesses would make their testimony questionable? Have they ever committed a crime? Are they mentally stable? Did they make inconsistent statements to the investigators? The pros and cons of each witness need to be weighed before they take the witness stand. The last witness should be the most important witness because the jury will remember the last witness the most. In some instances, you might be the last witness. In other instances, an expert may be the last witness. If you have a credible witness that totally contradicts the prosecutor's case, you may decide to have that witness be the last to testify.

Evidence for Defense Attorneys

Your attorney will usually introduce evidence to the jury by having the witness that discovered the evidence describe it. You and your attorney need to be careful and vigilant in finding evidence that contradicts the government's evidence. For instance, if the investigator finds your hair fiber at the crime scene, you need to point out that hair fibers were found from eleven different people. Furthermore, all of the problems with circumstantial evidence must be spotlighted by your attorney over and over again.

You and your attorney must carefully show the jury how the prosecutor's case is weak because it does not prove each element of each criminal count. Recall that if the prosecutor proves every element of a crime except for one element, the law says the jury cannot convict you on that count. It is your job to work with your attorney to show that at least one element of the alleged crime is doubtful.

The Defense Finishes

After your defense attorneys have called their last witness and presented their last evidence, they will announce: "The defense rests its case."

Tales from the Courtroom

A very famous case occurred several decades ago: A woman was murdered. A man was spotted nearby that same night. He was eventually charged with first degree murder. He pled not guilty and went to trial. There were no eyewitnesses to the actual murder itself and no physical evidence linking the defendant to the crime scene. One lawyer, assisted by a law student, defended the suspect.

The trial ended in a mistrial because the jury could not reach a unanimous verdict. After overhearing a juror's comment, the law student realized the defendant's facial features played a role in some of the juror's decisions. At least one of the jurors was suspected of voting guilty based on the defendant's appearance.

The prosecutor decided to retry the case in front of a second jury. No new evidence or witnesses were found for the second trial. Again, the case was entirely circumstantial. It was based completely on inferences. The defendant was in the wrong place at the wrong time.

By the time the second trial started, the law student had graduated from law school and became the lead defense attorney in the case. Prior to the second trial, the defense attorney gave a single, simple instruction to his client. The trial went on for several weeks. The defendant was found not guilty.

What was the simple instruction the defense attorney gave his client?

The attorney instructed his client to stare at his shoes during every minute of the trial. This simple instruction won the case and saved an innocent man's life. The defense attorney became one of the best defense attorneys in the United States.

CHAPTER 15:

Trial – The End

Introduction

After both the government and your defense team have finished calling all of their witnesses and introduced all of their evidence, the judge will verify that both sides are ready to rest their case. They will ask if any of the expert witnesses have anything to add. Recall that experts can be called to the witness stand several times and out of sequence.

Each side will be given an opportunity to make closing arguments. The government gets to go twice while the defense team only gets to go once. It is unfair. The sequence is as follows:

1. Government

2. Defense

3. Government

Motions

After the closing arguments are complete, the jury will be excused from the court room. Both sides will then have an opportunity to introduce legal motions. Each motion is an attempt to get the judge to rule in their favor using federal law as a basis.

For example, defense attorneys typically make a motion for a Rule 29 ruling. A Rule 29 motion asks the judge to review the evidence to see if it is sufficient to obtain a conviction on each count based on federal law. A Rule 29 ruling is essentially a sufficiency ruling. Of particular note is you need to have your attorney make a Rule 29 motion on *each element of each alleged crime.*

For example, your alleged crime requires elements A, B, and C for a conviction. In this example, element A is *possession* of an illegal gun. Element B is that you *knowingly* possessed the gun. Element C is the gun was bought or transported across state lines (*interstate commerce*). Your attorney must ask for separate Rule 29 motions on elements A, B, and C. This is important because you may need that ruling on each element of each alleged crime in your appeal if you are convicted. The federal appeals judges can deny part of your appeal if your attorney fails to make a Rule 29 motion on each element of each alleged crime. There is a way to try to get around this in an appeal but it is difficult, time-consuming, and expensive. It's far simpler to have your attorney ask for a Rule 29 motion on each element of each crime.

You and your attorney need to consider a motion to drop double jeopardy charges, if applicable. Keep your eyes and ears open. Read your indictments carefully. If you are getting charged in separate indictments with both attempted burglary and completed burglary on the same date at the same location, your judge should throw out one of the charges.

You and your attorney should consider if your case merits an instruction to the jury to consider you innocent by reputation. If your case is a circumstantial case and you are a pastor, school teacher, nurse, police officer, counselor, Red Cross official, etc., the judge can instruct the jury to give you the benefit of the doubt if you had a number of witnesses speak on behalf of your good character.

Jury Instructions

The jury will be called back into the court room. Your judge will give them a handout of jury instructions and will also read through them aloud. The rules of jury deliberation will be discussed. Each criminal count will be read out loud. The jury will be instructed to discuss each witness' testimony and each piece of evidence. The jury will be asked to discuss everything prior to taking a vote on guilt or innocence.

Jury Deliberations

The jury will be excused to start deliberations in private. If they have any legal questions, they will have the jury foreman write the questions down. The questions will be given to the bailiff, who will give the questions to the judge. The judge will give typed answers back to the bailiff to give to the jury. In some instances, the judge will speak directly with the jury.

Jury deliberations may only take fifteen minutes or as long as several weeks. Longer jury deliberations are generally better for defendants. If the jury comes back with a verdict in one or two hours, there is a high chance it is a guilty verdict. If they take several days, the chances of either a not guilty verdict or a hung jury increase. A hung jury refers to a jury that is split on its decision. Some jurors vote guilty while one or more jurors vote not guilty. You cannot be convicted of a crime with a hung jury. However, you can face another trial in the future with a new jury. Alternately, the prosecutors can drop the charges against you.

FOOD FOR THOUGHT

"If you want to achieve a high goal, you're going to have to take some chances."

Alberto Salazar

The Verdict

The judge will call everyone back into the court room to hear the verdict. The jury foreperson will be asked to read each count out loud and then read the verdict of guilty or not guilty after each count.

If you are found not guilty…great! Congratulations! This book is over for you. Stay out of trouble. Have a nice day.

If you are found guilty on one or more charges, keep reading. Your attorney should be bright enough to now request a poll of the jury. A jury poll is conducted by the judge. Each count is read one by one again. Each member of the jury is asked if they voted guilty or not guilty. Your defense attorney is looking for one of several issues:

1. If the jury foreperson lied about the voting results.

2. If a member of the jury actually voted not guilty, but the foreperson mistakenly counted the vote as guilty.

3. If a member of the jury felt bullied into making a quick decision or if a member of the jury feels uncertain about their vote. (Remember: Guilt is supposed to be beyond a reasonable doubt.)

Remanding Into Custody Versus Self-Reporting

After you are found guilty, your judge and prosecutor will discuss whether you should be immediately remanded into custody (locked up) or if you can self-report to the BOP. The BOP is a national government agency in charge of locking up federal inmates in prisons. In most instances, self-reporting to the BOP is preferable to being remanded into the U.S. Marshals' custody immediately. If you self-report, you get some time to prepare to serve time in prison. You can take care of your affairs. The judge will consider if you have any of the following reasons for not self-reporting:

1. You are convicted of a violent or sexual crime.

2. You are a flight risk.

3. You are going to be sentenced to a minimum mandatory of five or more years.

4. You have had previous problems on bail and bond, probation, parole, or supervised release.

If you have any one or more of the above issues, you will be locked up immediately by the U.S. Marshals.

If you are allowed to self-report to the U.S. Marshals or BOP, the judge will tell you when you are required to do so. A few important notes:

1. You must report on that date or a day or two before. If not, you can be charged with escape, which carries an additional five year prison sentence.

2. The BOP has to officially designate a spot for you in a prison. The judge's date is not the only date that has legal power. The BOP can designate that you arrive at prison on the judge's date or a week or two *earlier*. If the judge orders you to report to the BOP no later than March 30th and the BOP says you are designated to report on March 20th, you must report on March 20th. That's the law.

3. If the date to report arrives but the BOP has not designated a spot for you, then you must report to the U.S. Marshals on that date. They will take you into custody until the BOP designates a spot for you.

4. If you self-report, choose a non-holiday, Monday through Thursday. The BOP has many departments (for example: clothing department, medical clinic) that are closed or very understaffed on Fridays, Saturdays, Sundays, and federal holidays. If you arrive on a weekend or holiday, you will be neglected by the staff for several days. You may not get the clothes, medical care, or paperwork you need until several days later. It's better to just arrive a day or two early and get it over with.

FOOD FOR THOUGHT

"Self-assurance is two-thirds of success."

Author Unknown.

The Perp Walk

After you are convicted, you will either leave the courthouse with the U.S. Marshals or your defense attorneys. The press may be set up on the sidewalk to take your photo or video tape you. If they ask you questions just smile and say, "No comment" or "I am appealing." Don't discuss your case. You will never win with the press. Do not hide your face.

CHAPTER 16:

Federal Detention Centers/ County Jails

FOOD FOR THOUGHT

"Survival is nothing more than recovery."

Dianne Feinstein

Introduction

After you are arrested or convicted, you may spend anywhere from a day to several years in a FDC or county/city jail. The bad news is most detention centers and jails are horrible places. The good news is federal prisons are typically better. If you end up in federal prison, you will trade horror stories about where you previously served time. You will feel like a refugee from a war zone.

Anytime you are locked up, you will get a lot of advice. Beware; half of the advice and rumors you hear are wrong. You need to get in the habit of asking the same question to two or three different inmates or CO's. If all of them agree, then you can probably believe them. If there is a disagreement, ask another inmate or CO. Over time, you will learn whom you can semi-trust and who doesn't give accurate advice. Information in this book is as accurate as possible.

Safety and Security

Your safety is of paramount importance. Think before you go anywhere, say anything, or do anything.

Most fights behind bars occur because of one or more of the following reasons:

   1. Stealing: Don't steal. You will get into a fight.

2. Accusations of stealing: Be careful who you blame for stealing. Whether they are guilty or not, some people fight over the mere accusation.

3. Don't make it easy for someone to steal your belongings. Don't leave your belongings sitting around in plain view. Put them in your locker and lock them up.

4. Disrespect: Always be respectful. If you mess up, say, "My bad," which means "I'm sorry." "Excuse me" should cross your lips several times per day. Don't be rude.

5. Overcrowding: Realize that overcrowding puts pressure on everyone. You will spend several hours a day just waiting around. Be patient. Don't expect to be first all the time.

6. TV's: Don't try to control the TV all the time. Don't change the channel unless the majority agrees to it.

Realize violence begets violence. Try to de-escalate situations. Additional suggestions are detailed in "Chapter 17: General Prison Security Policies" and "Chapter 18: Inmate Safety Issues." You should stop and read both of these chapters now unless you already have substantial experience being locked up.

Most places require that you take random urine drug tests and breathalyzers for alcohol. You can also be tested if you act suspicious. Refusing to take a test typically gets you thrown in Solitary Confinement (Disciplinary Segregation or "Seg").

FOOD FOR THOUGHT

"If the leader is filled with high ambition and if he pursues his aims with audacity and strength of will, he will reach them in spite of all obstacles."

Carl von Clausewitz

Moves

When an inmate goes from one part of a detention center/jail to another, it is referred to as a "move." Most movement is controlled. You can only move from one area to another when a CO authorizes it. If you go somewhere without authorization, it's called "out of bounds." You can be charged with an attempted escape or thrown in Solitary Confinement for being out of bounds.

When you are in a move:

1. Get permission before you move.

2. Don't run. The CO's will assume you are trying to escape.

3. Don't dawdle.

4. Never go in an area not authorized for inmates, such as a CO's office. If a CO gives you permission to enter, do your business and leave immediately.

5. When you are on an elevator, face the rear wall.

6. In some places, you have to face the wall when you stop in a hallway.

7. You should walk in front of CO's, not directly behind them.

Food

The food in detention centers/jails is usually awful. It is a 2-4 on a scale of 1-10. A 10/10 is gourmet food. A 1/10 is pig slop. Try to eat something from every tray. Eat something from the Commissary a couple of times per day, if possible.

Strip Searches

You are subject to being strip-searched at any time anywhere. You will get used to the searches. In some cases, you will be allowed to keep your undergarments on. Other cases will require you to remove everything, turn around, and bend over. It depends on the CO and your risk level. Whether you are male or female, some CO will eventually ask you to lift your private anatomy or belly out of the way so they can check under it. These searches should go quickly. In routine situations, male CO's perform strip searches on male inmates while female CO's perform them on female inmates. Rectal cavity searches with a rubber glove are rare unless you are in a maximum security place (U.S. Penitentiary) or you are acting suspicious.

Shakedown

A shakedown is a search of your cell, bag, or clothes for contraband. The term shakedown comes from old cartoons in which CO's lifted inmates upside down and shook them to get all of the stolen property to fall out of their pockets.

You can be shaken down any time for no reason whatsoever. Expect this to happen periodically. Don't take it personally. If the CO's find major contraband (illegal narcotics or a weapon), expect to be thrown in Solitary Confinement and get new criminal charges. If the CO's find limited minor contraband (paper clips, unauthorized pens, old newspapers, a stolen piece of fruit, etc.), they usually just confiscate it. If you have a lot of minor contraband, you may get written up and lose Commissary or phone privileges for a period of time.

Some CO's will totally trash your cell. Some will steal from you or trash your legal documents. If something is important for your case, make sure your attorney has a copy of it.

FOOD FOR THOUGHT

"There are many teachers who could ruin you. Before you know it you could be a pale copy of this teacher or that teacher. You have to endure on your own."

Bernice Abbott

Federal Detention Center/Jail Policies

Whether you are in a FDC or a jail, you should get an inmate handbook, which describes the policies you are supposed to follow. If you don't have one, keep politely asking for one until you get it. Once you read the handbook, you need to realize that prison politics exist. Policies are listed in various memos. The policies written will often contradict each other. Whenever you are in a situation with a CO or Warden, they will use whichever memo is in their best interest. Plan on the staff making up the rules as they go along.

Some CO's are reasonable, hard-working, and honest, some are not. The BOP staff are statistically more professional than most jail/detention center CO's.

Many FDC's and jails are operated by private companies, such as the GEO Group and CCA. These companies run prisons for profit and often make money by neglecting inmates. GEO operates over 100 facilities in the U.S. and abroad. GEO lost a wrongful death lawsuit in Texas because an inmate died unnecessarily in its custody. The inmate's family was awarded over $40 million. GEO appealed the case and lost.

Custody Designation

If you are placed in a jail, the policies on custody will differ from one city or county to the next. If you are in a FDC, theoretically the center must comply with all standards of the U.S. Marshals. Generally, they will designate your danger level and place you in a group with a similar or almost similar risk level. (In some instances, inmates indicted on first degree murder live with low-risk inmates. This is not supposed to happen.) Most inmates are low-risk and live in General Population (GP). If you are very dangerous, very disruptive, or you are vulnerable to getting hurt, you will live in Segregation ("Seg"). Inmates that are disruptive or violate prison rules live in a part of

Seg known as Disciplinary Seg. This is usually Solitary Confinement. Inmates that are former cops, prosecutors, politicians, judges, sex offenders, or snitches live in a part of Seg called Protective Custody (PC). Inmates in PC may live in multiple-occupant cells or Solitary Confinement.

FOOD FOR THOUGHT

"The brain is like a muscle. When it is in use, we feel very good. Understanding is joyous."

Carl Sagan

Most FDC's will allow visitation with a window between you and your family. You have to speak into a phone. The conversation is recorded. Do not say anything you don't want used in court against you. Most visits are limited to 20 or 30 minutes. You may be allowed longer visits if your visitor lives a great distance away. Ask the CO's for details prior to the day of your visit.

You will have to submit a list of visitors for approval. Your alleged victims and accomplices will generally not be approved. Be careful: Before you submit the list, make sure it is complete and accurate. Some detention centers only allow you to make additions or changes to your list once every six months, choose wisely.

How to Spend Your Time

Some suggestions for how to spend your time include:

- The Law Library: Ask if you can visit the Law Library. Read through your case documents. Make notes for your attorney. Read about similar cases.

- The Recreational Library: Read. Have your family ship you a few books every other week. Get a magazine or newspaper subscription.

- Education/GED: Some facilities will let you take courses or work on your GED (Graduate Equivalence Diploma).

- Jobs: An inmate who works in a jail or detention center is referred to as a trustee. Sample jobs include: kitchen workers, custodians, maintenance staff, commissary staff, etc. Jobs usually don't pay much if anything at all. You might get $5 to $40 per month. Some places pay you by giving you an extra tray of food at meal times.

- Recreation Yard: This is a type of playground surrounded by fences, barbed wire, and CO's. Most places have a covered patio for chess, checkers, and cards.

- Watch TV.
- Listen to the radio.
- Chapel: Most places offer some type of religious service.
- Write letters and make phone calls (see below).

Mail

Mail policies will differ slightly from one place another. Generally, rules consist of the following:

- Your incoming and outgoing mail can be opened and read. Don't write anything you don't want a jury to read. Don't discuss the details, witnesses, evidence, or your strategy.
- Any contraband will be removed and the mail may be returned to the sender or confiscated. Contraband typically includes stamps, blank stationary, blank envelopes, multiple forms, money, drugs, dangerous letters, nudity/sexually graphic material, profanity, etc.
- Before you seal your envelope, check to see if you are allowed to seal it or if you should leave it open for inspection.
- There is a limit on how many photos you can receive in the mail. Ask for information.
- Most places do not accept hard back books. Ask about the policy on receiving books – what types are acceptable, etc.
- Legal mail/attorney mail must be marked "Attorney-Client Privilege." Additional words may be required. You generally have to place legal mail in a separate mail box.
- Generally, you cannot correspond with other inmates without first getting permission from the Warden.
- You cannot operate a business using mail service.

MAIL TIPS:

- Use certified receipt/registered mail for important documents.
- Generate an address list and have one of your contacts update it periodically.
- Write several letters every week. You need help while you are locked up. You will also need help fighting your case. Lastly, you will need help when you get out of prison. You cannot get help unless you keep relationships alive.
- Set up and use a Power of Attorney, Medical Power of Attorney, etc.

- Establish a safe inmate contact. It will take you a couple of months to determine which inmates you consider to be safe. Give one of these inmates a list of your family member's addresses. Instruct them to write your family if you go to Solitary Confinement or get a transfer unexpectedly. They should also write them if you go to the hospital emergency room or if you die.

FOOD FOR THOUGHT

"Be courteous to all, but intimate with few, and let those few be well tried before you give them your confidence."

U.S. President George Washington

Phones

Most places have phone policies similar to the following:

- You can only call people on a pre-approved list. This list cannot include any of your victims, co-conspirators, or other inmates.
- No illegal activity or threats can be done over the phone.
- You cannot conduct a business.
- Everything is recorded. Don't speak about your case unless you want the prosecutors to use your statements in court.
- Attorney phone calls must be made using separate phones, ask the CO's for procedure and permission.
- Calls are expensive, as in several dollars to connect and a high per minute rate.
- Some area codes just do not work with all inmate phones. To get around this, get a family member in a different area code to relay messages to your family. Alternatively, have your family get a cell phone from a different area code.
- Some places will not allow you to place calls to cell phones. Don't discuss cell phones over the phone.

Showers

Always wear shower shoes in prison showers. While thirty inmates have good hygiene in the showers, there is at least one crazy inmate that will do something disgusting in every shower every day, enough said.

Commissary

Inmates purchase items for themselves through a prison store known as the Commissary. Most places have a limit on how much you can order per week. Most places only allow you to place an order once per week. You should be given some type of an order form.

COMMISSARY TIPS:

- Make three lists - Low, Medium, and High Priority - to help you prioritize your purchases.

- When you get your Commissary order, don't announce it to the world or leave it sitting around. For your own protection, place it in your locker as soon as possible.

Good Behavior Time

If you are convicted of a federal offense and you are serving time in the BOP, you can get good behavior time by following the rules, working, and completing your GED. Good behavior time is time off from your total sentence. However, you cannot get good behavior time while you are in a detention center or jail.

FOOD FOR THOUGHT

"One of the characteristics of successful people is that they are action-oriented. One of the marks of average people is that they are talk-oriented."

Brian Tracy

Oversight and Complaints

If you believe you have been seriously mistreated in prison, you have a legal right to file an administrative appeal, also known as a grievance. (This is different from a criminal appeal.) The first one or two administrative appeals go to a local prison administrator (Counselor, Case Manager, Captain, Warden, etc.). The Warden typically has to answer either your first or second level administrative appeal. If you are unhappy with the Warden's answer to your administrative appeal, you can file an administrative appeal to an outside authority, such as a Regional Warden, etc.

If the above process fails and you are in a FDC, contact the U.S. Marshals. They have authority over FDC's. The U.S. Marshals generally treat inmates more humanely than detention center CO's. See "Appendix D: U.S. Marshals Service" for a list of agency addresses and phone numbers.

Another appeal route involves getting your state prison agency involved. They have jurisdiction over city and county jails. See "Appendix E: State Prison Commissions" for a list of agency addresses and phone numbers.

If all of the above fail, get your politicians involved. Have your family contact your state and federal congressmen; they sometimes carry more weight than your Warden. For a list of federal congressmen, see "Appendix B: U.S. Congressmen."

Tell your family to open an independent investigation if you die while in custody. Negligence in prisons is rampant. The staff will frequently try to cover it up. Facilities are legally required to provide for your *complete* safety and *all* of your medical needs.

Before you file any appeal, make sure you pick and choose your battles carefully. If your complaint is on a minor issue or you file too many complaints, you may find yourself in a freezing cell or trying to sleep while the CO's radio is blaring all night. All of your Commissary food might be declared contraband and confiscated. Your visitors may have to wait three hours to see you. When you complain, you better have a good reason. It's better to just "tough it out" in minor cases.

FOOD FOR THOUGHT

""Without risk, faith is an impossibility."

Soren Kierkegaard

Tales from the Cage

Segregation units in FDC's are supposed to be extremely secure environments. Highly trained professionals make sure nothing goes on without their consent. The inmates serve their time in one person cells. Three walls make up the cells with a set of bars at the exit. Some facilities have a fourth wall or a sheet of Plexiglas over the bars at the entrance to prevent the inmates from causing mischief.

One day, Raul sat in his segregation cell, waiting for lunch. The smell of chicken from the kitchen was driving him crazy. He really loved to eat chicken.

The CO's brought in the lunch trays. Raul was excited, "You know, CO, they released cell number nine this morning. That means the kitchen sent us an extra tray. I really love chicken. Do you think I could have that tray?"

"Well, that wouldn't be fair to all the other inmates here. Let me tell you what I'm going to do. Since you love chicken that much, I'm going to set this tray on the table here. You can have it if you can get it. Ha! Not just that tray – I will bring you two trays of chicken next week if you can get this chicken. If not, I'm going to eat your chicken next week."

The table was four feet from the bars at the entrance of Raul's cell. The CO set the tray at the opposite end of the table, a good eight feet from the bars on Raul's cell. The CO left laughing.

Raul was determined to get that chicken. He tied two of his bed sheets together. He threw the tied sheets like a rope. It took several tries until he managed to get the sheets exactly on top of the tray.

Continued on next page

Tales from the Cage

Continued

He slowly pulled the tray to the edge of the table. Then, he used his meal tray as a platform while he pulled the second tray off the table with his sheets. He balanced one tray on top of the other, making sure not to drop his prize.

Raul ate his first serving of chicken. He hid the second serving under his blanket. He placed the lid back on the second tray. He skillfully used his first tray to lift the second tray back on the table. While climbing on top of his bed, he reached out of his cell and grabbed a five foot long paper utensil he had previously made. He used the utensil to push the second tray across the table back to its original location. Then he sat patiently on his bed.

The CO came back after lunch to pick up the trays. He looked at the second tray on the table and shook his head. "I guess I'm going to be eating well next week. Too bad you won't be eating so well."

Raul replied, "Actually, your girlfriend wrote me a letter. She said you're fat and she wants me to put you on a diet." Then, Raul threw off the blanket, picked up his extra chicken, and started eating it with a smile on his face.

The CO turned around, went to the second tray on the table, removed the lid, and found that the chicken was missing. The CO's eyes got really big as he dropped his jaw. "Oh, my God!" he said. He started cursing as Raul's laughter erupted.

CHAPTER 17:

General Prison Security Policies

Introduction

The following procedures and schedules are standard in the BOP. The procedures and schedules in each FDC and county jail will differ slightly.

Official Head Counts

The CO's have to do head counts at least five times per day. A head count is a census of the inmates. If you interfere with the head count or you are out of place, you will get a shot (inmate disciplinary reprimand). You should be in your cell for each head count unless you are instructed otherwise. You must be in the proper location for the head count at least fifteen minutes before the count begins. For example, be in your cell before 3:45 P.M. for the 4:00 P.M. head count. If you are supposed to be at work during a head count, you will be placed on an out count list by the Control Center Officer (CCO). The CCO generates all census lists that are used during each head count. No inmate movement occurs during head counts.

There are three types of head counts. They are referred to as:

1. Stand Up
2. Bed Book
3. Leisure

You are expected to stand up quietly during a Stand Up head count. Your entire body must be visible to the CO's so don't stand behind a locker. The CO's will call your housing unit level instructing everyone to stand up. Once they count you, you can relax.

Bed Book head counts occur randomly. The CO brings a bed book with each inmate's bed assignment, name, register number (U.S. Marshals number/UM number), and photograph. When the CO's enter your cell, they will ask you for your last name and register number. The information will be verified with the bed book.

You can relax or sleep during Leisure head counts. The head counts at midnight, 3:00 A.M., and 5:00 A.M. are Leisure head counts.

During each head count, the CO's have to count living flesh, not just a blanket or a pile of clothes. This means you may get a flash light in your face to awaken you if you are asleep. Your door will be kicked, or knocked on, or you will get yelled at if you are completely covered up with a blanket. Just pull the blanket down and move around. The CO's will leave.

Routine Head Counts are usually scheduled as follows:

12:00 Midnight	Leisure head count. Every night.
3:00 A.M.	Leisure head count. Every night.
5:00 A.M.	Leisure head count. Every night.
10:00 A.M.	Stand up head count. Every weekend and federal holidays.
4:00 P.M.	Stand up head count. Every day.
10:00 P.M.	Stand up head count. Every night.

The 4:00 P.M. and 10:00 P.M. head counts are a national ordeal. These two head counts are transmitted to the Central Office of the BOP. The other head counts are mandatory but they are not transmitted to the Central Office of the BOP. If someone is missing, the U.S. Marshals and local law enforcement are notified immediately.

FOOD FOR THOUGHT

"We need every human gift and cannot afford to neglect any because of artificial barriers of sex, race, class, or national origin."

Margaret Mead

Lockdown

A lockdown refers to time during which inmates are locked in their cells or housing units. Housing unit lockdowns occur if there is a riot, bad weather, certain inspections, or the jail staff has a party. (No joke.)

During a housing unit lockdown, you can watch TV, make phone calls, send e-mail, play cards, etc. Cell lockdowns are more troublesome. You can be locked down in your cell for an hour or for several weeks. This happens if there is a riot or a massive fight. Brief lockdowns occur every day during head counts.

If you are around during a riot or a fight, vacate the immediate area of the fight or riot. You do not want to be blamed for being involved in the incident. When the CO's arrive in a camp, low-security, or medium-security prison, be prepared to face the wall and kneel down. If you don't kneel down and face the wall, you can be charged with failing to obey an order. You can also get pepper-sprayed, hand cuffed, shot, etc. There are even instances when the CO's shoot innocent bystanders in serious fights. You don't want to be caught in the cross fire, move out of the way.

If you are in a United States Penitentiary (USP) or a Super-Max prison during a riot or fight, your responsibility in the situation is different. An emergency bell will ring. The first ring is a warning. You should immediately respond by laying flat on the ground. Your hands must be visible and you cannot be holding anything. Stay quiet and don't move. If you are not lying down flat, quiet, and still, the CO's have orders to shoot you. They are that serious.

Disciplinary Action

In the BOP, the staff issues written reprimands called "shots." FDC's and jails differ in their wording of each of the following but the concepts are similar:

- Shots are numbered according to the severity of the alleged offense. (100, 200, 300, or 400 series shots.)

- A series 100 shot is most serious while a series 400 shot is the least serious. (A series 400 shot is like a parking ticket.)

- Series 100 shots include murder, rape, possessing a weapon, etc.

- Series 100 shots are always forwarded to the Regional BOP for review.

- Series 100 shots frequently result in not only BOP disciplinary action, but also criminal legal charges.

- Series 100 and 200 shots almost always result in time in the Hole (Special Housing Unit/Segregation).

- Series 100 and 200 shots almost always result in a pay reduction to maintenance pay ($5.25/month) for one year.

Disciplinary Hearings

The following policies refer to disciplinary hearings in the BOP. Each FDC or jail will have slightly different policies.

- If you get a series 100 or 200 shot, you will have a disciplinary hearing. If you get a minor shot (series 300 or 400), you may simply get a minimal punishment (i.e. no phone or commissary privileges for 30 days). A minor punishment can be issued without a disciplinary hearing.

- DHO: A Disciplinary Hearing Officer (DHO) presides over your disciplinary hearing. He or she writes up the decision in your case.

- Disciplinary hearings usually take place within three business days from when your shot is written up. The DHO can delay the disciplinary hearing for another five days without any reason. Additional delays can be obtained from the Warden if a valid reason is stated.

- You can and should get a BOP representative for your side of the case. You have to ask for one.

- Inmates get to call for a list of inmate witnesses.

- Inmates may not directly question a witness. In fact, the DHO can require the defendant inmate to leave the room for security reasons while each witness is questioned. However, your BOP representative can stay in the room and question all the witnesses.

- All inmates are required to leave the hearing room while deliberations occur. The DHO then writes up the decision on your case. In some instances, you may get a warning with a suspended sentence. In other cases, you may end up in the hole.

FOOD FOR THOUGHT

"Success is falling nine times and getting up ten."

Jon Bon Jovi

Appealing Shots

If you get a shot, you can appeal it. The following forms are used in the BOP in appealing shots. Each FDC or jail uses its own set of forms and policies. In some facilities, an appeal is known as a "grievance."

Form BP-8 (BP-228):
(Request for Administrative Remedy BP-228)

You get this form from your Counselor. You turn it into your Correctional Counselor, who answers it.

Form BP-9 (BP-229):
(Request for Administrative Remedy BP-229)

If your BP-8 fails, you can get a BP-9 (BP-229) from your Correctional Counselor. A BP-9 is answered by your Warden.

Form BP-10 (BP-230):
(Request for Administrative Remedy BP-230)

If your BP-9 fails, you can file a BP-10. BP-10's are answered by the Regional Director's Office.

Confidential Form BP-10:

You get this form from your Correctional Counselor. You answer it and then the form is sealed and sent to the BOP's Regional Director's office, where it is answered. You can only use this form if there is a sensitive private issue (such as rape) or if you can prove that the local staff in your prison might retaliate against you for filing a BP-8 or BP-9.

Form BP-11 (BP-231):
(Request for Administrative Remedy BP-231)

If your BP-10 fails, you can file a BP-11. BP-11's are answered by the General Counsel in the Central Office of the BOP.

Note: When you are dealing with a dispute with the CO's, tell your family not to call the Warden unless it is a life or death situation. Remember, the CO's can make your life really awful. Do not get into a dispute over a minor issue.

For more information on shots, see "Chapter 21: Oversight and Complaints."

Moves

Inmate movement from one part of a prison to another is referred to as a "move." A few notes on moves:

- When a move is in progress, the compound or prison is referred to as an "open compound" or "open move."

- When a move is finished, the compound or prison is referred to as "closed" to further movement.

- When a CO personally escorts you across the compound, it is referred to as a "super-controlled move." This occurs when fog or darkness limits visibility or when a riot occurs. The CO's keep close control of everyone.

- If you have to go somewhere when the compound is closed, you have to ask the Unit Officer for a pass. You carry the pass from one building to the next. The CO in each building will ask to see your pass if you get there when the compound is closed.

- Ask for permission from a Unit Officer before going into a housing unit other than your own. You can get a shot for being out of bounds.

Contraband

Contraband is anything you shouldn't have, including anything that is modified from its original form or purpose. You can get punished for having contraband. In some circumstances, you will not get punished for having minor contraband, such as extra newspapers, a hi-lighter, extra fruit, etc. Most CO's just confiscate the minor contraband. More serious contraband, such as a shank (homemade knife), cell phones, or drugs will definitely get you a shot.

The more trouble you cause, the more often you will get shaken down. Those who cause fewer problems will get searched less often.

FOOD FOR THOUGHT

"Don't simply retire from something, have something to retire to."

Harry Fosdick

CO's

A few notes on the CO's:

- Some CO's are good people. Some are not. Some are more dangerous than the inmates they guard.

- They are offended if you use the word "guard." They prefer to be called "officers."

- Some are hard-working, some are not.
- Some are polite, some are not.
- Don't challenge a CO just to challenge them, they usually win.
- Stay "off the radar." This expression means you should lay low. Operate quietly in the background while letting more troublesome inmates keep the CO's busy. If you "get on a CO's radar," they can confiscate your belongings, write up a false shot, destroy your mail, have you transferred to a job you will hate, etc.
- Don't stare at women/men. Don't flirt. Don't hang around CO's.
- Don't go in a CO's office without their permission. If you do go in, get out quickly.

Prison Security Levels

BOP Security Levels Include:

1. Minimum-Security or Federal Work Camps or just "camps."
2. Low-Security or just "Lows."
3. Medium-Security or just "Mediums." They are only for men, females don't have any.
4. U.S. Penitentiary or USP or just "the pen."
5. MAX-ADX or "Super Max." These are for dangerous inmates, located in Florence, Colorado.
6. Administrative Prisons or Federal Medical Centers (FMC's).

FDC's:

These are usually operated at a mix between a BOP USP and a BOP medium-security prison.

Restraints

You will inevitably be handcuffed. The officers are supposed to double-lock the cuffs with a key. The double-lock not only increases security but also keeps you from accidentally locking the cuffs even tighter on your wrists, which can be quite painful. A plastic black box may be inserted over the chain between the hand cuffs. This decreases your mobility and thus decreases your chances of escape. The bigger or more violent you are, the more likely you will get a black box.

Officers also use a "zip-tie." It's a piece of plastic similar to what you use to tie off a trash bag. The zip-ties are used in riot situations, and they have to be cut off of you.

You may experience the joy of a belly chain. A belly chain goes around your waist and connects to your hand cuffs. This limits your mobility. Because of this, make sure your belly chain is put on high enough so you can use your hands to eat. (Place the chain above your belly, not below it.)

If you are particularly violent or you are in a maximum-security (a USP), you will have an electronic custody control belt placed on you when you travel. This belt has a built-in stun feature. The CO walks around with a remote control. All the CO has to do is press the button to shock you. The policy states they can shock you if you threaten someone or you attempt to escape. Do not make jokes about the CO's spouse in this situation, you may find the result too electrifying.

On a similar note, a technology company has developed a laser that can be used to stun inmates up to one hundred feet away. The laser allegedly causes the inmate pain without permanently damaging tissue.

FOOD FOR THOUGHT

"Show class, have pride, and display character."

Bear Bryant

Serious Tools

The staff inside of prison usually does not carry weapons because the weapons create a temptation for the inmates. The staff carries stun guns during a riot. The staff also carries clubs with built-in tasers.

The anti-riot strike force consists of a team of CO's armed with stun guns, tasers, hand guns, shot guns, and/or mace. Each CO wears body armor, a helmet, and a face shield. (They look like a group of Ninja turtles.) Get out of their way when you see them coming. If you do not obey their commands immediately, you may find yourself getting maced, tased, or shot. They don't mess around.

A group of these Ninja turtles is called a cluster. A cluster typically consists of eight to twelve CO's in riot gear. At least four CO's carry a shield in a vertical orientation to protect the cluster - one CO faces in each of the four directions. This creates a box. One CO in front and one CO in back carry a shield in a horizontal orientation. Some CO's carry tasers, mace, or guns with rubber bullets or live ammunition.

Note: It's BOP policy to shoot any inmate attempting to escape. You can also be shot if you fail to cooperate in a fight or riot, though this is rare in a camp or low-security prison.

Employee Hostages

In the BOP, "any employee taken hostage is without any authority, regardless of rank or position."

Security Dogs

Many FDC's and jails have security dogs that search for drugs or explosives. You cannot approach, touch, feed, or communicate with the dogs. Leave them alone.

Ion Spectrometers

Ion spectrometers are devices used to search inmates and visitors for traces of narcotics.

FOOD FOR THOUGHT

"He that won't be counseled can't be helped."

Benjamin Franklin

Tales from the Cage

The DOJ oversees the BOP. These federal agencies hire the finest men and women in the nation. The BOP spends millions of dollars every year training this elite group of officers. One of the awesome responsibilities of these fearless officers is to keep track of all inmates at all times. To lose track of an inmate is to place the public's safety in jeopardy. That would never happen.

If an inmate is out of their housing unit during a census count, the CCO has to create an out-count list. This list contains the names of every inmate that is supposed to be at a specific location, such as the Chow Hall, Library, or Visitation Room.

One day, Officer Maxaft Cop and Officer Bad Cop were in charge of conducting a census count using an out count list. Officer Bad Cop got every inmate to stand in line quietly so they could concentrate on the great words of wisdom from Officer Maxaft Cop. As each inmate's name was read aloud, the inmate stated his register number in response.

Officer Maxaft Cop looked up to see an inmate raise his hand. "You skipped me. My name is John Doe, number 12345-678." Two other inmates chimed in, their names were left off the list.

Officer Maxaft Cop read through the entire list again only to realize the three inmates' names were still nowhere to be found. The inmates didn't want to be accused of being out of place or attempting to escape. One said, "Well, we're here."

Officer Bad Cop walked up and yanked the clipboard out of the first officer's hands. He huffed and he puffed his way down the list but he still could not find the names of the three unaccounted for inmates. This ordeal went on for six minutes. These dedicated cops were going to get to the bottom of this perplexing mystery.

Officer Good Cop finally showed up on the scene, wondering what was taking so long. He grabbed the clipboard. After finishing all of the inmates' names on page one, he simply turned the page to find the remaining three names on page two. He looked at Officers Maxaft Cop and Bad Cop. Mystery solved. All the inmates laughed.

For More Information

- For more information on your FDC's or jail's policies, please see the Inmate Handbook for that facility.

- For more information on the BOP's policies, please see the following BOP program statements:

- BOP Program Statement 1150.05: Office of Security Technology

- BOP Program Statement 1237.11: Information Security Programs

- BOP Program Statement 1237.13: Information Security Programs

- BOP Program Statement 5100.06: Security Designation and Custody Classification Manual

- BOP Program Statement 5100.08: Security Designation and Custody Classification Manual

- BOP Program Statement 5500.12: Correctional Services Procedures Manual

- BOP Program Statement 5521.05: Searches of Housing Units, Inmates, and Inmate Work Areas

- BOP Program Statement 5522.01: Ion Spectrometry Device Program

- BOP Program Statement 5538.05: Escorted Trips

- BOP Program Statement 5538.13: Stun Gun

- BOP Program Statement 5566.06: Use of Force and Application of Restraints

CHAPTER 18:

Inmate Safety Issues

Introduction

This chapter is dedicated to inmate safety and security issues. The government will publicly state it has safety and security policies to protect individual inmates and the public from any violence. The reality is violence occurs in prisons. Some USP's have 500 fights per year. Many fights are not reported. Camps will have a few fights per year. In some instances, the CO's will quickly break up the fights. In other cases, they will encourage the fighting and only enter the scene to pick up the body of the loser. On paper, they will write down that they "responded to the fight immediately." Inmates at the fight realize the CO's dragged their feet. It's in your best interest to avoid violence.

Respect

Respect is critical in prison. There are some key concepts you should learn about respect:

- In the free world, respect is usually unspoken. In prison, it's spoken of often as people are forced to live in close quarters.

- Respect should be mutual but sometimes it's not. If someone treats you disrespectfully, be the mature person by not escalating the situation.

- Always think if something is respectful or disrespectful before you act.

- Be friendly but not "happy-go-lucky." Try to get along with most people.

- Blend in but not to the point of being racist, mean, or participating in illegal activities.
- Don't look in other inmate's cells when you walk by.
- Don't read other people's mail.
- Don't look in other people's lockers.
- Respect people's personal space: In the U.S., people generally stand at least two feet away from other people. (Your immediate family members should be the only people you stand closer to.)
- Knock before you enter someone else's cell room.
- Ask for permission before you sit in someone else's chair.
- Respect other people's property: Don't steal, destroy, or eat it.
- Don't jump to conclusions.
- Don't try to be better than someone else: Don't mention your money, job titles, degrees, real estate property, etc. unless someone asks.
- Don't stare at people.
- Be somewhat generous but be careful what you loan because you may not get it back.
- Clean up after yourself.
- Respect others by taking care of your appearance (see below).

Your Appearance

- Confrontations have been started and then have escalated because of people's appearance.
- Stay off the radar. The radar is the public's focused attention. You are on the radar if you draw attention to yourself. You are off the radar if you blend in. Don't become Freaky Inmate.
- Take at least one shower every day. (Yes, this means you, smelly one.)
- Blue Shoes: Only wear the blue shoes from Receiving and Discharge (R&D) for one day, if possible. You will be picked on because of the blue shoes as they indicate you are a new inmate. The CO's will write you up if you wear blue shoes after your first couple of days in prison.
- Men should cut their hair.
- Shave or trim your beard every day.
- Men should *never* wear nail polish.

- If you are obese, lose weight.
- Normal glasses are o.k., not yellow, red, blue, purple, or green ones.
- Wear your uniform correctly.
- Pull up your pants.
- Making friends increases your safety.

Confrontations

No matter what you do, you will have confrontations. There are inmates who honestly have nothing to look forward to in the free world. They have no qualms about hurting or killing you.

When you've made a mistake, try to de-escalate it by saying "my bad" ("I'm sorry"). Count to ten before fighting. Think before you act: "Is it worth going to the hole (solitary confinement) over an apple?" Many inmates bluff. Their goal is to act macho to scare everyone off. They actually have no real intention of fighting.

FOOD FOR THOUGHT

"As I grow older, I pay less attention to what men say. I just watch what they do."

Andrew Carnegie

The Most Common Reasons for Fighting Are:

Stealing:

1. You steal from another inmate.

2. Another inmate stole from you and you try to get your stuff back.

3. Another inmate stole from you but you blame the wrong inmate.
   Solutions:

   a. Don't steal.

   b. If you do steal, don't steal from inmates. Some inmates suggest only stealing from the BOP.

   c. Prevent stealing by locking your locker when you are not close by it. Don't leave your belongings sitting around.

Lack of Respect:

Solutions:

    a. Be respectful.

    b. Think before you act.

    c. Learn to de-escalate confrontations.

    d. Learn to give and take.

Overcrowding: The overcrowding is like a pressure cooker: Sometimes, it's just going to blow.

Solutions:

    a. Be patient.

    b. Move out of other people's way.

    c. Be respectful.

Televisions: People want to control the channels on the TV's.

Solutions:

    a. Ask others before you change a channel.

    b. Watch TV with some of your friends.

    c. Don't sit in or move someone else's chair.

    d. Find something to read instead of watching TV.

FOOD FOR THOUGHT

"Woe to him who believes in nothing."

Victor Hugo

Stay Off the Radar

- Blend in.
- Cut your hair, shower, and shave.
- If you are a snitch, never admit it. Consider a cover story.
- If you are homosexual, don't discuss it. Don't practice it or only practice in a private room. Consider acting heterosexual.
- If you are a sex offender, don't discuss it. Consider a cover story.

Snitches

- If you snitch, never admit it. Consider a cover story.

- Inmates know general sentences for common crimes, like conspiracy to smuggle narcotics. If your sentence is too low, inmates will think you snitched. Some may attack you.
Solutions:

   a. Tell them you gave money from a drug deal back to the government as a part of a plea agreement for a shorter sentence.

   b. Change your name.

   c. Consider going into Protective Custody.

   d. Use the buddy system. *(See below)*.

Homosexuality/Cross Dressing

- Don't discuss your homosexuality or your cross-dressing hobby. It places you in danger. If you get caught in the act, you are at an even higher risk of violence. You can also get a shot (inmate written reprimand) known as a "205 Engaging in Sexual Acts."

- Don't cross dress or wear fingernail polish.

- If you do practice, do it in a locked cell at night after the CO's finish their head count.

- This is a personal choice. Most inmates in low-security prisons and work camps are tolerant. The problem is there is a percentage of inmates who are both intolerant and violent.

Sex Offenders

Any sexual offense places your safety at risk in prison. The more personal your offense was, the higher your risk of violence. For example, sex offenders that committed rape are at a higher risk than those people that only possessed child pornography.

Tips:

   1. Don't discuss your case.

   2. Stay off the radar. (Cut your hair, shower, shave, no fingernail polish.)

   3. Follow the rules of respect.

   4. Use the buddy system (see below).

   5. Consider Protective Custody.

   6. Use a cover story.

7. Change your name.

8. Transfer out of state.

FOOD FOR THOUGHT

"Go big or go home. Because it's true: What do you have to lose?"

Eliza Dushku

Gangs

Gangs are a group of people that commit organized criminal activity. Gangs in prisons are more of an issue in Texas, California, and Florida. Northern states have fewer gang issues. Some gangs are violent while others are not. Some typically non-violent gangs can become violent if they are threatened or someone tries to take over their territory. Most gangs have some territory. Most of them will leave you alone if you just stay out of their territory. Many members tend to bluff more than they fight.

If possible, make a friend or two from each gang by finding something in common. Be very respectful and it might pay off. However, stay out of their illegal activity.

There is a reason there aren't a lot of old people in gangs. Many of them have died violently. Tear drop tattoos beneath an inmate's eyes or to the side indicate they have served a prison sentence of five years for each tear drop. Try not to upset the inmate with several tear drop tattoos beneath his eyes.

The Buddy System

Most people in low-security prisons do not need a buddy, but if you are a vulnerable inmate, you should consider the buddy system. Take your buddy everywhere you go. Your buddy stands guard while you take a shower. Then you guard the entrance while your buddy showers. Go to eat, exercise, and watch TV together. You watch each other's cells when one of you is gone.

Mail Security Issues

Get a P.O. Box for your immediate family to use. It makes it harder for people to track them down.

- Shred your mail, legal documents, used envelopes, etc.
- Don't leave your mail or legal documents sitting around. Put them in your locker.

Your Financial Credit Score

A credit bureau is an organization that keeps track of your financial credit score. Those people who pay all their bills on time have a higher credit score than those who don't pay their bills on time. Your credit score is important to you because it can be used for you to get a loan for a house or a car when you get out. Even potential leasers look at your credit score before leasing to you. Potential employers may look at your credit score before deciding to hire you. If your score is too low, they may not hire you.

You are already at a disadvantage for getting a job or place to live because you have a felony conviction. If someone steals your identity while you are in prison and opens up accounts in your name that they have no intention of paying off, your credit score will go even lower. It is to your advantage to protect your credit score.

The problem is compounded in several ways:

1. You are stuck in prison without access to a private phone you can use.

2. You have no private e-mail.

3. You keep getting shipped around so your address keeps changing. If someone steals your identity, it's harder for you to learn about it.

4. It's hard to know if you can trust your significant other not to destroy your credit rating in your absence.

5. You worry about other inmates or the staff stealing your identity.

FOOD FOR THOUGHT

"Always desire to learn something useful."

Sophocles

In the BOP, you can pay your bills using money from your Commissary Account by using a BP-199.045 form (Request for Withdrawal of Inmate's Personal Fund). For more information, please see the "Withdrawal of Funds" section in "Chapter 30: Inmate Trust Fund."

Consider protecting your credit score by placing a freeze on each of your credit bureau files while you are serving time in prison. Once your credit bureau file is frozen, no new lines of credit (loans) can be opened under your identity without you first issuing a password to temporarily unlock your credit file. This reduces your risk of identity theft.

To request a security freeze on your credit bureau file, write to each of the credit bureaus listed below. Be sure to include your:

1. Full name

2. Address

3. Federal register number

4. Social Security number

5. Date of Birth

6. A photocopy of your prison ID badge

7. Some credit bureaus require a notarized letter of your identity. An identity letter verifies items 1-5 above. You sign it in front of a notary public after they look at your photo ID badge. (Your Education and Lieutenant's Offices should have a notary public.)

Equifax Credit Information
P O Box 740241
Atlanta, GA 30374

Experian
P O Box 9701
Allen, TX 75013

Trans Union
P O Box 6790
Fullerton, CA 92834

CHAPTER 19:

Preparing for Your Sentencing Hearing

FOOD FOR THOUGHT

"Procrastination is opportunity's assassin."

Victor Kiam

Your Convictions

Whether you were found guilty at trial or you are signing a plea agreement, you need to obtain a copy of the indictments and a list of which charges you were actually convicted of at trial or will be convicted of through the plea agreement process. Read "Chapter 9: Sentencing Guidelines" to see what your sentence range is.

Pre-Sentencing Interviews and Reports

Federal law requires you to go through a Pre-Sentencing Interview (PSI) before you are sentenced. Your PSI will be conducted with you and your PO. It is to your advantage to have your attorney present, taking notes on critical issues. Your attorney should attempt to set limits on how far the PO pushes you for information. There is a fine line between which information is considered required by federal law and which information is protected by privacy law and the Fifth Amendment to the U.S. Constitution.

A Pre-Sentencing Report (PSR) will be generated, consisting of sections on:

1. Your demographic information (i.e.: name, address, date of birth, etc.)

2. The criminal convictions (Your prosecutor generates this section.)

3. A description of each crime (Your prosecutor generates this section.)

4. Other criminal history: Both convictions and accusations without convictions (You and your prosecutor generate this section.)

5. Your childhood, family, education, upbringing, work history, military history, gang affiliations, etc.

6. Your Possible Sentence:

   a. Each base charge

   b. Enhancements on each charge

   c. Downward Departures on each charge

   d. Fines

   e. Special Assessments

   f. Restitution

You must be honest. Lying to your PO can get you charged with obstruction of justice, which will increase your time served.

PSI's and pre-plea PSI's are conducted by PO's who write a PSR. Once the rough draft of your PSR is done, it is sent to both your defense attorney and the prosecutor. You will get to review it for mistakes. Make a written list of the mistakes. Keep a copy for your records and send the original to your attorney. Your attorney should attempt to get the mistakes fixed. Your PO will fix simple issues, like typos. More complex issues will have to be argued directly with the judge during the sentencing hearing.

The rough draft of your PSR is due at least seven days before your sentencing hearing. This is supposed to give you time to review your PSR and submit changes to your lawyer, who sends the changes to your PO. The PO is supposed to send your attorney and the prosecutor a final draft of the PSR.

You are supposed to have an opportunity to read your final PSR before your sentencing hearing. In your sentencing hearing, your judge is required to ask you if you have read your final PSR and if you agree with it. If there is a mistake, politely point it out: "Your Honor, I have read it. There is one mistake – My correct address is 1001 Main Street…. Other than that, it is accurate."

If you have not had a chance to read your PSR, let the judge know: "Your Honor, I have not had a chance to read my PSR. I politely request a chance to review it." You are legally accountable for what's in your PSR. The judge knows this. The judge also knows you have a legal right to review your PSR. If not, the contents of your PSR can be appealed, though this is costly and time-consuming.

If you are signing a plea agreement, make sure you have completed a pre-plea PSR and you have read and understand your pre-plea PSR *before* you sign the plea agreement. Realize part of your sentence is based on your past Criminal History and enhancements as they are described in your pre-plea PSR. If you sign a plea agreement and the prosecutor or PO subsequently adds enhancements or erroneous Criminal History to your pre-plea PSR, you may receive a higher sentence than you agreed to in the plea agreement.

For example, you are signing a plea agreement for possessing cocaine. You agree to a maximum sentence of five years. After you sign the plea agreement, the prosecutor adds on enhancements for possessing a weapon because you had a pocket knife in your pocket. Then they add a past crime, consisting of a stereo you allegedly "stole from your girlfriend." The judge sentences you to ten years in prison, not the five years you agreed to. You must protect yourself by reading your pre-plea PSR *before* you sign a plea agreement.

FOOD FOR THOUGHT

"Life is not the way it's supposed to be. It's the way it is. The way you cope with it is what makes the difference."

Virginia Satir

The Pre-Sentence Investigation and Your Close Contacts

After your PSI, your PO will contact some or all of your references. This may include your family, friends, and recent employers. The PO will ask questions about your:

1. Demographical Information
2. Criminal History (both convictions and simple accusations)
3. Medical History
4. Alcohol and Drug History
5. Family History
6. Education
7. Military History
8. Work History
9. Upbringing
10. Gang Affiliations

Enhancements

Your base sentence may be increased because of enhancements. You must read your PSR carefully to understand which enhancements you are being charged with. Try to obtain the federal statutes concerning each enhancement in your case. The law requires specific evidence before an enhancement can be applied to your sentence. In some cases, prosecutors will try to enhance your sentence without the necessary evidence. In other cases, prosecutors will try to apply repetitive enhancements to your sentence. While you can be given an enhancement, getting two enhancements for the same issue may be illegal in some circumstances. (You can get an enhancement for issue A *or* issue B but not both A *and* B.) Your attorney should file a written motion to fight the enhancements, if they are legally inappropriate.

Downward Departures

The U.S. Sentencing Commission issues sentencing guidelines that federal judges use when sentencing defendants. The sentencing guidelines state certain reasons for a downward departure. Additionally, in the U.S. Supreme Court case known as *U.S. v. Booker (2005)*, the Supreme Court ruled that the sentencing guidelines were just guidelines, not absolute rules that federal judges have to follow. This ruling allows federal judges to give a sentence that is a downward departure from the sentence recommended in the sentencing guidelines. For example, if the sentencing guidelines recommend a ten-year sentence, the judge can sentence you to five years.

The judge has to have a specific legal reason to give you a downward departure. Part of the Title 18 U.S. Code § 3553 outlines some of these reasons. *U.S. v. Booker (2005)* lists additional reasons. See if any of the following reasons apply to your situation. Talk to your lawyer on how to use this information in your sentencing hearing.

- Age 55 years or older
- Educational and vocational skills
- Mental conditions
- Medical conditions
- Drug or alcohol dependency
- Employment history
- Family responsibilities (especially if you are a woman with children)
- Community responsibilities
- Race
- Gender

- National Origin
- Creed
- Religion
- Socioeconomic status
- Military service
- Civic or charitable service
- Record of private good works
- Poor upbringing
- You didn't knowingly harm or injure a victim
- Your victim's conduct provoked or contributed to the harm you did. (This does not apply to criminal sex abuse.)
- You committed a lesser crime, such as a mercy killing.
- Your conduct was innocent, such as a police officer who had an illegal weapon at home that was supposed to be used for training at an academy.
- You committed a crime under blackmail or duress.
- You enter into and make significant progress in rehabilitation.
- You committed the offense under severely reduced mental capacity. However, your judge cannot give you a downward departure if:

    a. Your decreased mental capacity was caused by the voluntary use of drugs or alcohol.

    b. The facts and circumstances of your offense reveal a need to protect the public because the offense involved actual violence or a serious threat of violence.

    c. Your Criminal History indicates a need to lock you up to protect the public.

    d. You have been convicted of an offense listed in Title 18, U.S. Code, Chapter 71, 109A, or 117.

- You voluntarily reported the crime to law enforcement and the crime was unlikely to have been discovered otherwise.
- Aberrant behavior. If your offense was out of your character, it may be the basis for a downward departure. You can only use this argument if your crime was a single occurrence, was of short duration, and was a deviation by you in an otherwise law-abiding life. You cannot use this argument if:

    a. The offense involved serious bodily injury or death.

    b. The offense involved a dangerous weapon.

   c. You committed a serious drug trafficking offense.

   d. You have more than one Criminal History point.

   e. You have a prior state or federal felony conviction.

   f. Your offense involved a minor under section 1201, 1591, or Title 18, U.S. Code, Chapter 71, 109A, 110, or 117.

Any one of the above is unlikely to get you a downward departure. However, if you have several of the above, you may have a better chance at being successful.

While defendants accused of non-sexual crimes can use any of the above reasons to argue for a downward departure, defendants accused of sexual crimes may or may not be able to use each reason listed above. A law known as "The Feeney Amendment" narrowed the list of reasons defendants of sexual crimes can use to argue for a downward departure. *U.S. versus Booker* and other court cases have questioned the legality of "The Feeney Amendment". Ultimately, you will have to make a list of reasons for a downward departure and discuss the legal merits of each reason with your lawyer.

FOOD FOR THOUGHT

"Virtually nothing on earth can stop a person with a positive attitude who has his goal clearly in sight."

Denis Waitley

A special note about family responsibilities (from § 5H1.6 of the Guidelines Manual): The defendant has to prove:

   i. The defendant's service of a sentence within the applicable guideline range will cause a substantial, direct, and specific loss of essential caretaking, or essential financial support, to the defendant's family.

   ii. The loss of caretaking or financial support substantially exceeds the harm ordinarily incident to incarceration for a similarly situated defendant. For example, the fact that the defendant's family might incur some degree of financial hardship or suffer to some extent from the absence of a parent through incarceration is not in itself sufficient as a basis for departure because such hardship or suffering is of a sort ordinarily incident to incarceration. [For example, you are scheduled to donate a kidney to your child. You are the only donor match. Without the kidney, your child could die. The judge might allow you to serve your sentence on probation instead of in prison.]

iii. The loss of caretaking or financial support is one for which no effective reme-
dial or ameliorative programs reasonably are available, making the defendant's
caretaking or financial support irreplaceable to the defendant's family.

iv. The departure effectively will address the loss of caretaking or financial support.

Minimum Mandatory Sentences

A distinction must be made between the sentencing guidelines and minimum mandatory sentences. Sentencing guidelines are *optional* sentences recommended by the U.S.
Sentencing Commission. The U.S. Sentencing Commission makes independent recommendations. Minimum mandatory sentences are *required* sentence lengths created
by federal Congress in the laws. While your judge has the option to give you a downward departure from the sentencing guidelines, he or she must give you a minimum
mandatory sentence, if the law requires it.

Other Criminal Conduct

In determining your sentence, your judge will consider your current criminal allegation
as well as your past Criminal History. This includes both crimes you were convicted of
and crimes you were accused of but never convicted of.

A clarification must be made between the level of evidence used in a criminal trial and
the level of evidence used in a sentencing hearing. In a criminal trial, the government
must prove its case "beyond a reasonable doubt." There is a high standard of evidence.
When you are sentenced, the judge uses a standard of "the preponderance of the evidence." This is a low standard of evidence that can hurt you. A mere verbal accusation
made by a reputable person can be used in your sentencing hearing to give you a longer
sentence. Your lawyer can try to fight this, but you may find yourself serving a longer
sentence because of a "he said, she said" situation.

The Walsh Act

The Walsh Act is a federal law that allows the government to hold dangerous sex offenders in a civil commitment after they finish their prison term. In other words, a sex
offender can be convicted and sentenced to serve ten years in prison. When the ten
years is up, they can be released only to find themselves being confined to a Community
Corrections Center (CCC). A CCC, which is also known as a Halfway House (HH)
or Residential Re-entry Center (RRC), is a type of community prison. The amount of
evidence the government must use to obtain a civil commitment is relatively minimal.
The legality of the Walsh Act was upheld by the U.S. Supreme Court in *U.S. v. Com-
stock (2010)*.

Fines, Special Assessments, and Restitution

For information on fines, special assessments, and restitution, please refer back to "Chapter 11: Plea Bargains." Recall that most defendants will get to keep one average house and one average automobile. If you own an extravagant house or automobile or you own multiple houses or automobiles, be prepared for the judge to seize your property to pay off money you will owe for fines, special assessments, and/or restitution.

Of special note on your money: You cannot hide your money from the government. You can get charged with obstruction of justice. However, you *can* pay your legitimate bills with your money. If you get a bill for $10,000 from a credit card company, you have a legal right to pay the entire bill from your assets. The downside is the DOJ may freeze all of your assets and then nitpick over how the assets are utilized.

Witnesses and Supporters

Alleged victims can be called to testify for the prosecutors in your sentencing hearing. You can call witnesses to testify on your behalf. Government witnesses and supporters sit behind the prosecutors while defense witnesses and supporters sit behind the defense team.

You should have as many well-behaved, well-dressed supporters as you can in the courtroom. The prosecutors want to make you out to be an evil felon, deserving of ten life sentences. Your supporters will show the judge you are a warm human being – someone's spouse, parent, child, friend, or co-worker. Every bit helps.

Men should wear dark suits with dark ties. If women testify, they need to call your attorney in advance and find out if the judge requires women to wear long dresses with hemlines below the knee or suits. Long dresses or skirts may be required in one courtroom and forbidden in the next. Your judge decides, not the court of public opinion.

Everyone should stand when the judge enters and leaves. Everyone should be quiet during the proceedings. No one should enter or leave the courtroom unless they are given permission.

You need to let everyone know that cameras of any kind (including cell phone cameras) are forbidden in courthouses. All cell phones and pagers should be turned off. Weapons are forbidden, including mace, knives, guns, and weapons possessed by law enforcement.

You and your family cannot communicate with each other. If the bailiffs catch you communicating with them, they will ask them to leave. Let your family know this in advance so they are not offended. The most you can do is glance at them when entering or leaving. Once in a while, a bailiff will give you permission to speak to your family for one minute after the judge is finished.

FOOD FOR THOUGHT

"Sow a thought, reap an action; sow an action, reap a habit; sow a habit, reap a character; sow a character, reap a destiny."

Samuel Smiles

Character Letters

You should consider having your supporters write character letters to the judge. The purpose of the letters is to persuade your judge that you are generally not a bad person. In some instances, character letters will give the judge just enough of a reason to be lenient on you. Sometimes it works; sometimes it doesn't. The good news is they are cheap. They just cost one postage stamp and ten minutes of someone's time.

The letters themselves should be addressed to your judge ("Dear Judge") but mailed to your attorney. Set a deadline several weeks before your sentencing hearing. This gives time for your attorney to read each letter. Those letters that contain profanity, severe anger, or other unflattering comments will be screened out by your attorney. The better letters will be mailed to the judge in advance of your sentencing hearing.

Character Letters Should Include:

1. Your identity (name, federal registration number/ U.S. Marshals number)

2. How long the supporter has known you.

3. Your good character and examples that show your character and good deeds: i.e. volunteer work, taking care of family members, church work, military service, etc.

4. Your low-risk for posing a safety risk to the community in the future.

5. Possibly your innocence, if you were convicted at trial. Innocence claims may anger a judge, who only saw what the prosecutors wanted him or her to hear at trial. Your attorney needs to decide in advance if your innocence should be discussed or avoided in the letters.

Tell your supporters to:

1. Avoid angry comments or foul language.

2. Never threaten anyone.

3. Type the letters.

4. Have someone else read the letter to check for typos, clarity, etc.

Do the character letters and supporters at the sentencing hearing really help?

Sometimes. In some cases inmates got nothing out of it at all. In other cases several inmates were told by their judge that they were getting a lenient sentence because of their supporters. One inmate put it this way: "The judge told me, 'Before we started today, I was planning on giving you a five to seven year sentence. Because of the 120 letters I received and the presence of dozens of your family members and friends, I'm giving you a three year sentence.'" It was a drug case, which means he was allowed to participate in the Residential Drug and Abuse Program (RDAP). If he has good behavior and completes the RDAP, his potential of a five to seven year sentence turned into less than a two year sentence.

Character letters are generally worth the minimal effort if you are a first-time offender.

Military Service

It's been said that the DOJ no longer allows federal inmates to serve time in the military instead of in prison. While this is mostly true, it is not always the case. One inmate facing a ten year drug sentence that did a plea bargain avoided serving prison time by serving in the U.S. Army for twenty years. It doesn't hurt to ask your attorney if this is an option for you.

FOOD FOR THOUGHT

"If you feel like it's difficult to change, you will probably have a harder time succeeding."

Andrea Jung

Your Speech

After the prosecutors have listed as many reasons as they can think of to have you locked up for one million years, your attorney gets to speak on your behalf. Then you get a chance to speak. Your speech should be less than one minute long. You should practice it with your attorney. Your attorney should give you tips on your allocution (public speech delivery). For example, look directly at the judge. Don't curse or use slang. Speak clearly.

If you are truly guilty, express deep remorse and apologize. If you are innocent, express concern for the victim(s), but do not express personal remorse. In any case, express what you have lost, what you have learned, and how the process has changed you.

Your Prison Preference

You should tell your attorney in advance which prison you would prefer to serve your time in. Your attorney will inform the judge. The judge may recommend you serve your time anywhere they want you to. Furthermore, the BOP does not have to obey any order your judge issues in regards to where you serve your time. Some defendants get their first choice while others do not.

In general, the BOP attempts to keep inmates within 500 miles of their home address, although this occurs only half the time.

You need to read "Chapter 29: Entering the BOP" twice: Once before your sentencing hearing and once after it. Chapter 29 contains the prison security Federal Custody Classification Table. Go through the Federal Custody Classification Table before your sentencing hearing to determine which security level of prison you will be locked in (work camp, low, medium, U.S. Penitentiary). Then read "Appendix F: "Federal Prisons and Federal Bureau of Prisons Offices." Decide which prison you prefer and notify your attorney.

Go back through the Federal Custody Classification Table after your sentencing hearing. At that point, you will know how long your sentence is and which enhancements were added or dropped by the judge. Either of these items can change your prison security classification. For instance, if you are sentenced to twenty to twenty-nine years, you cannot serve your initial time in a work camp or low-security prison. You have to go to a medium-security prison until your security points decrease over time.

Many inmates won't get to go to their first prison choice. Why not?

1. If you had co-defendants in your case, you cannot serve time in the same prison. For example, if there are twelve co-defendants, they will be sent to twelve different prisons, regardless of what the defendants chose.

2. Likewise, you cannot serve time in a prison that has a co-defendant from a previous case you were involved in.

3. You cannot serve time in a prison that is the wrong security level for you. If you chose to serve your time in a work camp, but your security points are too high, you won't get to go to a work camp initially.

4. You will be unlikely to serve your time in a prison that is more than 40% overcrowded. Most federal prisons have an extra 30-40% overcrowding. If you

choose a prison that is more than 40% overcrowded, you will find yourself in another location. (Note: As of the writing of this chapter, there are only three low-security prisons on the entire west coast.) Prisons usually don't publicize their statistics on overcrowding.

CHAPTER 20:

Your Sentencing Hearing

Process

You will be awoken at 4:00 A.M. or 5:00 A.M. the day of your sentencing hearing. You will be taken to a holding tank and searched. You will then take a trip to the federal court house, where you will be searched again and locked in another holding tank. You and five to ten other defendants will be taken into the court room for sentencing.

Your judge will have read your records prior to the hearing. He will have also read statements from you, your supporters, and your alleged victims. A ballpark sentence will be on the judge's mind. Your goal is to lower that sentence as much as possible.

The judge will ask you if you have read and agree with your Pre-Sentencing Report (PSR). Speak up if there are errors. Otherwise, you will have to live with the mistakes in your PSR. Everything from your biographical information, criminal history, and medical history will be quoted back to you by a future prosecutor, CO, or prison medical staff member. Getting your PSR fixed later is a real hassle. No one will believe you. You will hear, "Your PSR says A, B, and C.... You agreed to your PSR."

The judge will verbally discuss certain parts of your PSR as well as each base charge for each count you were convicted of. Your Criminal Conduct History will also be discussed. The judge will then discuss the Offense Level you are starting at as well as each enhancement proposed by the prosecutor. If your attorney wrote motions to request a downward departure and/or to defend you against each enhancement, the judge will discuss the motions.

After the judge and both attorneys have discussed the base offenses, proposed enhancements, and proposed downward departures, the judge will declare the modified Offense Level you are at prior to any allocution by either side.

The prosecutors will then get an opportunity to call their witnesses followed by your witnesses.

Each legal team then gets to speak on their side's behalf, starting with the prosecutors. This process is commonly referred to as allocution. Your attorney will then get a chance to speak, followed by you. You need to speak slowly and annunciate carefully. Look directly at the judge, and have the salient points of your remarks well-thought out in advance. If you pleaded guilty (as 97% of criminal defendants do), don't say anything at all suggesting that you are not guilty. Rather, accept responsibility – and express regret – for your criminal misconduct.

FOOD FOR THOUGHT

"A good head and a good heart are always a formidable combination."

Nelson Mandela

Your sentence will be issued verbally. Your prison preference may or may not be discussed, though the attorneys have usually notified the judge of your preference in advance.

After you leave, your judge has to write the final Judgment and Commitment (J&C) orders. J&C orders state how long you will serve in prison, your fines, special assessments, and restitution. It will also list how long you will be on supervised release and which rules you will be expected to follow. The judge's verbal comments in your sentencing hearing and the written J&C may differ in some respects. While some of the rules will be similar to rules other defendants have in their J&C's, other rules will be unique. Because the J&C orders differ and you are legally bound to follow them, you must get a written copy of your J&C orders, even if it takes several months to get them. The last thing you want to do is get arrested while you are on supervised release because you did not follow an unknown rule in the J&C orders.

When you leave the court house, you may go through a "perp walk". A "perp walk" is a walk directly in front of the press. Walk calmly and don't answer questions. Generally speaking, any attempts to cover your face will only make the situation worse. Photographs or video footage of you covering your face tend to get more publicity.

CHAPTER 21:

Oversight and Complaints

FOOD FOR THOUGHT

"The best remedy for anger is delay."

Brigham Young

Inmate Requests to Staff

What happens if you make a request to the FDC staff and they deny it? You may consider appealing. Some places call it an "appeal." Other places call it a "grievance." You usually have to ask the staff for a form to start the process. The first appeal is usually made to the head of the Department you need help from, such as the Laundry Department. If that fails, you usually go on to file an appeal to the Warden. You can then appeal to the Regional Warden. Be careful. There are time limits for filing each form. Ask for details.

You will notice that some of the FDC staff are honest, hard-working professionals and many are not. You will meet Officers Bad Cop, Maxaft Cop, Corrupt O. Cop, and Creepy Cop along the way. They work at every location of every FDC. If you thought the Department of Motor Vehicles in your state was a nightmare, multiply it by a factor of a thousand to understand the FDC.

U.S. Marshals Service

You should consider contacting the U.S. Marshals if you encounter staff engaged in:

1. Fraud, extortion, bribery

2. Theft

3. Physical or sexual abuse

4. Possession or selling illegal drugs

5. Waste

6. Unprofessional conduct (disorderly conduct or abusive language)

7. Failure to respond to an emergency

8. Violations of security regulations

9. Other violations of standards of Employee Conduct

While fraud, physical and sexual abuse, and illegal drug activity in the FDC are relatively rare, instances of waste, unprofessional conduct, failure to respond to emergencies, and violations of security regulations occur several times an hour.

FOOD FOR THOUGHT

"Happiness is not a state to arrive at, but a manner of traveling."

Margaret Lee Runbeck

American Correctional Association

Another avenue that can be used to report a serious issue is the American Correctional Association (ACA). The ACA is an accreditation organization for prisons. The ACA will not change the ruling on a case in a FDC nor will they independently investigate your case. However, you may cause the ACA to demand a better investigation into the prison issue. Remember, if the ACA does not approve a prison's procedures for handling complaints, they may not give their seal of approval to the prison, causing the entire prison to shut down, leaving all the staff without jobs. What's more likely to happen is the ACA will not give the prison its highest stamp of approval, causing the prison staff to take your case more seriously. The FDC may have trouble sweeping something under the rug if the ACA is now asking questions about the issue. The ACA can be reached at:

American Correctional Association
Standards and Accreditation Department
206 North Washington Street, Suite 200
Alexandria, Virginia 22314
703-224-0000

Your Medical Record

You are allowed access to a copy of your medical records but you must often submit a Freedom of Information Act request to get the records *(see below)*.

Freedom of Information Act

The Freedom of Information Act of 1974 (FOIA) forbids the release of information from agency records without a written request or by a prior written consent of the individual except for specific instances. The law is codified in Title 5 U.S. Code § 552. This type of request can be used to get a copy of your prison records or your medical records.

A FOIA Request Must:

1. Be addressed to the Regional Warden of the FDC, Attention: FOI Request.

2. State the nature of the records wanted.

3. State the approximate dates covered.

4. Include the inmate's register number (U.M. number) and date of birth.

Joint Commission on Accreditation of Healthcare Organizations

The Joint Commission on Accreditation of Healthcare Organizations oversees the operation of health clinics in the FDC. If your healthcare is seriously jeopardized, you can contact the Joint Commission. Their phone number is 1-800-994-6610. It is best for your family to file the report to protect your privacy, if possible.

Pick and Choose Your Battles Carefully

You and your family should pick and choose your battles carefully. You should think about who you are filing a complaint on and how they might retaliate. You do not want to become a grievance hungry inmate, who files one complaint after another. You will get on the staff's radar. If you get on their radar, they can write you up for the smallest of issues. They can have diesel therapy initiated. During diesel therapy, you are arbitrarily shipped using the least efficient route. You will end up across the country after taking a very long trip.

For More Information

For more information, see: Title 5 U.S. Code § 552.

CHAPTER 22:

Your Significant Other

FOOD FOR THOUGHT

"Have a very good reason for everything you do."

Lawrence Oliver

Introduction

Whether you are a man or woman, an inmate or significant other in the free world, young or old, you must understand some issues about serving time in prison:

Inmates feel isolated from their loved ones. You feel like you are in a prison on an island in a foreign war. You feel dehumanized. You have a loss of dignity, a loss of privacy, and a loss of respect. You are a number, not a person. You feel as though you are an animal in a cage at the zoo and the zookeepers taunt you instead of care for you.

Messages come to the island in a bottle. Some messages are lost or not returned. Most romantic relationships break up if you serve several years in prison. The result is overwhelming hopelessness.

On a day-to-day basis, inmates have only a few things to look forward to: visits, mail, e-mail, phone calls, and commissary food.

Visits with Your Significant Other

Inmates look forward to visits just like when they were going out on a date on a Saturday night in high school, they are that important. Some inmates spend one hour grooming themselves, one hour pressing their uniforms, and one hour shining their boots.

Bring money for the vending machine. The vending machine food is better than the food in the prison's cafeteria.

The time spent in a visit is like time spent outside the prison. One CO asked an inmate, "Don't you get bored with your wife after the first two hours of talking? Haven't you said all that you have to say to her?" The inmate said, "You don't understand, when I'm with my wife in the Visitation Room holding her hand, it's like I'm back home sitting on the couch in front of the fireplace. I can sit there for seven hours just holding her and never saying a word. My time with her means that much." The CO just looked at the inmate in disbelief. The CO had no clue what long-term isolation feels like.

Contacting Your Significant Other

Whether you are an inmate or significant other in the free world, you need to communicate with each other several times per week. Write letters or send e-mails several times per week.

Mail call usually occurs each evening, Monday thru Friday. Mail call is one of the better parts of the day. There is a great sense of sadness when you realize that no one sent you any mail. You can visibly see the pain on an inmate's face when they realize they have no mail. Even the smallest of notes with just a few sentences is uplifting. During phone calls, both sides need to learn to talk and listen equally. Make a phone topic list.

FOOD FOR THOUGHT

"Conversation is an exercise of the mind; gossip is merely an exercise of the tongue."

Author Unknown

Some Tips

Money: If you are in the free world, try to send your significant other some money every month, even if it is just twenty dollars. It's the thought that counts. Realize that most inmates are unable to pay full alimony or child support while they are locked up, most inmates don't earn enough.

Photos: If you are in the free world, send photos once or twice per month to your significant other. Consider pictures of family events, religious events, holidays, concerts, sporting events, and meetings. Have your partner mail them back to you and build a photo album. Include the date of each photo. Your partner is going to have to rebuild their life when they get out. Having a few photo albums in chronological order will help them.

Magazines: Buy some magazines if your partner is locked up. Write to the following companies for a free catalog. Inmate Magazine Service offers extremely cheap deals.

Inmate Magazine Service	Tradewinds Publication
P O Box 2063	P O Box 219247
Fort Walton Beach, FL 32549	Houston, TX 77218

Compliments: For every one critical remark you make of your spouse, make sure you give at least ten positive comments. (i.e. "I love you." "You're beautiful." "You're the best." etc.)

Outside Problems: Couples tend to want to discuss their day-to-day problems. This isn't always good for inmates because inmates have no control over what goes on in the free world. Likewise, inmates should not discuss every problem they have in prison. Both parties should think twice before worrying their partner.

Your Intervention

If your partner encounters a problem in prison, don't contact the Warden unless it is life or death. If you do contact them, be very calm and polite. No yelling, no cussing, be reasonable in your request. The inmate can get punished severely over minor issues. Your partner's personal belongings can get confiscated. Your partner can get thrown in the hole (solitary confinement) for arbitrary reasons. Your partner can get shipped two thousand miles away, etc.

Let the inmate try to solve the problems first – internally. If the informal resolution fails, the inmate should go through the appeals process (BP-8, BP-9, BP-10, BP-11). If that fails, then a U.S. Congressman should be contacted.

CHAPTER 23:

Divorces and Marriages

FOOD FOR THOUGHT

"I searched the world over and thought I'd found true love. You met another and plutttt you were gone".

Song from Hee Haw

Divorces

In general, half of all marriages in the United States end in divorce. In prison, the vast majority of all marriages do not survive. Risk factors for a divorce while you are in prison include:

1. Your spouse was a victim of your crime.

2. You are under age forty. (Older inmates are more successful at maintaining their marriages.)

3. You have a prison sentence of more than three years. (Many spouses are willing to wait a few years. The longer your sentence, the less likely your spouse will wait for you.)

4. You were convicted of a violent crime or sex crime.

5. You cannot provide financial security for your family. (When you are poor and in prison, many spouses will kick you to the curb.)

When you get a "Dear John" letter or phone call, your world will be shattered. Realize that the other inmates are not your enemy. Take some time to spend by yourself so you don't end up getting in a fight over some minor inmate issue. Exercise is a healthy way to relieve some stress.

Attorneys that practice Family Law handle divorces. For general help with hiring an attorney, see "Chapter 5: Hiring a Criminal Defense Attorney". Before you hire an attorney, you need to consider each of the following:

1. Do you have a Contested or Uncontested Divorce? Your attorney is going to want to know if you and your spouse are going to contest (disagree on) various issues:

   a. The Divorce Itself: If both of you agree to a divorce, it will cost less.

   b. Assets and Liabilities Division: If both of you agree to split up the assets and liabilities equally, your divorce costs less.

   c. Child Custody: If both of you agree that the parent living in the free world should get custody of your children, your divorce costs less.

   d. Child Support: If both of you agree on a child support amount, your divorce will cost you less. (In Texas, most judges will not make most average inmates pay child support until they are released from prison. While judges in Texas may not hold you in contempt of court for failing to pay child support while you are in prison, and only earning a trivial amount of money, they can assign you child support that will accumulate in arrears (late payments). If you have a lot of financial assets, be prepared to pay child support while you are locked up.) For more information on child support, please see "Chapter 24: Your Children".

   e. Child Visitation Schedule: If both of you agree on a visitation schedule with your children, your divorce will cost you less.

   f. Alimony: If both of you agree on an alimony amount (if required in your state), your divorce will cost less. (Texas does not allow alimony.)

   g. Spousal Maintenance: If your spouse is disabled, you may have to pay spousal maintenance until your spouse is no longer disabled or until your spouse remarries or cohabitates with someone else. (That's the law in Texas.)

   If you disagree with your spouse on one or more of the above issues, your attorney will have to contest the issue in front of the judge. This will force your attorney to spend time collecting evidence, interviewing witnesses, and researching your legal side of the issues. This is why contested divorces cost so much. If possible, try to work out some of the above issues before you hire an attorney that costs $300 per hour.

2. Your Reasons for a Divorce: "Felony conviction" and "insupportability" are common reasons for inmates to get a divorce.

3. Asset and Liability Division List: Make a list of your assets, liabilities, and personal belongings. Your attorney will need this.

FOOD FOR THOUGHT

"Never look down to test the ground before taking your next step; only those who keep their eye fixed on the far horizon will find their right road."

U.N. Secretary-General Dag Hammarskjold

In trying to hire a Family Law attorney to represent you in a divorce, it is most effective for you to have someone meet personally with an attorney on your behalf. Many attorneys will not answer letters from inmates. You need to send this person a Limited Power of Attorney, which gives this person your legal permission to meet with the attorney on your behalf.

Following is a sample of a letter that can be written to the family law attorney authorizing the person you selected to meet on your behalf.

Limited Power of Attorney

Dear Sir/Madam:

I hereby authorize Mr. John Doe to meet with you on my behalf. I am in need of an attorney to represent me in a divorce. I understand you practice Family Law in XYZ County. Please inform Mr. Doe of the cost of your services so I can make financial arrangements.

If you want to save a little money and speed up your divorce at the same time, see if your spouse will agree to file a Waiver of Notification for a Divorce. In Texas, the law requires one spouse to hire an officer of the court (i.e. a constable or sheriff's deputy) to deliver a Notice for a Divorce. This takes some time and cash. It may also embarrass your spouse at work as he or she is served with divorce papers from a law enforcement officer. If your spouse agrees to it, have your attorney mail a Waiver of Notice for a Divorce to your spouse. Your spouse should sign it and take it to the court house. This saves money and time.

If you have children, there are four possible outcomes:

1. Managing conservatorship (the best)

2. Possessory conservatorship

3. Extremely limited rights

4. No rights at all (the worst)

Managing conservators have custody of the children and full rights to make all decisions regarding the children. Since you are in prison, it is rare that you would get a managing conservatorship. Possessory conservators have limited rights, including the rights to visits, communication, and access to medical, educational, and financial records. Possessory conservators have the right to make some decisions while the children are visiting, such as discipline, religious instruction, some types of medical care, etc. Both managing conservators and possessory conservators have the responsibility to provide food, shelter, clothing, medical care, etc. to the children when they are in their possession. The rights and duties of managing conservator and possessory conservators vary from one state to another. If you don't get to be a full possessory conservator, you may get extremely limited rights, such as communication rights only. In the worst case scenario, you get no rights at all.

If you are fighting in a divorce to maintain a managing conservatorship or possessory conservatorship, keep a log of all communication you have with your spouse and kids. Include the date, time, who you communicated with, and the issues discussed. This log may be helpful for your lawyer.

Since you are in prison, you are very vulnerable during a divorce. Your spouse will look like a saint while you are a prisoner. If you are having trouble getting visits with your children while you are in prison and your parents can afford it, ask your parents if they would join the divorce lawsuit to protect their grandparent rights and your rights. (In Texas, see § 153.433.) The legal argument is that your children are being hurt by not being able to see you or their grandparents. If this petition is granted, your parents and your children will get visitation with each other and with you. By getting your parents involved in the divorce, you can actually level the playing field with your spouse.

Marriages

Enough talk about divorces. There is good news out there. Despite the horrors of going through a divorce while you are locked up, there are people that will start a new relationship with convicted felons. Many inmates have gotten married or engaged after they were convicted. There are even people who find convicts attractive no matter what the inmate was accused of. There are convicts that were accused of the most serious crimes who had new romantic relationships.

A few key points on starting a new relationship:

1. Work on you before looking for love. Lose weight, work out, get clean, etc. They say if you get your life in order, love will eventually find you.

2. Many surveys are done on people starting new long-term relationships. On most surveys, both men and women agree the number one characteristic they

are looking for in a new partner is kindness. Think about this: You can become a "hardened criminal" in prison or you can become a better person. It's your choice. Don't let other inmates convince you to become hateful or commit new crimes. (For those of you who are curious about the other characteristics commonly sought after in a new partner, a sense of humor, good looks, financial security, intelligence, and confidence were high on the lists.)

3. You will have to build relationships over time. "Say what you do, do what you say."

4. You can get married while you are locked up in the BOP:

   - You have to send the Warden a cop-out (Form BP-S148.055 Inmate Request to Staff), requesting permission to get married. You will receive two copies of a form to fill out – one for you and one for your fiancé.

   - You must be mentally competent.

   - You must have a letter from your fiancé discussing his or her intent to marry you. It must include your full name and register number. If you or your fiancé has ever been married before, you will have to submit proof that a divorce was finalized.

   - You must pay for all of the expenses. The law prevents the BOP from paying for any of it.

   - One federal prison only allowed marriage ceremonies one month out of the six. You and your spouse were allowed a maximum of four guests total.

   - The wedding ceremony may be held in the visitation room or the chapel, depending on your prison's policy.

   - Unfortunately, there is no way for you to consummate the marriage while you are on BOP property.

   - You may be able to get a furlough to get married if you are a low-risk inmate in a low-security prison or camp.

For More Information

For more information, see:

- Chapter 5: Hiring a Criminal Defense Attorney
- Chapter 22: Your Significant Other
- Chapter 24: Your Children

CHAPTER 24:

Your Children

FOOD FOR THOUGHT

"The more sand that has escaped from the hourglass of our life, the clearer we should see through it."

Jean Paul

Introduction

Your relationship with your children is very special. If you are allowed to communicate with your children and they come visit you, consider yourself lucky. Many inmates are not so fortunate. Don't brag about your visits as some inmates will resent you. Try to stay involved with your children's lives. That continuity is important for your children as well as for you.

Visits With Your Children

If you are allowed visits with your children, make sure you save enough visitation points each month to accommodate them. (Some FDC's and prisons ration visits using a point system.) Interact with them. Build them paper animals out of the napkins. Don't let them just stare at the TV. Some prisons are more permissive than others. In some prisons, inmates can sit on the floor and play games with their children. Progressive prisons even have visitation days when only children and their free-world parents can visit. (This is rare.)

Communicating With Your Children

You should plan on communicating with your children on a routine basis:

- Pick one, two, or three evenings a week to call them. Make it a routine, scheduled event.

- Write them a letter every week. Draw them a picture or mail them a picture of you. Send them articles from newspapers or magazines that you know they have an interest in.

- E-mail them most days of the week or e-mail them on the days you don't call them.

Some suggested discussion topics include:

- Their classes.

- What they are learning in and out of class.

- What they are reading.

- What exercises they are doing. (Most children naturally love to watch TV and play video games. You must politely remind your children to read and exercise.)

- What field trips they are looking forward to.

- Instill a sense of ethics in your children.

- Send them greeting cards.

- Encourage them to do their chores.

- Encourage them to pray or meditate.

- Look up topics for them in the encyclopedias in the library. Teach them.

- If your children send you art work, thank them and praise their work.

Parenting Support Classes

Many prisons offer parenting support classes. They offer suggestions on different styles of parenting. They will offer approaches to dealing with problems children face, especially problems that are common to children that have a parent serving time in prison.

Project Angel Tree

Some prisons participate in Project Angel Tree. Project Angel Tree is a national Christmas campaign to help children get a couple of Christmas gifts from their inmate mom or dad. A church from your home town has to participate to make this happen. Each inmate's child is placed on a list, if the inmate requests it. Members of congregations in your home town will purchase and deliver the gifts to your child. The important part is that the gifts come with the inmate's parent's name on them. This helps you maintain a relationship with your children. Ask about this in late November of each year.

For more information, please write:

    Angel Tree Christmas
    P O Box 1478
    Bartlesville, OK 74005-1478

FOOD FOR THOUGHT

"We don't accomplish anything in this world alone. Whatever happens is the result of the whole tapestry of one's life-all the weavings of individual threads from one to another that create something."

Supreme Court Justice Sandra Day O'Conner

Child Support

When you arrive in the BOP, you realize it may be difficult to pay for full child support while you are in prison. If possible, you should make some kind of monthly child support payments, even if it is just twenty bucks. It's the thought that counts. If you don't make any payments, your spouse, future judges, and future prosecutors may refer to you as a "deadbeat parent". If you make some type of payment, you will gain respect from your family and any future prosecutors or judges.

You can make one time payments or predetermined monthly payments. Ask for form BP-199.045 Request for Withdrawal of Inmate's Personal Funds ("BP-199") from your Unit Manager. If your prison has Trust Fund Limited Inmate Computer System (TRUL-INCS), you can access it there. When you are done filling out the form, you must submit it to your Unit Manager. Don't hold your breath: The process takes 4 to 8 weeks.

A list of addresses for each child support agency is listed at the back of this book in "Appendix C: Child Support Agencies."

You should write your child support agency and see if they have an informational handout for incarcerated parents. In Texas, the packet is called "Incarcerated Parents and Child Support." It will answer many common questions you may have.

Please consult your family law attorney for details. However, here are a few issues you should consider if you live in Texas:

You can request a document, known as "Inquiry Form for Incarcerated Parents". This document will allow you to find out:

    1. Information on your child support case.

2. The addresses and phone numbers of the child support offices handling your cases.

3. A request for a modification to see if you can have your child support payments reduced while you are in prison. (A modification form may also be called a "Review and Adjustment Form" in some states. Ask for both forms and determine the difference between the two forms.)

4. Information on how you can determine paternity on a child. (If you believe you are not the parent of a child but the court is requiring you to make child support payments, you can request a DNA test.)

5. You can send a letter to your child once, if you don't know his or her address. The letter will be screened and mailed to the custodial parent.

A few notes:

- If you have a child support case before you are incarcerated, you may get all or most of your child support payments reduced while you are in prison, if you don't have a significant outside source of funding.

- The state of Texas considers $500 or more of monthly income as a sufficient reason for you to make child support payments. This income includes income from your prison job, your free-world income, and donations from your family into your commissary account. The Attorney General of Texas has a program that identifies inmates with $500 or more in income per month. These inmates are then investigated to see if a judge will order them to make child support payments.

- In Texas, there are two ways child support can be set up during a divorce:

  a. Active case.

  b. Private Registry-Only.

FOOD FOR THOUGHT

"The most serious mistakes are not being made as a result of wrong answers. The truly dangerous thing is asking the wrong question."

Peter Drucker

In an active case, the Attorney General's Office opens an official investigation. The amount of child support is established by the law. A judge orders the child support payments and the Attorney General's Office oversees the payments. In a private registry-only case, you and your spouse agree to an amount of child support, which your judge endorses. You make payments to a private registry, which then sends 100% of the payments to your children. The Attorney General's Office does not open an active case unless there is a need for it.

There is a fine print in "BOP Program Statement 5380.08: Inmate Financial Responsibility Program (IFRP)," stating that inmates may be held responsible for child support or alimony if the Unit Team gets "appropriate documentation." However, this is contradicted by two personal observations:

1. A spokesman for the Texas Attorney General's Office stated that the state of Texas cannot currently forcibly deduct child support payments out of a federal inmate's trust fund account unless an order is issued by a federal judge. (Child support issues are dealt with under state jurisdiction, not federal.)

2. In one case, an inmate owes child support for three children. The BOP is not able to automatically take money out of his Inmate Trust Fund Account without his permission. To his credit, the inmate signs a Request for Withdrawal of Inmate's Personal Funds (BP-199.045), which allows money from his Inmate Trust Fund Account to be mailed to the Texas Attorney General's Office.

If you need documentation of how much money you have paid in child support, request an affidavit of payments. It will list how much you paid on specific dates.

Texas law sets the following general guidelines for child support payments if you earn at least minimum wage and you work at least forty hours a week.

- 20% for one child

- 25% for two children

- 30% for three children

- 35% for four children

- 40% for five children

- Not less than 40% for six or more children.

If you don't earn at least minimum wage in Texas and you don't work at least forty hours a week, then a different part of Texas law applies.

If the court believes you are not making as much money as you should, the child support amount may be based on your potential earnings.

If you are incarcerated and indigent, most Texas judges will assign you child support as though you were earning minimum wage and working forty hours per week. The unpaid balance (arrears) will accumulate. If you are indigent and incarcerated, you can file a motion at the end of your prison sentence, stating you are incarcerated and indigent. Some judges will write off a portion of your arrears.

There are two cases in Texas involving uncontested paternity where the judges assigned paternity to inmates by default. The way Texas law works, any woman can claim that a male inmate is the father of her child. She files a child support case with the Attorney General's Office. The father has three or four years to contest the paternity issue. The problem is you may never be notified of the paternity case. This is more likely if you are in prison. You could wake up one day finding out you owe child support for twenty-one years even though you are not the father of the child. The bad news is you can only contest the paternity in the first three or four years. Otherwise, the court assigns you paternity by default and you cannot appeal your case. To get around this, you have to contact the Attorney General's Office in each state where you have lived and get them to see if they have new child support cases involving you. You should check every year just to be safe.

For More Information

For more information, see:

- BOP Program Statement 5380.08: Inmate Financial Responsibility Program (IFRP)

CHAPTER 25:

Your Business: Keeping or Closing It?

Deciding to Keep Your Business Open or to Close It

You must consider several issues when you decide whether to keep your business open or close it while you are locked up.

The Nature of Your Crime

The more serious your crime, the less likely you will get to keep your business. People convicted of murder or armed robbery usually have to close their businesses. Even if you can legally keep the business open, you may lose all of your clients. Also, if you owned a pharmacy that manufactured prescription narcotics and you were convicted of distributing illegal narcotics, you will have to close your business. If you were convicted of a lesser crime, such as tax evasion, illegal fruit importation, or illegal gambling, you may be able to keep your business open in certain situations. If you do keep it open, you need to consider how many clients or customers you will lose to your competitors.

You will need to read your supervised release restrictions very carefully. They are listed in your J & C Orders from your sentencing hearing. The judge may actually prohibit you from working in the previous career you had. For example, you were a firearms dealer, but you are prohibited from being around firearms. This is another reason you must get a copy of your J & C Orders, even if it takes you a year.

Power of Attorney (POA)

If you keep your business open, you will need to have a POA drawn up if you don't already have one. The POA is a legal document that allows someone else to operate your business in your absence. Most FDC's have a generic POA form. All you have to do is fill in the blanks. Your FDC should also have a notary public. Most states require you to sign a POA in front of a notary public. Even if you close your business, you will need a POA to give someone the authority to close your business down. (Note: A general POA is not valid at banks in Texas. You need a special POA developed by the attorneys at your bank. Request one from your bank.)

Business Operation

In addition to a POA, your business needs to have the necessary staff to perform the day-to-day operations of the business. If you were self-employed, this may be impossible. (You physically cannot do your job because you are locked up.) In some cases, you may be lucky enough to have employees or sub-contractors who will agree to work for your company while you are locked up.

FOOD FOR THOUGHT

"Vision without action is merely a dream. Action without vision just passes the time. Vision with action can change the world."

Joel Arthur Barker

Operating a Business from Prison

You need to realize a distinction the BOP makes: You can own a business while you are in the BOP's custody but you cannot operate a business. You can get a shot (inmate disciplinary reprimand) for running a business while you are in prison. The good news is it is only a 300-series shot, which is minor. You don't have to go to the hole (disciplinary segregation) and you won't face actual criminal charges as long as the business is legal. Follow the prison's policy.

The main purpose of the BOP's policy is to prevent any one inmate from getting in everyone else's way. For instance, you cannot run a mail order company out of your cell because there isn't enough space in your cell to store the stock. Likewise, the CO's that work in the Mail Room do not have the time to process a slew of mail order forms, it's not their job. The BOP wants to prevent any one inmate from monopolizing the prison's resources. Another example involves an inmate that tries to iron clothes as a side job while in prison. This would work a lot better if the inmate could buy his or her own iron and ironing board, that is not the case. In reality, some Housing Units in the BOP only have one iron and one ironing board creating a struggle over limited resources.

E-Mail and Snail Mail

E-mail is stored by the BOP for ten years after you leave prison. The use of code words is forbidden.

The mail you send out from a low-security prison is rarely read unless it is suspicious, you are a gang leader, or you have a history of manipulating the mail (mail fraud). Average inmates in a low-security prison are allowed to seal their envelopes before the letter is mailed. If you are in a medium or high-security prison, you must leave your envelopes unsealed so the staff can read your mail before they mail it.

Incoming mail is a different story. All of it is opened and inspected for contraband. Samples of mail are read periodically. To be safe, follow the prison's rules.

Telephone

Your calls are recorded and saved. Your calls will be randomly reviewed by the staff. Your calls are more likely to be reviewed if you are a gang leader or if you have a history of telephone fraud. To be safe, follow the prison's rules.

FOOD FOR THOUGHT

"Luck is a dividend of sweat. The more you sweat, the luckier you get."

Ray Kroc

Visits

Visits are monitored less closely than e-mail, mail, or phone calls. However, there are cameras and microphones in every Visitation Room. To be safe, follow the prison's rules.

If You Decide To Close Your Business

Minimize your liability. Even though you are incarcerated, you still have liability for your business. Each of the following steps listed below will hopefully minimize some of your liability.

1. Send a letter to your clients/customers telling them your business is closing.

2. Notify your clients/customers if there is a transfer in power or ownership.

3. Store your records properly. Check with your Certified Public Account (CPA) to see how long you need to keep your tax records. Check with your attorney or state regulatory agency for specific professional requirements.

4. Pay your taxes – all of them. Check with your CPA.

5. Consider surrendering your professional licenses, permits, and memberships. (See Chapter 26: "Surrendering Your Licenses, Memberships, and Permits".)

6. Attempt to refer your clients to one of your competitors who has a good reputation.

Your Private Finances

While the BOP and FDC's do not allow you to operate a business from inside of prison, you do have the right to manage your own private finances. You can get your bank statements while you are locked up. (This is not advisable, as your privacy may be violated. If you are wealthy, your safety may be jeopardized.)

You can use the phone or e-mail to tell your family to buy or sell a piece of real estate, as long as you personally own it and it is not owned by a company. Likewise, you can have money transferred from one of your personal bank accounts to another personal account. It's not illegal nor does it violate any BOP policy.

(Note: As this book goes to press, the ability for inmates to make personal profits from certain types of investments is being reviewed by the BOP.)

(Note: In Texas, you cannot sell your real estate property if you are given a life sentence or death sentence.) However, you can have money transferred from one of your personal bank accounts to another personal account. It's not illegal nor does it violate any BOP policy.

Whichever the case may be, you need to make it clear to whoever is listening in or reading your e-mail that you are using your personal assets, not operating a business or other organization. You also need to be as quiet about your finances as possible when speaking with others for your own protection.

FOOD FOR THOUGHT

"It does not matter how slow you go, as long as you do not stop."

Confucius

Tales from the Cage

You will meet some incredibly assertive entrepreneurs in prison. An inmate named "Josh" had two businesses prior to getting locked up. One of his businesses was a retail company, which one of his daughters operated. His second business was operated by his other daughter. She helped him develop and patent electronic devices.

Prior to being incarcerated, Josh took one of his inventions to a major U.S. company. They declined to buy the patent on his product.

After Josh was locked up, he officially had both of his daughters installed as Chief Executive Officer of the businesses they ran. They visited him a couple of times each month. During one of their visits, they informed their father that his patented idea for an electronic device had been stolen by the company he had presented the device to a couple of years before. Josh wrote a number of law firms, looking for one that would take his case. He found one of the best copyright infringement law firms in the U.S. After losing his case initially, Josh eventually won his copyright infringement case and was awarded a large financial sum.

One daughter developed, tested, patented, and marketed another electronic device while Josh served his sentence. Josh's other daughter was a hard worker and had good business sense and she expanded the retail business.

By the time Josh left prison, he had two booming businesses that were run by his daughters, and his net worth increased several times. He did all of this without violating a single law.

CHAPTER 26:

Surrendering Your Licenses, Permits, and Memberships

A Few Issues to Consider

Make a list of every license, permit, or membership you have. This should include simple issues, like driver's licenses, fishing licenses, or gym memberships. It should also include more complex issues, such as law licenses, medical licenses, pharmaceutical licenses, etc.

Write Each Organization

Write each organization letting them know you were convicted of a felony, state what the felony was. It is better for you to inform the organization than for the organization to figure it out on its own. You may be accused of concealing the felony conviction. The failure to report the conviction is worse than the felony itself in the eyes of some organizations.

Consider Legal Counsel

You probably don't need to involve an attorney if you are dealing with a fishing license. In many states, you can keep your fishing license or driver's license, unless your crime involved the realm of the license itself, such as driving dangerously while escaping the police. If you are dealing with a professional license, you may want to get an attorney involved. Your defense attorney may help you. Have him or her call the organization on your behalf. The attorney can tell them you were convicted of a felony and you are considering self-surrender of your license/permit. Self-surrender of your license means you voluntarily give up your license without a fight. Why is it better to self-surrender your license than to have it revoked? Because some organizations do not hold any prejudice for anyone self-surrendering their license. Your record reflects that you voluntarily resigned or retired rather than having your license revoked. A revocation on your record would look worse.

Social Security

If you collect Social Security payments and you are incarcerated, you legally must report it to the agency. You cannot get Social Security payments while you are incarcerated. You can resume it as soon as you get out. They cannot remove the Social Security benefits you earned just because you were convicted of a crime unless you falsified your work history to the Social Security Administration.

FOOD FOR THOUGHT

"Either you decide to stay in the shallow end of the pool or you go out in the ocean."

Christopher Reeve

Disability

You cannot file for disability just because you were incarcerated. This common myth runs rampant in prisons. You must have an appropriate diagnosis to file a claim. The average disability claim takes three attempts and eighteen months before it is approved. If you are walking and talking, the likelihood of getting disability approved is low.

Medicare/Medicaid/Private Medical Insurance

While you are in a Federal Detention Center (FDC), your Medicare, Medicaid, or private medical insurance can be billed for your health care. Once you are in prison, the prison is legally responsible for paying for all of your health care. The exception to this is when you leave to go to a halfway house.

Regaining Your Professional License/Permit

After you finish serving your time in prison and you finish your supervised release, you may consider attempting to get your license or permit back. Before you fill out an application, it is best for you to talk to other people who have lost their license and tried to get it back in your state. In some states, you simply cannot get your license back. However, don't give up right away. Check the internet and call around. Check with an attorney that represents professionals in your state. They will most likely know how easy it is for you to get your license back in your state. They will also know of states that have more lenient criteria on regaining your license. You may have to move out of state to get your license back. If you want to practice in your home state, consider getting your license back in another state and practicing there for a year or two. Then, apply to get a license in your home state. Many states allow licenses to be transferred from one state to another by reciprocation. This may help you bypass the hurdle.

CHAPTER 27:

Your Weight

FOOD FOR THOUGHT

"A friend to all is a friend to none."

Aristotle

If you are out of shape, you now have a lot of time to get back in shape. This chapter will help you determine your ideal body weight.

- To maintain your body weight, you should consume no more than 15 calories per pound per day.

- To lose weight, you should consume no more than 14 calories per pound per day. Try this number of calories for two weeks. If you still cannot lose weight, try consuming 13 calories per pound per day.

- For instance, if you weigh 250 pounds, you should consume 3,500 calories per day to lose weight.

    250 pounds x 14 calories (per pound per day) = 3,500 calories (per day)

- If consuming only 3,500 calories per day for two weeks does not cause you to lose weight, cut back to 3,250 calories per day.

    250 pounds x 13 calories (per pound per day) = 3,250 calories (per day)

FOOD FOR THOUGHT

"The greatest thing in this world is not so much where we are, but in what direction we are moving."

U.S. Supreme Court Justice Oliver Wendell Holmes, Jr. Wilson Mizner

---

Body Mass Index (BMI)

BMI = **Mass in Kilograms** (Height in Meters)^2

		120	130	140	150	160	170	180	190	200	210	220	230	240	250
							Weight in Pounds								
	4'6	29	31	34	36	39	41	43	46	48	51	53	56	58	60
	4'8	27	29	31	34	36	38	40	43	45	47	49	52	54	56
	4'10	25	27	29	31	34	36	38	40	42	44	46	48	50	52
	5'0	23	25	27	29	31	33	35	37	39	41	43	45	47	49
Height in Feet and Inches	5'2	22	24	26	27	29	31	33	35	37	38	40	42	44	46
	5'4	21	22	24	26	28	29	31	33	34	36	38	40	41	43
	5'6	19	21	23	24	26	27	29	31	32	34	36	37	39	40
	5'8	18	20	21	23	24	26	27	29	30	32	34	35	37	38
	5'10	17	19	20	22	23	24	26	27	29	30	32	33	35	36
	6'0	16	18	19	20	22	23	24	26	27	28	30	31	33	34
	6'2	15	17	18	19	21	22	23	24	26	27	28	30	31	32
	6'4	15	16	17	18	20	21	22	23	24	26	27	28	29	30
	6'6	14	15	16	17	19	20	21	22	23	24	25	27	28	29
	6'8	13	14	15	17	18	19	20	21	22	23	24	25	26	28

Key:	Underweight	Healthy Weight	Overweight	Obese

Note: This chart is for adults (≥ 20 years old)

For your information, walking burns 5 calories/minute while running burns 10 calories/minute. So walking 10 minutes burns 50 calories while running 10 minutes burns 100 calories.

CHAPTER 28:

Interesting Miscellaneous Resources

Introduction

This chapter is an assortment of resources you can utilize as you go through the system.

Library

Every FDC is required to have a library. They are also required to have a law library, which is usually a sub-section of the library. In some FDC's, the library is referred to as "Education."

Photocopiers: These are often located in the library. If not, you have to submit a cop-out (Inmate Request to Staff form S148.055 in the BOP. Alternatively, you can submit an electronic Inmate Request to Staff on the Trust Fund Limited Inmate Computer System (TRULINCS) by clicking on Request to Staff) to use one.

Typewriters: These are often located in the library. If not, you have to submit a cop-out to the staff to use one.

Office Supplies: Tape, scissors, staplers, and postage scales are often located in the library.

Boxes: If you need a box, check with the Trustees that work in the kitchen or library. You may need to get permission from a CO before you take it. Also, don't seal the box closed; a CO has to inspect the box's contents. In some cases, you may have to fill out a permission form to obtain approval for sending the box.

Notary Public: They are usually located in the library and/or Lieutenant's office. You usually have to submit a cop-out to the staff requesting an appointment to get a document publicly notarized.

FOOD FOR THOUGHT

"We must realize that no arsenal, no weapon in the arsenals of the world, is so formidable as the will and moral courage of free men and women. It is a weapon our adversaries in today's world do not have."

U.S. President Ronald Reagan

Contacts

A few helpful contacts:

Faith Ministry:
Located in Fort Worth, Texas, Faith Ministry provides assistance and training to help inmates obtain a new start. Phone - 972-870-7308

Prison Entrepreneurship Program:
This program teaches inmates in the Texas Department of Corrections how to successfully open and operate their own small businesses. 48% of the first 600 graduates obtained full-time employment.

Project Angel Tree:
This program provides free Christmas gifts to your children in selected cities. (For more information on Project Angel Tree, see "Chapter 24: Your Children.")
Angel Tree Christmas
P O Box 1478
Bartlesville, OK 74005-1478

www.abine.com:
Abine is a privacy organization that fights to protect your online privacy. The problem with online data brokers is that they will sell not only your criminal history and home address, but also your family member's names, your past and current addresses, your personal financial information, your family's financial information, your e-mail address, your civil legal issues (such as bankruptcies, liens, and judgments), and a whole lot

more. Abine offers a yearly subscription service. Abine will have your data profile removed from twenty of the largest data broker's websites. Abine offers a free web browser program called "DoNotTrackMe" which attempts to block data mining from websites you visit.

www.bop.gov:
Use the "Locator" feature on this BOP website to locate an inmate and determine his or her federal register number (ID number). Note: You must use the inmate's correct full name.

www.CollectionBully.com:
A website run by consumer protection attorneys. The attorneys fight collection companies which violate federal debt collection laws. This website can assist you if collection companies are harassing you.

www.DefyVentures.org:
This New York organization runs a series of MBA-like seminars that teach entrepreneurial ex-felons how to successfully open and operate their own small businesses. At the end of the course, students get an opportunity to compete for financial capital to actually fund their business idea. Contact CEO Catherine Rohr at 917-342-2371.

www.DuckDuckGo.com:
Every time you search a term in Google, Google stores that search term in a unique profile about you. Data from that profile is sold to marketing agencies and is occasionally turned over to law enforcement. DuckDuckGo allows users to enter a search term at www.DuckDuckGo.com, which in turn uses Google to search the term. Google sends the results back to DuckDuckGo, which strips out the data mining from Google. DuckDuckGo does not allow any data to be collected about you.

www.PrisonTalk.com:
This website allows your friends and family to discuss prison/jail issues with other people who know someone that is locked up. All users create a user name to protect their privacy. Note: Prosecutors and law enforcement agents visit this website as well. Don't say anything in the public area you don't want them to know. Use the private messaging feature.

www.Reagan.com:
A private e-mail service that does not data mine the contents of your e-mail for the purpose of selling it to marketing agencies.

www.ReentryRoundTable.net:
This organization is located in Austin, Texas. It offers an abundance of employment resources, housing resources, substance abuse referrals, and policy reform.

www.Reputation.com:
This website allows you to find out about your online reputation. For a fee, the company will help clean up your online reputation by helping you put your best foot forward.

www.StartMail.com:
A private e-mail service that does not data mine the contents of your e-mail for the purpose of selling it to marketing agencies.

www.StartPage.com:
Every time you search a term in Google, Google stores that search term in a unique profile about you. Data from that profile is sold to marketing agencies and is occasionally turned over to law enforcement. StartPage allows users to enter a search term at www.StartPage.com, which in turn uses Google to search the term. Google sends the results back to StartPage, which strips out the data mining from Google. StartPage does not allow any data to be collected about you. Once you leave StartPage, there is no permanent record left behind.

www.thomas.gov.com:
This website tracks every bill that is being considered by the U.S. Senate and U.S. House.

www.txrs.org:
Texas Re-Entry Services offers case management, medication vouchers, substance abuse counseling, anger management, financial management, support housing, employment searches, GED classes, and much more.
Texas Re-Entry Services
3001 Race Street
Fort Worth, TX 76111
817-834-2833

CHAPTER 29:

Entering the Federal Bureau of Prisons

FOOD FOR THOUGHT

"I never wanted to be famous. I only wanted to be great."

Ray Charles

Introduction

You undoubtedly will have a lot of questions as you prepare to enter the BOP. If you are in a FDC, you will run into people that have served time in the BOP. Some inmates will answer your questions accurately while others will only confuse you. One rule you need to keep in mind: *Half* of what you hear from inmates is false. You need to be in the habit of getting your information from two or more trustworthy inmates. Compare their answers. You will learn which inmates are not worth asking future questions.

Inmates have their own code they live by in prison. Part of it is based on respect. Part of it is based on how you clean up after yourself.

You are in one of the following four situations:
1. Out on bail and bond, waiting to self-surrender.
2. In a FDC.
3. In a county or city jail.
4. In a state prison.

Most inmates go to a BOP facility based on their security level.
- Minimum-Security: Federal Prison Camp (FPC) or Federal Work Camp (FWC).
- Low-Security: Low Federal Correctional Institution (FCI)

- Medium-Security: Medium Federal Correctional Institution (FCI)
- High-Security: U.S. Penitentiaries (USP's)
- ADX: Super Max Security. The most secure federal prison. It is located in Florence, Colorado.

Some inmates will be assigned to an administrative prison, such as a Federal Medical Center (FMC).

Federal prisons are overcrowded by 40% to 100% of their original authorized maximum capacity. New inmates that are just arriving in the BOP get first priority at open positions in camps and low-security FCI's. If you are at a medium-security or USP, you have to wait until an opening occurs before you can be transferred.

If you qualify for a medium-security prison and they are all full, the BOP may try to get you to sign a waiver to allow them to put you in a USP. Do not allow them to do that. It is dangerous. USP's are several times as violent as medium-security prisons. Medium-security prisons are several times as violent as low-security prisons.

Initial designations to BOP institutions are usually made by the Designation and Sentence Computation Center (DSCC) in Grand Prairie, Texas. The designation is based on information from your judge, the U.S. Marshals Service, the U.S. Attorney's Office, and the U.S. Probation Office. Your security points are determined. You are assigned to a prison that has an appropriate security level. In addition to security points, you may also be assigned to a prison based on Public Safety Factors (PSF's or Management Variables (MGTV's).)

FOOD FOR THOUGHT

"Ideas are easy. It's the execution of ideas that really separates the sheep from the goats."

Sue Grafton

Prison Security Levels

Prison Security Level	Male	Female
Minimum	0–11 points	0–15 points
Low	12–15 points	16–30 points
Medium	16–23 points	No medium security prisons for women
High	24+ points	31+ points
Administrative	All point totals	

Prison Custody Classification Table

		Score Tally
1. Judge:		No Points
2. Rec Facility:		No Points
3. Rec Program:		No Points
4. USM Office:		No Points
5. Voluntary Surrender Status:	0 = No −3 = Yes	
6. Months to Release:		No Points
7. Severity of Current Offense:	0 = lowest 5 = high 1 = low–moderate 7 = greatest 3 = moderate	
8. Criminal History:	0 = 0–1 points 6 = 7–9 points 2 = 2–3 points 8 = 10–12 points 4 = 4–6 points 10 = 13+ points	

9. History of Violence:

	< 5 years	5–10 years	10–15 years	> 15 years
None				
Minor 0	5	3	1	1
Serious 0	7	6	4	2

10. History of Escape Attempts:

	< 5 years	5–10 years	10–15 years	> 15 years
None				
Minor 0	3	2	1	1
Serious 0	3	3	3	3

		Score Tally
11. Type of Detainer:	0 = none 5 = high 1 = lowest/low moderate 7 = greatest 3 = moderate	
12. Age:	0 = 55 and over 4 = 25 through 35 2 = 36 through 54 8 = 24 or less	
13. Education Level:	0 = Verified High School Diploma or GED 1 = Enrolled in and making progress in a GED Program 2 = No verified High School Diploma/GED and not participating in a GED Program	
13a. Highest Grade Completed: _____		
14. Drug/Alcohol Abuse: years.	0 = Never/>5 1 = <5 years	

	Score Tally
15. **Security Point Total:** #5 + #7 + #8 + #9 + #10 + #11 + #12 + #13 + #14	

FOOD FOR THOUGHT

"Success is achieved by developing our strengths, not by eliminating our weaknesses."

Marilyn von Savant

Notes on the Federal Custody Classification Table:

1. **Judge**: Your sentencing judge's last name will be entered here.

2. **Recommended Facility**: Your judge may recommend a specific prison or geographical region for you. However, the BOP can send you wherever they want to, regardless of a judge's order.

3. **Recommended Program**: Any program recommended by your sentencing judge will be entered here. (i.e. RDAP).

4. **USM Office**: Your U.S. Marshals Service Office is listed.

5. **Voluntary Surrender**: You get a three point deduction if you voluntarily surrender/self-surrender. For this item, voluntary surrender means you were not escorted by a law enforcement officer to either the U.S. Marshals Office or the place of confinement. This item applies only to post-sentencing voluntary surrender, and does not include the circumstance where you surrendered to the U.S. Marshals on the same day as your sentencing. Voluntary surrender credit only applies to your initial confinement, not any subsequent return to custody for a violation of parole, mandatory release, or supervised release.

6. **Months to Release**: This item reflects the total number of months you have left to be incarcerated. For classification purposes, consecutive federal prison sentences are added together. Based on your J&C Order, federal sentences may have different beginning dates. Enter the total number of months remaining less 15% (for sentences greater than twelve months), and give credit for any time served in a FDC. (Note: The time you spent in a city or county jail doesn't always get credited by the BOP. If it is not credited, you will have to file a motion to give you credit once you are in a federal prison.)

The security point total is not impacted by this item but it does influence the Sentence Length Public Safety Factor. Example: If you are sentenced to eight years for breaking and entering, the length of incarceration is expected to be 96 months x 85% = 81.6 months or 82 months. Subtract any time served in a FDC.

If you were sentenced with a death penalty, life sentence, or parolable life sentence and a parole date has not been set yet, enter 540 months.

7. **Severity of Current Offense**: The appropriate number of points that reflect the most severe documented intent offense behavior regardless of the current conviction offense should be entered. The highest score will be utilized in scoring the current offense for multiple offenses. All sentences will be considered, including federal sentences that have a future beginning date or a previous DC or state sentence if there was not physical release from custody.

The severity will be determined by using the Offense Severity Scale.

If your PSR says you were charged with a more serious crime but you plead guilty to a less serious crime, you will get assigned points of the more severe documented behavior unless your sentencing judge sentences you to less time and clearly indicates this in his or her Statement of Reasons (SOR).

The security point total is not impacted by this item but it does influence the Sentence Length Public Safety Factor. Example: If you are sentenced to eight years for breaking and entering, the length of incarceration is expected to be 96 months x 85% = 81.6 months or 82 months. Subtract any time served in a FDC.

Procedures for Supervised Release, Mandatory Release, Special Parole Term, or Parole Violators:

If your violation involved new criminal conduct, the new criminal conduct will be used for rating the severity of the current offense. If you had a technical violation, the severity of the current offense will be low to moderate.

Your original criminal offense behavior which happened before the violation is considered past behavior and is not used in determining the severity of the current offense.

Procedures for Violators of Probation:

Your original offense behavior that caused you to end up on probation should be used for scoring the severity of the current offense. However, if your new violation behavior is more severe than the original offense behavior, then this new behavior is used for rating the severity of the current offense. The most serious documented behavior between the original offense and the violation behavior will be used for scoring the severity of the current offense.

8. **Criminal History Score**: You will enter your Criminal History Points, which are derived from the U.S. Sentencing Guidelines Criminal History Points, or

they will be entered in your J&C Orders and your SOR. If your Criminal History Points are not found in your J&C Orders or SOR, the points in your PSR will be used.

In some instances, the Criminal History Points are not accessible (i.e. in offenses committed prior to November 1, 1987, state cases, DC Code and military offenders, or when the PSR is waived). In such instances, the Criminal History Score will be derived from the Criminal History documented in the NCIC III Report using the following protocol:

a. Add 3 points for each of your prior sentences of imprisonment exceeding one year and one month;

b. Add 2 points for each of your prior sentences of imprisonment of at least sixty days not counted in (a);

c. Add 1 point for each of your prior convictions not counted in (a) or (b), up to a total of 4 points for this item; and,

d. Add 2 points if the current offense is a revocation accompanied by a new state or federal conviction, or if the current offense occurred while under federal supervision including incarceration, probation, parole, or supervised release.

9. **History of Violence:** The total number of points that reflect any history of violence will be included if there are documented findings of guilt (i.e. DHO, Court, Parole, Supervised Release, or Mandatory Release violation.) (The DHO is the Discipline Hearing Officer in the BOP.) State disciplinary findings must be recorded unless there is documentation that the state disciplinary hearings did not give you due process protection.

Prior periods of incarceration will be considered as a "history" item if you were released from custody and then returned to serve either a violation or a new sentence. Information from a District of Columbia Youth Rehabilitation (DCYRA), Youth Correction Act (YCA), or juvenile cases can be used against you unless the case is expunged or vacated.

Minor History of Violence: Aggressive or intimidating behavior which is unlikely to cause serious bodily harm or death (i.e. fights, verbal threats, simple assault, etc.). A finding of your guilt is mandatory.

Serious History of Violence: Aggressive or intimidating behavior which is likely to cause serious bodily harm or death (i.e. domestic violence, aggravated assault, intimidation with a weapon, incidents including arson, rape, or explosives, etc.). A finding of guilt is mandatory.

10. **History of Escape or Attempts**: Enter your points for escape history only if there is documentation of a finding of guilt (i.e. parole, court, DHO,

mandatory release, or supervised release violation). Escape history includes your entire background of escapes or attempts to escape, or absconding from community supervision, excluding your current term of confinement. If you were in state prison and you were disciplined for escape activity, it will be included unless you were not given due process.

Failure to appear for a traffic violation, fleeing or eluding arrest, running away from foster homes, and absconding from a judicial hearing or sentence imposed by a judge should not be rated under the escape history but they can be the basis for the "greater security" Management Variable.

If a violation occurred while in YCA, DCYRA, or as a juvenile, the record has been expunged or vacated.

Minor History of Escape: This includes escape from an open institution or program (i.e. minimum security facility, furlough, CCC) not involving any actual or threat of violence. It includes flight to avoid prosecution, military AWOL, Bail Reform Act, and absconding from community supervision. You must be found guilty except as noted above.

Serious History of Escape: If you escape from secure custody with or without threat of violence. This includes any escape from an open facility or program with a threat of violence. You must be found guilty.

11. **Type of Detainer**: You must enter the number of points that reflect the detainer status using Offense Severity Scale. The offense of the most serious detainer must be used.

If law enforcement officials indicate intent to file a detainer, consider it filed. Score a concurrent state sentence as a detainer only if it is expected that your state sentence will exceed your federal sentence. However, score consecutive state sentences, state detainees, and/or state parole violation terms/warrants as detainees.

Consecutive federal sentences are ordinarily not logged as detainees because federal sentences are calculated as they are received. The most severe offense will be used if you have more than one sentence.

No points will be assigned for U.S. Parole Commission warrants. However, the original offense behavior will be factored into the history points and the violation behavior.

No points are added if you have an Immigration and Customs Enforcement (ICE) detainer but you can get a PSF for deportable alien.

12. **Age**: Select your age category.

13. **Education Level**: Select your educational level.

14. **Drug/Alcohol Abuse**: Select the number of points that reflect your drug or alcohol abuse or lack thereof.

   Examples include a conviction of drug or alcohol-related offense, positive drug test, a DUI, detoxification, or a parole or probation violation based on drug or alcohol abuse. You can self-report the information as well.

15. **Security Point Total**: Enter the sum of items 5 and 7 through 14.

FOOD FOR THOUGHT

"We all lose our looks eventually. Better develop your character and interest in life."

Jacqueline Bisset

In addition to the security point total above, PSF's may be used to assign you to a different prison security level. PSF's include:

   A-None
   B-Disruptive Group
   C-Greatest Security Offense (males only)
   F-Sex Offender
   G-Threat to Government Officials
   H-Deportable Alien
   I-Sentence Length (males only)
   K-Violent Behavior (females only)
   L-Serious Escape
   M-Prison Disturbance
   N-Juvenile Violence
   O-Serious Telephone Abuse

FOOD FOR THOUGHT

"To acquire knowledge, one must study; but to acquire wisdom, one must observe."

Marilyn von Savant

A few notes on Public Safety Factors (PSF's):

A. Even though you have a low number of security points, you may still be assigned to a higher level of security because of a PSF.

B. Disruptive Group: If you get a Disruptive Group PSF, you will be going to a USP, unless the PSF is waived.

C. Greatest Severity: If you are a male and your offense falls in the Greatest Severity range on the Offense Security Scale, you have to go to at least a low-security prison, unless the PSF is waived.

F. Sex Offender: If you are a Sex Offender, you have to go to at least a low-security prison, unless the PSF is waived. A conviction is not required to get assigned a PSF if your PSR or other official documentation clearly indicates behavior occurred warranting a PSF. For example, if your PSR indicates you were involved in a sexual assault but you signed a plea bargain for only a simple assault, you can still get assigned a Sex Offender PSF.

H. Deportable Alien: If you are a Deportable Alien, you have to go to at least a low-security prison.

I. Sentence Length:

- If you are a male and you have at least ten years remaining to serve, you will have to go to at least a low-security prison, unless the PSF is waived.

- If you are a male and you have at least twenty years remaining to serve, you will have to go to at least a medium-security prison, unless the PSF is waived.

- If you are a male and you have at least thirty years remaining to serve, you will have to go to a USP, unless the PSF is waived.

K. Violent Behavior: If you are a female whose current term of confinement or history involves two convictions (or findings by the DHO) for serious violent incidents within the last five years, you will have to go to at least a low-security prison, unless the PSF is waived.

L. Serious Escape:

- If you are a female who has been involved in a serious escape within the last ten years, including your current term of confinement, you will have to live in the Carswell Administrative Unit, unless the PSF has been waived.

- If you are a male who has escaped from a secure facility (currently or in the past) with or without the threat of violence or who escapes from an open institution with a threat of violence, you will serve your time in at least a medium-security prison, unless your PSF is waived.

29. **M. Prison Disturbance**: If you are a male and you are involved in a serious incident of violence within a prison involving engagement in a riot, encouraging a riot, or acting in furtherance of a riot, you will serve time in a USP, unless your PSF is waived. If you are female, you will serve time in Carswell Administrative Unit, unless your PSF is waived.

N. Juvenile Violence: If you are a juvenile who has any documented single instance of violent behavior, past or present, which resulted in a finding of guilt, a conviction, or a delinquency adjudication, you will get this PSF. Examples include aggressive behavior causing serious bodily harm or death or aggressive or intimidating behavior likely to cause serious bodily harm or death.

O. Serious Telephone Abuse: You will be assigned this PSF if you use a phone to further criminal activities, promote illicit organizations, you are a leader/organizer, communicate threats, death, assaults, or homicides, attempt or commit fraud, arrange narcotic/alcohol smuggling into prison, federal agents or U.S. Attorneys want your phone calls monitored, you are convicted of a 100 or 200 series shot (inmate disciplinary reprimand) for telephone abuse, or the BOP has reasonable suspicion supporting telephone abuse.

Note: Items D, E, G, and J are PSF's the BOP no longer uses.

FOOD FOR THOUGHT

"I don't pay good wages because I have a lot of money: I have a lot of money because I pay good wages."

Robert Bosch

The following Security Designation Tables combines your Security Point Total and Public Safety Factors to determine your Inmate Security Level. The Inmate Security Level is the type of prison you are eligible for. For instance, low-security, medium-security, etc.

Security Designation Table (Males)

Inmate Security Level Assignments Based on Classification Score and Public Safety Factors

Security Point Total	Public Safety Factors	Inmate Security Level
0–11	No Public Safety Factors	Minimum
	Deportable Alien	Low
	Juvenile Violence	Low
	Greatest Severity Offense	Low
	Sex Offender	Low
	Serious Telephone Abuse	Low
	Threat to Government Officials	Low
	Sentence Length Time remaining > 10 Yrs Time remaining > 20 Yrs Time remaining > 30 Yrs (includes non–parolable Life and Death penalty cases)	Low Medium High
	Serious Escape	Medium
	Disruptive Group	High
	Prison Disturbance	High
12–15	No Public Safety Factors	Low
	Serious Escape	Medium
	Sentence Length Time remaining > 20 Yrs Time remaining > 30 Yrs (Includes non–parolable Life and Death penalty cases)	Medium High
	Disruptive Group	High
	Prison Disturbance	High
16–23	No Public Safety Factors	Medium
	Disruptive Group	High
	Prison Disturbance	High
	Sentence Length Time remaining > 30 Yrs (Includes non–parolable Life and Death penalty cases)	High
24+		High

Security Designation Table (Females)

Inmate Security Level Assignments Based on Classification Score and Public Safety Factors

Security Point Total	Public Safety Factors	Inmate Security Level
0–15	**No Public Safety Factors**	**Minimum**
	Deportable Alien	Low
	Juvenile Violence	Low
	Serious Telephone Abuse	Low
	Sex Offender	Low
	Threat to Government Officials	Low
	Violent Behavior	Low
	Prison Disturbance	High
	Serious Escape	High
16–30	**No Public Safety Factors**	**Low**
	Prison Disturbance	High
	Serious Escape	High
31+		**High**

Offense Severity Scale: Greatest Severity

Aircraft Piracy – placing a plane or passengers in danger
Arson – substantial risk of death or bodily injury
Assault – serious bodily injury intended or permanent or life threatening bodily injury resulting
Carjacking – any
Drug Offense – see criteria below*
Escape – closed institution, secure custody, force or weapons used
Espionage – treason, sabotage, or related offenses
Explosives – risk of death or bodily injury
Extortion – weapon or threat of violence
Homicide or Voluntary Manslaughter – any
Kidnapping – abduction, unlawful restraint, demanding or receiving ransom money
Robbery – any
Sexual Offenses – rape, sodomy, incest, carnal knowledge, transportation with coercion or force for commercial purposes
Toxic Substances/Chemicals – weapon to endanger human life
Weapons – distribution of automatic weapons, exporting sophisticated weaponry, brandishing or threatening use of a weapon

* Any **drug offender** whose current offense includes the following criteria shall be scored in the Greatest Severity category:

The offender was part of an organizational network and he or she organized or maintained ownership interest/profits from **large-scale** drug activity,

AND

The drug amount equals or exceeds the amount below:

    Cocaine – greater than or equal to 10,000 gm, 10 K, or 22 lb
    Cocaine Base "Crack" – greater than or equal to 31 gm
    Hashish – greater than or equal to 250,000 gm, 250 K, or 551 lb
    Marijuana – greater than or equal to 620,000 gm, 620 K, or 1,367 lb
    PCP – greater than or equal to 100,000 mg, 100 gm, or 20,000 dosage units
    Heroin or opiates – greater than or equal to 2,000 gm, 2 K, or 4.4 lb
    Methamphetamine – greater than or equal to 16,000 gm, 16 K, or 35 lbs
    Other illicit drugs – Amphetamine, Barbiturates, LSD, etc. – greater than or equal to 250,000 dosage units

Offense Severity Scale: High Severity

Arson – other
Cruelty to Children – any
Drugs (For Females only):
    Cocaine – greater than or equal to 10,000 gm, 10 K, or 22 lb
    Cocaine Base "Crack" – greater than or equal to 31 gm
    Hashish – greater than or equal to 250,000 gm, 250 K, or 551 lb
    Marijuana – greater than or equal to 620,000 gm, 620 K, or 1,367 lb
    PCP – greater than or equal to 100,000 mg, 100 gm, or 20,000 dosage units
    Heroin or Opiates – greater than or equal to 2,000 gm, 2 K, or 4.4 lb
    Methamphetamine – greater than or equal to 16,000 gm, 16 K, or 35 lb
    Other illicit drugs – Amphetamine, Barbiturates, LSD etc. – greater than or equal to 250,000 dosage units
Explosives – other
Extortion – other
Involuntary Manslaughter – includes vehicular homicide
Residential Burglary – with evidence that occupants were in dwelling during the commission of the offense
Rioting – any
Sexual Offenses – sexual exploitation of children, unlawful sexual conduct with a minor, pornography
Stalking – any
Threatening Communications – with conduct evidencing intent to carry out such threat
Toxic Substances/Chemicals – other

Offense Severity Scale: Moderate Severity

Assault – other
Auto Theft – any
Breaking and Entering – any
Burglary – other
Child Abandonment – any
Contempt of Court – criminal contempt
Drugs:
    Cocaine – greater than or equal to 400 gm, 0.4 K, or 0.88 lb
    Cocaine Base "Crack" – greater than or equal to 1 gm
    Hashish – greater than or equal to 11,000 gm, 11 K, or 24 lb
    Marijuana – greater than or equal to 25,000 gm, 25 K, or 55 lb
    PCP – greater than or equal to 4,000 mg, 4 gm, or 0.14 oz
    Heroin or Opiates – greater than or equal to 80 gm, 0.08 K, or 0.18 lb
    Methamphetamine – greater than or equal to 667 gm, 0.67 K, or 1.4 lb
    Other illicit drugs – Amphetamine, Barbiturates, LSD, etc. – greater than or equal to 10,000 dosage units, 0.05 K, or 0.11 lb
Escape – walking away from an open institution, failure to appear/bail reform act, no threat of violence involved
Immigration Offenses – transportation of unlawful aliens
Obstruction of Justice – any
Property Offenses – over $250,000, includes theft, fraud, tax evasion, forgery, currency offenses
Sexual Offenses – other
Weapons – other

Measurement Conversion Table

1 oz = 28.35 gm	1 gm = 1 ml (liquid)
1 lb = 453.6 gm	1 liter = 1,000 ml
1 lb = 0.4536 kg	1 kg = 1,000 gm
1 gal = 3.785 liters	1 gm = 1,000 mg
1 qt = 0.946 liters	1 grain = 64.8 mg

Offense Severity Scale: Low–Moderate Severity

Bigamy – Polygamy
Drugs:
    Cocaine – less than 400 gm, 0.4 K, or 0.88 lb
    Cocaine Base "Crack" – less than 1 gm
    Hashish – less than 11,000 gm, 11 K, or 24 lb

Marijuana – less than 25,000 gm, 25 K, or 55 lb
PCP – less than 4,000 mg, 4 gm, or 0.14 oz
Heroin or Opiates – less than 80 gm, 0.08 K, or 0.18 lb
Methamphetamine – less than 667 gm, 0.67 K, or 1.47 lb
Other illicit drugs – Amphetamine, Barbiturates, LSD, etc. – less than 10,000 dosage units, 0.05 K, or 0.11 lb
Indecent Exposure – indecent acts, lewd behavior
Immigration Offenses – other
Post-Release Supervision Violation – technical, administrative
Property Offenses – valued between $2,000 and $250,000

Offense Severity Scale: Lowest Severity

Drugs – personal use
Gambling Law Violation – any
Liquor Law Violation – any
Property Offenses – less than $2,000
Suspicion – any
Traffic Laws – any
Vagrancy – any
Vandalism – any

Marijuana Equivalent Chart

Drug	Marijuana Equavalent
1 gm of Heroin	1,000 gm
1 gm of Cocaine powder	200 gm
1 gm of Methamphetamine	2,000 gm
1 gm of LSD	100,000 gm
1 gm of "crack" cocaine	20,000 gm*
1 gm of Hashish Oil	50 gm

For other drug equivalents, refer to the Drug Equivalency Table on page 24(change with book text)

*In 2010, U.S. Congress changed the ratio of "crack" cocaine to powder cocaine from 100:1 to 18:1.

Special Notes

- The BOP is not allowed to release information on where you are being sent until after you arrive there. This is a security issue.

- In some instances, you can be designated to go to a FCI for six months while they study your behavior. After the study is complete, they decide where to send you.

- You are supposed to get assigned to a prison within 500 miles of your legal residence. However, the prison may be full, causing you to get assigned far away. Also, if you cause problems along the way, you may get assigned to a prison on the other side of the country.

- The Office of Medical Designations Transportation (OMDT) reviews all cases where inmates have medical or mental health issues.

- See Appendix F, "Federal Prisons and Federal Bureau of Prisons Offices" for a complete listing of facilities.

FOOD FOR THOUGHT

"Don't be fooled by the calendar. There are only as many days in the year as you make use of."

Judge Charles Richards

Packing Out

Once you are sentenced, you need to learn how to pack out quickly. "Packing Out" is short for "packing up your belongings and shipping out." Some inmates call it "packing out" while others call it "B&B". "B&B" refers to packing up your "bedding and baggage" on the day you leave a jail or prison. Leaving jail to go to prison is referred to as "catching chain." (In the old days, inmates were literally chained up to a chain gang that marched to prison. Hence, you "caught the chain".)

You need to quickly down-size your belongings. Some of your belongings will be stolen or trashed by the CO's when you leave. If you have legal documents or special letters or photos, mail them home before you leave the jail. The legal papers of many inmates "disappear." Clothes purchased from Commissary may also just "disappear" when you "catch the chain."

When it's time to leave, you will not be warned very long in advance. Some inmates get a one hour warning while others only get five minutes to pack out. The less you have to pack, the better off you are. Many inmates are told "you have B&B" at 4:00 A.M. They have to pack out immediately. Because you don't get much of a warning when you get B&B, you usually will not have a chance to call your family. There are several things you can do to help your family know what is going on:

1. Write a brief letter to your family in advance. Give the letter to an inmate you trust in your cell block. The inmate keeps it until you get B&B. The inmate will mail the letter to your family once he or she realizes you are gone. In your letter, tell your family:

   a. You are leaving.

   b. Deposit money in the BOP's Inmate Trust Fund for you. (See "Chapter 30: Inmate Trust Fund".)

   c. Check the Inmate Locator at www.BOP.gov to see which BOP facility you arrive at.

   d. You are OK and you will contact them ASAP.

2. Call your family every night at 8:00 P.M. or at any other agreed upon time each evening to let them know you still have not caught the chain. They will know you caught the chain the night you don't call home.

3. Have your family check the Inmate Locator at www.BOP.gov to see which BOP facility you arrive at. It will also list your Register Number.

As you are packing out, realize you will not be able to keep all of your food that is open. Your jail uniforms and food can be used by other inmates. Pass out your food and uniforms quickly. Use the bathroom because you may not get a chance to for several hours. Think carefully about what you eat or drink because many CO's don't care if you have to go to the bathroom.

As you travel, you will be secured in hand cuffs, an abdominal chain, and ankle shackles. If you are especially violent, you will also get a box cuff. A box cuff fits between your wrists to further immobilize your arms.

Once you leave your local jail, FDC, or prison, you will be taken to the nearest U.S. Marshals holding tank, which is usually at the federal court house in your district. You will be turned over to the U.S. Marshal Service. Your identity will be verified. You will be searched. Again, use the bathroom when you have a chance and be mindful of what you eat.

You will be transported to an airport, where an inmate swap takes place. Federal prisoners fly on ConAir airplanes. (ConAir is the nickname given to the airplanes used by the U.S. Marshals to fly federal convicts around the country.) After the plane lands, each bus or van with inmates will surround the plane on a service runway. U.S. Marshals with semi-automatic weapons will provide security. All of the inmates will exit the plane, buses, and vans. Everyone will be searched again. Your identity will be verified. Most inmates will fly on ConAir. A few inmates will bypass ConAir and the Federal Transfer Center (FTC) and go directly to a BOP facility. All vehicles wait on the side of the runway until the plane takes off. This ensures all the inmates are properly accounted for.

FOOD FOR THOUGHT

"If you want to be happy, put your effort into controlling the sail, not the wind."

Author Unknown

Federal Transfer Centers

Most federal inmates will travel to the FTC in Oklahoma City. Some will go to the FTC in Atlanta, which is severely overcrowded. Once there, you will be assigned to the General Population (GP) or the Special Housing Unit (SHU). Average-risk inmates go to the GP while high-risk individuals go to the SHU.

Candidates for the SHU include:

1. Extremely violent offenders.
2. Inmates that came from a SHU in another prison.
3. Moderately ill inmates that require certain medical care.
4. Vulnerable inmates, such as former police officers, prosecutors, judges, sex offenders, snitches, etc. These inmates are housed in what is referred to as protective custody (PC).

Most inmates stay at the FTC for one to four weeks. You can call your family to let them know where you are. You can call them collect.

Most inmates do not get to shop at the Commissary. You can if you are a trustee. Volunteer to be a trustee (janitor, kitchen worker, maintenance, etc.) so you can shop at the Commissary.

Sick Call at the FTC is at 6:00 A.M. three days per week. You sign up at breakfast. Don't miss it by sleeping in because you won't get healthcare until the next day. You get your medicines refilled by going to Sick Call. Be prepared to skip breakfast, if necessary.

You get clean clothes every Monday, Wednesday, and Friday. You get clean linen once a week.

Hygiene products are dispersed on Tuesdays and Thursdays. You get three packs. Each pack contains a razor, shaving cream, toothbrush, and toothpaste.

There are three TV rooms for entertainment. The TV's actually have sound with volume controls. There are book carts for reading. You can play chess, checkers, and cards.

Self-Surrender

When you are sentenced, you are either remanded into custody or allowed to self-surrender to prison authorities at a later date. If you self-surrender, you won't have to go through a FTC, such as Oklahoma City or Atlanta.

When a judge issues you a self-surrender date, you have to report to the prison by that date or earlier, if the BOP tells you to. The BOP will assign you to a prison. The designation process will take anywhere from a few days to a few weeks. Once they designate you to report to a specific prison, they can legally force you to report their earlier than the date the judge told you. You must comply. You are responsible for the travel costs, if you self-surrender.

If the date the judge assigned to you comes but the BOP has still not designated you to a specific prison, you must turn yourself in to the nearest U.S. Marshals Office. They will place you in a FDC or county/city jail until the BOP finishes assigning you to a prison.

Self-surrendering on a business day on Monday through Thursday is superior to a Friday through Sunday or a holiday. You need clean clothes and a lot of processing which simply cannot get done on a Friday, weekend, or federal holiday. Turn yourself in a day or two early, if you have to.

Mail your money order for the Inmate Trust Fund (Commissary Fund) after you are designated by the BOP and about four business days before you have to self-surrender. (See "Chapter 30: Inmate Trust Fund"). That way, your Commissary money arrives in Des Moines, Iowa the same day you self-surrender.

Diesel Treatment/Freezer Treatment

Be careful not to cause too many problems. Be respectful to the staff even if they are rude or foolish. If you are a trouble maker, you can get diesel treatment or freezer treatment. Diesel treatment is where you get to take the longest route to get from point A to point B. The CO's know how to make your life a living hell by keeping you traveling eighteen hours a day every day a week for ten days. You will not get to eat, sleep, or use the bathroom often. When you finally get off the bus, you realize you are two thousand miles away from your family.

You can also get freezer treatment. If you cause trouble, you may find yourself in a freezer cell with no coat or long sleeves.

FOOD FOR THOUGHT

"They that will not apply new remedies must expect new evils."

Francis Baron

Your Safety

Think before you act or speak. Be patient. Don't steal or accuse others of stealing. Show respect to everyone. Don't stand out in a crowd. If you have never served time in prison before, make sure you read "Chapter 17: General Prison Security Policies" and "Chapter 18: Inmate Safety Issues".

BOP Policies

You will be frustrated by the seemingly contradictory instructions you will be given by the BOP staff. You will see signs that contradict each other. One CO will instruct you to do things completely different from the next CO. You will learn which policies are followed and which policies are ignored by which staff. Do not let this frustrate you. In time, you will learn the CO's preferences. Some care about the policies. Some don't.

Expect every CO to follow every rule when the Warden, Captain, Lieutenant, or an outside inspector (Region) is around. Be on your best behavior because a CO that is usually lenient will become unusually strict. Remember: The CO's have to cover their own hides first even if that means getting you in trouble.

What the BOP Allows You to Bring into Prison

- Prescription Eyeglasses: If you are reading this in advance of being locked up, get an eye exam and a new pair of eyeglasses. It takes 6 to 36 months to get the BOP to issue you eyeglasses.
- Wedding Band without a Stone: It's value must be less than $100.00.
- Plain earrings for ladies worth less than $50.00. Men cannot possess earrings.
- Certain Medical Devices: Nebulizers, crutches, CPAP machines, wheel chairs, dentures.
- Cash: $700 limit.
- Prescription meds for that first day (possibly).

What the BOP Won't Allow You to Bring into Prison

- Weapons.

- Alcohol and drugs.

- Your own clothes or shoes of any kind (unless it is shipped by your previous Warden from your previous prison).

- Your watch.

- Your PSR (Pre-Sentencing Report).

- Your addresses (usually not).

- Your paperwork (unless it is shipped by your previous Warden from your previous prison).

- Food.

For More Information

For more Information, see:

BOP Program Statement 5100.06: Security Description and Custody Classification.

CHAPTER 30:

Inmate Trust Fund

FOOD FOR THOUGHT

"Patience is never more important than when you are at the edge of losing it."

O.A. Battista

Introduction

Your financial account in the BOP is known as the inmate trust fund or Commissary fund.

Depositing Funds

No one can put money into your inmate trust fund until they know your inmate name and federal register number. Your family can locate this information using the inmate locator at www.BOP.gov. (They need to enter your real name, not a nickname.) No one can deposit money into your account until your register number shows up and you are in the custody of the BOP or in transit to the BOP.

There are four basic ways of depositing money into an inmate trust fund in the BOP:

1. Money Orders

2. Western Union

3. MoneyGram

4. Cash. (Only if you self-surrender.)

Money Orders

All funds for the inmate trust fund should be mailed in the form of a money order to the lockbox in Des Moines, Iowa, *not* the prison where you are staying. The address is:

> Federal Bureau of Prisons
> Inmate Name
> Inmate Register Number
> P O Box 474701
> Des Moines, Iowa 50947-0001

- If you have a question about the lockbox, you can call 1-202-307-2712 between 8:00 A.M. and 4:30 P.M. ET.

- You must use a money order as they do not accept personal checks or cash. Try to use the U.S. Postal Service money orders because they are deposited immediately. Private bank money orders are held for two weeks to make sure they clear the bank.

- The person's name that is sending the money order does not have to be on the money order.

- Your account can hold a maximum of $99,999.

- Money orders take four-to-seven days to show up on your account. Plan ahead and save money. A U.S. Postal Service money order for $400 costs $1.10. Check with the U.S. Postal Service for current rates.

- To send money even faster, use Western Union or MoneyGram.

Western Union

- You can place an order with Western Union by calling 1-800-634-3422, press option #2. You can also send it by Western Union over the internet: www.westernunion.com
  Enter:
  1. Inmate Register Number Inmate Last Name (No spaces or dashes)
  2. Attention: Inmate Name
  3. Code City: FBOP, DC
  Example:
  1. 12345678smith
  2. Attention: John Smith
  3. Code City: FBOP, DC

- Money sent over the Internet by Western Union hits your books in 3 to 6 hours. This is the fastest but most expensive method.

- You can only send up to $300 per month by Western Union.

- Western Union charges $6.95 to send less than $100 and $9.95 to send more than $100 using the online service. They charge $11.95 if you call in an order. This is expensive. The cheaper method is to send a U.S. Postal Service money order to the lockbox in Des Moines, Iowa.

- Some credit cards will charge a cash advance fee for ordering a money order. Check before you waste money.

FOOD FOR THOUGHT

"A pat on the back, though only a few vertebrae removed from a kick in the pants, is miles ahead in results."

Bennett Cerf

MoneyGram

- To locate an agent, call 1-800-976-9400 or visit www.moneygram.com.
- A MoneyGram money order costs up to $9.95 for a transfer up to $5,000.
- To fill out a MoneyGram order:

    1. Enter your name, address, and telephone number.

    2. Sign your name.

    3. Under "Company Name", enter "Federal Bureau of Prisons (FBOP)".

    4. Under "City and State", enter "Washington, DC".

    5. Under "Receive Code", enter "7932".

    6. Under "Inmate Register Number Last Name", enter the inmate's eight digit federal register number and the inmate's last name without a space in between. For example, "12345678Jones".

    7. Under "Message to Biller or Beneficiary Name", enter the inmate's first and last names.

- MoneyGram offers a three day service for $15.00.
- MoneyGram offers a same day service known as the "Money Express Payment Program." Money sent via this route takes two-to-four hours to reach your account if it is ordered between 7:00 A.M. and 9:00 P.M. EST, seven days per week, including holidays. Funds received after 9:00 P.M. EST are posted by 9:00 A.M. the following morning. MoneyGram charges $39.99 for its same day service. Western Union is cheaper if you really need same day service. (See "Western Union" above.)

Cash

If you self-surrender, you can take cash to the prison. They will credit your account. Call the prison in advance to see what their limit is.

How much money do I send?

Consider depositing $838.00. Here's how it breaks down:
- $320 initial Commissary spending
- $320 one month's routine Commissary spending
- $69 one month's phone calls
- $69 one month's reserve phone calls
- $30 TRU-Units for e-mail and printing
- $30 TRU-Units for reserve e-mail and printing

The reserve money is used every September and March when all inmate trust fund accounts are frozen for one to two weeks during inventory.

In the past, you could place funds on a debit card for vending machines at some institutions. However, a change in policy forced all vending machines to be removed except for the ones in the Visitation Rooms.

Inmate Trust Fund Account Balance

How to check your account balance:

1. TRULINCS (Trust Fund Limited Inmate Computer System):
   Sign on to an inmate e-mail computer using your register number (8 digits), 9 digit Phone Account Code (PAC number), and 4 digit Personal Identification Number (PIN). (Get your PAC number and PIN from your Counselor.) (Note: Your PAC number is the same as your ITS# (Inmate Telephone System number).)

2. Dial 118 on an inmate telephone: Enter your PAC number (9 digits). Select option #2 to check your balance.

3. TRUFACS (Trust Fund Account and Commissary System): It uses an Automated Inquiry Machine (AIM). This is like an ATM only it does not dispense cash. If your prison has the TRULINCS e-mail system, your TRUFACS will be disabled. To sign on to the AIM, enter your register number (8 digits) and your PIN (4 digits).

For your security, don't discuss your account balances. If someone asks you for your account balance, say something like, "I'm filing bankruptcy. My house got foreclosed on. I'm broke. My attorney took all my money. I have to pay a fine…"

You can only spend $69.00 per month in actual phone calls on the Inmate Telephone System. You can deposit *more* money in the ITS, but you can only make 300 minutes worth of phone calls per month.

Your Commissary spending limit renews once per month, depending on the fifth digit of your eight digit federal register number. The day of the month when your Commissary spending limit renews is calculated by multiplying the fifth digit by three and adding one. For instance, if your federal register number is 12345-678, your Commissary spending limit renews on the 16th of each month (5x3+1=16). So if you arrive at the BOP on the 15th of the month, you can spend $320 on your initial trip to the Commissary that day and your spending limit renews on the 16th, allowing you to spend another $320. (Note: One prison allowed inmates to routinely spend only $160 from the 1st-14th of the month and $160 from the 15th-31st. However, you could spend all $320 on your first trip to the Commissary.)

FOOD FOR THOUGHT

"If you want to see the true measure of a man, watch how he treats his inferiors, not his equals."

J. K. Rowling

Indigent Inmates

If you have less than $6.00 in your account for the past 30 days or more, you may be declared indigent. Depending on your local prison policy, you may qualify for:

- A few free postage stamps and envelopes to correspond with your family.
- Free toothpaste, toothbrushes, soap, and combs.
- Certain free over-the-counter medicines at the Commissary if you have an order from the Health Service Unit (HSU).
- No co-pay at the HSU for office visits.
- Free printing on the Electronic Law Library (ELL) if you submit the proper form.
- An occasional free phone call.

Withdrawal of Funds

You can have the BOP pay some of your bills using your inmate trust funds. If your prison does not have the TRULINCS e-mail system, you have to fill out a green form known as the BP-199.045 Request for Withdrawal of Inmate's Personal Funds. If your prison has the TRULINCS e-mail system, sign on to a designated inmate e-mail computer using your federal register number (8 digits), your PAC (9 digits), and your PIN (4 digits). Then, click on the button labeled "Send Funds (BP-199)." When you are finished filling out the form, press "Print". You must then log out of the computer by clicking on the "Exit" button. Then, sign on a printing kiosk computer using your federal register number, PAC number, and PIN. Press the "Print" button. You will be shown a list of all the print jobs you have not printed out in the last 21 days. Click the box next to each BP-199 you want to print out. (Printing BP-199's is free.) Make sure you sign out.

You must sign your BP-199 form. Then submit it to your Unit Manager. It takes three to eight weeks for the recipient to get your check.

For More Information

For more information, see:

- BOP Program Statement 2010.05: Accounting for the Trust Fund Inmate Debit Card Vending Programs
- BOP Program Statement 4500.01: Trust Fund Accounting and Commissary Systems – Deposit Fund
- BOP Program Statement 4500.02: Trust Fund Accounting and Commissary Systems – Trust Fund
- BOP Program Statement 4500.03: Trust Fund Management Manual
- BOP Program Statement 4500.04: Trust Fund/Warehouse/Laundry Manual
- BOP Program Statement 4500.05: Trust Fund/Deposit Fund Manual
- BOP Program Statement 4500.06: Trust Fund/Deposit Manual
- BOP Program Statement 5265.13: Trust Fund Limited Inmate Computer System (TRULINCS) – Electronic Messaging

Tales from the Cage

Every week in the BOP, a couple of memos get posted on the bulletin board in each Housing Unit. The inmates gather around to read the new edict from the King. Memos are written by the Warden, Captain, department heads, etc. Two inmates decided they would have a little mischievous fun with the Warden's authority. They stole a memorandum and photocopied the top portion with the Warden's name and signature. They blanked out the subject and the rest of the memo. They took the blank memo and typed the following:

"Every Christmas it is our policy to issue each inmate a holiday gift bag that is paid for by the inmate trust fund. Due to a clerical mistake, we have accidentally ordered 600 extra holiday gift bags. If you would like an extra gift bag, please line up in front of the Captain's Office on Friday at noon."

On Friday, the two inmates each bought a pint of ice cream and sat down across the compound in full view of the Captain's Office. They ate their ice cream as the entertainment unfolded. About 800 inmates lined up in front of the Captain's Office. They enjoyed watching the Captain and Lieutenant argue with the inmates about where the extra gift bags had gone.

CHAPTER 31:

The Worst Things About Prison

FOOD FOR THOUGHT

"The times are bad. Very well, you are there to make them better."

Thomas Carlyle

The Worst

People often want to know exactly what is it that makes the entire prison experience so bad? Which of the rumors are true?

A series of inmates were asked the following question: "What are the three worst things about being locked in prison?" Here are their answers:

Separation: You are separated from your family and friends. You cannot be there to watch them grow up or grow old. You cannot be there when they are sick. You cannot go to their ball games or recitals. You miss out on their weddings or funerals.

Deprivation of Freedom: One inmate described it as "the subjugation of time and control." You are told when to go to eat lunch. If you are fifteen minutes late, you simply miss lunch. You are told when to go into your cell so the staff can do a census count. You cannot walk to the library unless it is the right time of the day. You can only drop off your laundry at a very specific time or your clothes won't get cleaned.

Lack of Privacy: The staff will read your mail. They will spread gossip about you at some point. You will have to use the commode in front of other people at times. There is no private space to just sit and think or sit and write. The staff will look through every item in your cell at one point. You will be strip searched and patted down countless times. The staff will learn your scars, your tattoos, and the details of your case.

The Idiots: You will meet some really idiotic people in prison. Many are downright rude and dangerous. Some are inmates, some are staff members. In the free world, if you were treated rudely by them, you would never go back to their place of business. You wouldn't associate with them publicly or privately. In prison, you have to deal with them day in and day out. One inmate described it as "the clash of overbearing egos." Some of the officers have a real ego problem, so do some of the inmates. Everyone else just kind of sits back and watches them butt heads.

Overcrowding: No matter where you go, there is a line of people in front of you. You wait in a line to eat. You wait in a line to use the phone, check your e-mail, or take a shower.

One inmate went to the clinic one day to see the doctor. After waiting all day, he was finally sent back to his cell at 3:30 P.M. He returned to the clinic the next morning. He waited all day again only to be told, "Come back tomorrow." He was finally seen the third day.

Another inmate described it as, "They want us to live like Lilliputians. They put us in a cell the size of a closet. We have to cram everything we own into a locker the size of one suitcase."

FOOD FOR THOUGHT

"We will either find a way or make one."

Carthaginian General Hannibal

Lack of Opportunities for Real Advancement: Prison will teach you how to steal. They will teach you how to perform a really low-paying job, such as sweeping the floors or placing a sticker on a law enforcement vehicle. They will teach you to trim the trees or wash clothes but they won't teach you to be an office manager, chief financial officer, or a marketing director. If you don't have a high school diploma, the staff will force you to attend GED classes. (This is probably a good thing.) But some of the very same staff will often take steps to discourage you from getting an advanced degree. They don't want felons learning how to become engineers, architects, or physicists.

Ironically, many inmates get locked back up in prison after being released because they cannot find a way to make a good living in a lawful way. Felons who do get legitimate jobs may often earn only nine bucks per hour. Felons are tempted to steal drugs or rob banks in order to earn a lot of money fast.

Since most inmates are locked up for a long time, why isn't there a real push to rehabilitate and highly educate inmates during their incarceration so they can get a legal high-paying job when they get out? It seems like it would reduce the recidivism rate. (Recidvism is the habit of repeatedly committing a crime and returning to prison.) Additionally, keeping felons out of prison would sure save money on taxes. If felons got a good job when they got released, they would even boost the economy by spending the lawfully-earned money they made. This would be a win-win-win-win situation: a win for the felon, a win for the overcrowded prison, a win for the government, and a win for the rest of private society because the crime rates would decrease and the economy would be boosted.

Noise Pollution: There is constant noise from 5:00 A.M. to 11:00 P.M. every day. The chow hall is extremely loud, the library is loud, and the TV rooms are loud. The noise is a manifestation of the overcrowding problem.

The Food: The food quality varies from one facility to the next and from one meal to the next. You will find out what a 1/10 meal really tastes like. You will taste brands of food made in countries you have never visited. The brands of food are purchased by prisons because they are cheap. They are cheap because they are horrible.

The Boredom: Inmates complain about the boredom. You can only play so many games of cards, checkers, and chess. You can only watch so many reality TV shows or TV shows about gangs and prison. You can only walk around the track so many times.

Abuse: The bad news is inmates are abused more than the government would like to admit. Most inmates will be verbally abused and neglected in various ways. If you were verbally abused or neglected by your spouse in the free world, you would file for a divorce. If you were verbally abused at a job in the free world, you would resign and consider suing your boss. If you were verbally abused or neglected at a place of business in the free world, you would not return to that business. If you were neglected by your doctor, you would change doctors.

Unfortunately, some inmates will be physically or sexually assaulted in prison. (Most people are not.) The Bureau of Statistics estimates that twenty percent of prisoners are sexually assaulted. Always keep your personal business private unless you are with a trustworthy inmate you have known for several months. Always be aware of your surroundings. Learn to diffuse difficult or tense situations.

CHAPTER 32:

Conclusion

FOOD FOR THOUGHT

"There is only one corner of the universe you can be certain of improving and that's your own self."

Aldous Huxley

The Moment

If you have read this book, you have most likely shared the moment:

- When you are suddenly surrounded by law enforcement officers. You feel powerless. If you try to run, they will undoubtedly catch or shoot you.

- When your hands are being bound behind you, leaving you vulnerable to the whims of your captors.

- When the federal government unfurls the indictment against you for all the world to see.

- When some of your family and friends turn their backs on you, refusing to communicate with you.

- When you realize you have to decide between going to trial against the overwhelming feds or taking a plea bargain. Yet you have very little knowledge of whether a trial or a plea bargain is right for you.

- That if you do go to trial, it's when you recognize the dominion of the federal machine that is fighting you.

- That if you are found guilty at trial or you make a plea bargain, it's when you stand before everyone taking blows while your hands are chained.

- When you are losing control of your life because you are forced to enter the Federal Bureau of Prisons. It's a new journey in your life.

Our Hope for You

Our hope for you is that you will stay out of prison. The U.S. Bureau of Statistics reports that about 80% of prisoners who are released from prison will end up back in prison within 15 years from their release. About one-third of you will be sentenced to prison three or more times in your life.

Our hope is that you will make new friends when you leave prison. Spend time on your new career, your family, and at church. Avoid the troublemakers in your life.

No matter what you do, do it with your eyes open. Understand the pros and cons – the risks, benefits, and alternatives.

Make the right choices. Think two steps ahead – not to evade the law but to avoid situations that will come close to getting you in trouble again. In this delicate moment in your life, knowledge is power. Understand the perilous legal process.

APPENDIX A

Credit Bureaus

Equifax Credit Information
P O Box 740241
Atlanta, GA 30374

Experian
P O Box 9701
Allen, TX 75013

Trans Union
P O Box 6790
Fullerton, CA 92834

Please see "Chapter 18: Inmate Safety Issues" for more details.

U. S. Congressmen

U.S. House of Representatives

Alabama-1st, Republican
Bonner, Jo
2236 Rayburn HOB
Washington, DC 20515-0101
Phone: 202-225-4931

Alabama-2nd, Republican
Roby, Martha
414 Cannon HOB
Washington, DC 20515-0102
Phone: 202-225-2901

Alabama-3rd, Republican
Rogers, Mike
324 Cannon HOB
Washington, DC 20515-0103
Phone: 202-225-3261

Alabama-4th, Republican
Aderholt, Robert B.
2264 Rayburn HOB
Washington, DC 20515-0104
Phone: 202-225-4801

Alabama-5th, Republican
Brooks, Mo
1230 Longworth HOB
Washington, DC 20515-0105
Phone: 202-225-4801

Alabama-6th, Republican
Bachus, Spencer
2246 Rayburn HOB
Washington, DC 20515-0106
Phone: 202-225-4921

Alabama-7th, Democrat
Sewell, Terri A.
1133 Longworth HOB
Washington, DC 20515-0107
Phone: 202-225-2665

Alaska-At Large, Republican
Young, Don
1230 Rayburn HOB
Washington, DC 20515-0201
Phone: 202-225-5765

American Samoa-Delegate, Democrat
Faleomavaega, Emi F. H.
2422 Rayburn HOB
Washington, DC 20515-5201
Phone: 202-225-8577

Arizona-1st, Democrat
Kirpatrick, Ann
330 Cannon HOB
Washington, DC 20515-0301
Phone: 202-225-3361

Arizona-2nd, Democrat
Barber, Ron
1029 Longworth HOB
Washington, DC 20515-0302
Phone: 202-225-2542

Arizona-3rd, Democrat
Grijalva, Raul
1511 Longworth HOB
Washington, DC 20515-0303
Phone: 202-225-2435

Arizona-4th, Republican
Gosar, Paul A.
504 Cannon HOB
Washington, DC 20515-0304
Phone: 202-225-2315

Arizona-5th, Republican
Salmon, Matt
2349 Rayburn HOB
Washington, DC 20515-0305
Phone: 202-225-2635

Arizona-6th, Republican
Schweikert, David
1205 Longworth, HOB
Washington, DC 20515-0306
Phone: 202-225-2190

Arizona-7th, Democrat
Pastor, Ed
2465 Rayburn HOB
Washington, DC 20515-0307
Phone: 202-225-4065

Arizona-8th, Republican
Franks, Trent
2435 Rayburn HOB
Washington, DC 20515-0308
Phone: 202-225-4576

Arizona-9th, Democrat
Sinema, Kyrsten
1237 Longworth HOB
Washington, DC 20515-0306
Phone: 202-225-9888

Arkansas-1st, Republican
Crawford, Eric A. "Rick"
1408 Longworth HOB
Washington, DC 20515-0401
Phone: 202-225-4076

Arkansas-2nd, Republican
Griffin, Tim
1232 Longworth HOB
Washington, DC 20515-0402
Phone: 202-225-2506

Arkansas-3rd, Republican
Womack, Steve
1508 Longworth HOB
Washington, DC 20515-0403
Phone: 202-225-4301

Arkansas-4th, Republican
Cotton, Tom
415 Cannon HOB
Washington, DC 20515-0404
Phone: 202-225-3772

California-1st, Republican
LaMalfa, Doug
506 Cannon HOB
Washington, DC 20515-0501
Phone: 202-225-3076

California-2nd, Democrat
Huffman, Jared
1630 Longworth HOB
Washington, DC 20515-0502
Phone: 202-225-5161

California-3rd, Democrat
Garamendi, John
2438 Rayburn HOB
Washington, DC 20515-0503
Phone: 202-225-2511

California-4th, Republican
McClintock, Tom
428 Cannon HOB
Washington, DC 20515-0504
Phone: 202-225-2511

California-5th, Democrat
Thompson, Mike
2263 Rayburn HOB
Washington, DC 20515-0506
Phone: 202-225-3311

California-6th, Democrat
Matsui, Doris O.
2434 Rayburn HOB
Washington, DC 20515-0505
Phone: 202-225-7163

California-7th, Democrat
Bera, Ami
1408 Longworth HOB
Washington, DC 20515-0507
Phone: 202-225-5716

California-8th, Republican
Cook, Paul
1222 Longworth HOB
Washington, DC 20515-0508
Phone: 202-225-5861

California-9th, Democrat
McNerney, Jerry
1210 Longworth HOB
Washington, DC 20515-0509
Phone: 202-225-1947

California-10th, Republican
Denham, Jeff
1730 Longworth HOB
Washington, DC 20515-0510
Phone: 202-225-4540

California-11th, Democrat
Miller, George
2205 Rayburn HOB
Washington, DC 20515-0511
Phone: 202-225-2095

California-12th, Democrat
Pelosi, Nancy
235 Cannon HOB
Washington, DC 20515-0512
Phone: 202-225-4965

California-13th, Democrat
Lee, Barbara
2267 Rayburn HOB
Washington, DC 20515-0513
Phone: 202-225-2661

California-14th, Democrat
Speier, Jackie
211 Cannon HOB
Washington, DC 20515-0514
Phone: 202-225-3531

California-15th, Democrat
Sualwell, Eric
501 Cannon HOB
Washington, DC 20515-0515
Phone: 202-225-5065

California-16th, Democrat
Costa, Jim
1314 Longworth, HOB
Washington, DC 20515-0516
Phone: 202-225-3341

California-17th, Democrat
Honda, Mike
1713 Longworth, HOB
Washington, DC 20515-0517
Phone: 202-225-2631

California-18th, Democrat
Eshoo, Anna G.
241 Cannon HOB
Washington, DC 20515-0518
Phone: 202-225-8014

California-19th, Democrat
Lofgren, Zoe
1401 Longworth HOB
Washington, DC 20515-0519
Phone: 202-225-3072

California-20th, Democrat
Farr, Sam
1126 Longworth HOB
Washington, DC 20515-0520
Phone: 202-225-2861

California-21st, Republican
Valaxao, David
1004 Longworth HOB
Washington, DC 20515-0521
Phone: 202-225-4695

California-22nd, Republican
Nunes, Devin
1013 Longworth HOB
Washington, DC 20515-0522
Phone: 202-225-2523

California-23rd, Republican
McCarthy, Kevin
2421 Rayburn HOB
Washington, DC 20515-0523
Phone: 202-225-2915

California-24th, Democrat
Capps, Lois
2231 Rayburn HOB
Washington, DC 20515-0524
Phone: 202-225-3601

California-25th, Republican
McKeon, Howard R. "Buck"
2310 Rayburn HOB
Washington, DC 20515-0525
Phone: 202-225-1956

California-26th, Democrat
Branley, Julia
1019 Longworth HOB
Washington, DC 20515-0526
Phone: 202-225-5811

California-27th, Democrat
Chu, Judy
1520 Longworth HOB
Washington, DC 20515-0527
Phone: 202-225-5464

California-28th, Democrat
Schiff, Adam
2411 Rayburn HOB
Washington, DC 20515-0528
Phone: 202-225-4176

California-29th, Democrat
Cardenas, Tony
1508 Longworth HOB
Washington, DC 20515-0529
Phone: 202-225-6131

California-30th, Democrat
Sherman, Brad
2242 Rayburn HOB
Washington, DC 20515-0530
Phone: 202-225-5911

California-31st, Republican
Miller, Gary
2467 Rayburn HOB
Washington, DC 20515-0531
Phone: 202-225-3201

California-32nd, Democrat
Napolitano, Grace
1610 Longworth HOB
Washington, DC 20515-0532
Phone: 202-225-5256

California-33rd, Democrat
Waxman, Henry
2204 Rayburn HOB
Washington, DC 20515-0533
Phone: 202-225-3976

California-34th, Democrat
Becerra, Xavier
1226 Longworth HOB
Washington, DC 20515-0534
Phone: 202-225-6235

California-35th, Democrat
Negrete McLeod, Gloria
1641 Longworth HOB
Washington, DC 20515-0535
Phone: 202-225-6161

California-36th, Democrat
Ruiz, Raul
1319 Longworth, HOB
Washington, DC 20515-0536
Phone: 202-225-5330

California-37th, Democrat
Bass, Karen
408 Cannon HOB
Washington, DC 20515-0537
Phone: 202-225-7084

California-38th, Democrat
Sanchez, Linda
2423 Rayburn HOB
Washington, DC 20515-0538
Phone: 202-225-6676

California-39th, Republican
Royce, Ed
2185 Rayburn HOB
Washington, DC 20515-0539
Phone: 202-225-6676

California-40th, Democrat
Roylal-Allard, Lucille
2330 Rayburn HOB
Washington, DC 20515-0542
Phone: 202-225-1766

California-41st, Democrat
Takaro, Mark
1507 Longworth HOB
Washington, DC 20515-0541
Phone: 202-225-2305

California-42nd, Republican
Calvert, Ken
2269 Rayburn HOB
Washington, DC 20515-0542
Phone: 202-225-1986

California-43rd, Democrat
Waters, Maxine
2221 Rayburn HOB
Washington, DC 20515-0543
Phone: 202-225-2201

California-44th, Democrat
Hahn, Janice
404 Cannon HOB
Washington, DC 20515-0544
Phone: 202-225-8220

California-45th, Republican
Campbell, John
2331 Rayburn HOB
Washington, DC 20515-0545
Phone: 202-225-5611

California-46th, Democrat
Sanchez, Loretta
1114 Longworth HOB
Washington, DC 20515-0546
Phone: 202-225-2965

California-47th, Democrat
Louenthal, Alan
515 Cannon HOB
Washington, DC 20515-0547
Phone: 202-225-7924

California-48th, Republican
Rohrabacher, Dana
2300 Rayburn HOB
Washington, DC 20515-0548
Phone: 202-225-2415

California-49th, Republican
Issa, Darrell E.
2347 Rayburn, HOB
Washington, DC 20515-0549
Phone: 202-225-3906

California-50th, Republican
Hunter, Duncan D.
223 Cannon HOB
Washington, DC 20515-0550
Phone: 202-225-5672

California-51st, Democrat
Varges, Juan
2410 Rayburn, HOB
Washington, DC 20515-0551
Phone: 202-225-0508

California-52nd, Democrat
Peters, Scott
2410 Rayburn HOB
Washington, DC 20515-0552
Phone: 202-225-0508

California-53rd, Democrat
Davis, Susan A.
1526 Longworth HOB
Washington, DC 20515-0553
Phone: 202-225-2040

Colorado-1st, Democrat
DeGette, Diana
2335 Rayburn HOB
Washington, DC 20515-0601
Phone: 202-225-4431

Colorado-2nd, Democrat
Polis, Jared
501 Cannon HOB
Washington, DC 20515-0602
Phone: 202-225-2161

Colorado-3rd, Republican
Tipton, Scott R.
218 Cannon HOB
Washington, DC 20515-0603
Phone: 202-2225-4761

Colorado-4th, Republican
Gardner, Cory
213 Cannon HOB
Washington, DC 20515-0604
Phone: 202-225-4676

Colorado-5th, Republican
Lamborn, Doug
437 Cannon HOB
Washington, DC 20515-0605
Phone: 202-225-4422

Colorado-6th, Republican
Coffman, Mike
1222 Longworth HOB
Washington, DC 20515-0606
Phone: 202-225-7882

Colorado-7th, Democrat
Perlmutter, Ed
1221 Longworth HOB
Washington, DC 20515-0607
Phone: 202-225-2645

Connecticut-1st, Democrat
Larson, John B.
1501 Longworth HOB
Washington, DC 20515-0701
Phone: 202-225-2265

Connecticut-2nd, Democrat
Courtney, Joe
215 Cannon HOB
Washington, DC 20515-0702
Phone: 202-225-2076

Connecticut-3rd, Democrat
DeLauro, Rosa L.
2413 Rayburn HOB
Washington, DC 20515-0703
Phone: 202-225-3661

Connecticut-4th, Democrat
Himes, James A.
119 Cannon HOB
Washington, DC 20515-0801
Phone: 202-225-5541

Connecticut-5th, Democrat
Esty, Elizabeth
509 Cannon HOB
Washington, DC 20515-0705
Phone: 202-225-4476

Delaware-At Large, Democrat
Carney, John C., Jr.
1429 Longworth HOB
Washington, DC 20515-0801
Phone: 202-225-4165

District of Columbia-Delegate, Democrat
Norton, Eleanor Holmes
2136 Rayburn HOB
Washington, DC 20515-5100
Phone: 202-225-8050

Florida-1st, Republican
Miller, Jeff
2416 Rayburn HOB
Washington, DC 20515-0901
Phone: 202-225-4136

Florida-2nd, Republican
Southerland, Steve II
1229 Longworth HOB
Washington, DC 20515-0902
Phone: 202-225-5235

Florida-3rd, Republican
Yoho, Ted
511 Cannon HOB
Washington, DC 20515-0903
Phone: 202-225-5744

Florida-4th, Republican
Crenshaw, Ander
440 Cannon HOB
Washington, DC 20515-0904
Phone: 202-225-2501

Florida-5th, Democrat
Brown, Corrine
2111 Rayburn HOB
Washington, DC 20515-0905
Phone: 202-225-0123

Florida-6th, Republican
DeSantis, Ron
427 Cannon HOB
Washington, DC 20515-0906
Phone: 202-225-2706

Florida-7th, Republican
Mica, John L.
2187 Rayburn HOB
Washington, DC 20515-0907
Phone: 202-225-4035

Florida-8th, Republican
Posey, Bill
120 Cannon HOB
Washington, DC 20515-0908
Phone: 202-225-3671

Florida-9th, Democrat
Grayson, Alan
430 Cannon HOB
Washington, DC 20515-0909
Phone: 202-225-9889

Florida-10th, Republican
Webster, Daniel
1039 Longworth HOB
Washington, DC 20515-0910
Phone: 202-225-2176

Florida-11th, Democrat
Nugent, Richard
1727 Longworth HOB
Washington, DC 20515-0911
Phone: 202-225-1002

Florida-12th, Republican
Bilirakis, Gus M.
2313 Rayburn HOB
Washington, DC 20515-0912
Phone: 202-225-5755

Florida-13th, Republican
Young, C.W. Bill
2407 Rayburn HOB
Washington, DC 20515-0913
Phone: 202-225-5961

Florida-14th, Democrat
Castor, Kathy
205 Cannon HOB
Washington, DC 20515-0914
Phone: 202-225-3376

Florida-15th, Republican
Ross, Dennis
229 Cannon HOB
Washington, DC 20515-0915
Phone: 202-225-1252

Florida-16th, Republican
Buchanan, Vern
2104 Rayburn HOB
Washington, DC 20515-0916
Phone: 202-225-5015

Florida-17th, Republican
Rooney, Tom
221 Cannon HOB
Washington, DC 20515-0917
Phone: 202-225-5792

Florida-18th, Democrat
Murphy, Patrick
1517 Longworth HOB
Washington, DC 20515-0918
Phone: 202-225-3026

Florida-19th, Republican
Radel, Trey
1123 Longworth HOB
Washington, DC 20515-0919
Phone: 202-225-2536

Florida-20th, Democrat
Hastings, Alice L.
2353 Rayburn HOB
Washington, DC 20515-0920
Phone: 202-225-1313

Florida-21st, Democrat
Deutch, Ted
1024 Longworth HOB
Washington, DC 20515-0921
Phone: 202-225-3001

Florida-22nd, Republican
Frankel, Lois
1037 Longworth HOB
Washington, DC 20515-0922
Phone: 202-225-9890

Florida-23rd, Democrat
Wasserman Schultz, Debbie
118 Cannon HOB
Washington, DC 20515-0923
Phone: 202-225-7931

Florida-24th, Democrat
Wilson, Frederica
208 Cannon HOB
Washington, DC 20515-0924
Phone: 202-225-4506

Florida-25th, Republican
Belart, Mario
436 Cannon HOB
Washington, DC 20515-0925
Phone: 202-225-4211

Florida-26th, Democrat
Garcia, Joe
1440 Longworth, HOB
Washington, DC 20515-0926
Phone: 202-225-2778

Florida-27th, Republican
Ros-Lehtinen, Ileana
2206 Rayburn HOB
Washington, DC 20515-0927
Phone: 202-225-3931

Georgia-1st, Republican
Kingston, Jack
2372 Rayburn HOB
Washington, DC 20515-1001
Phone: 202-225-5831

Georgia-2nd, Democrat
Bishop, Sanford D., Jr.
2429 Rayburn HOB
Washington, DC 20515-1002
Phone: 202-225-3631

Georgia-3rd, Republican
Westmoreland, Lynn A.
2423 Rayburn HOB
Washington, DC 20515-1003
Phone: 202-225-5901

Georgia-4th, Democrat
Johnson, Henry C. "Hank", Jr.
2240 Longworth HOB
Washington, DC 20515-1004
Phone: 202-225-1605

Georgia-5th, Democrat
Lewis, John
343 Cannon HOB
Washington, DC 20515-1005
Phone: 202-225-3801

Georgia-6th, Republican
Price, Tom
100 Cannon HOB
Washington, DC 20515-1006
Phone: 202-225-4501

Georgia-7th, Republican
Woodall, Rob
1725 Longworth HOB
Washington, DC 20515-1007
Phone: 202-225-4272

Georgia-8th, Republican
Scott, Austin
516 Cannon HOB
Washington, DC 20515-1008
Phone: 202-225-9893

Georgia-9th, Republican
Collins, Doug
513 Cannon HOB
Washington, DC 20515-1009
Phone: 202-225-9893

Georgia-10th, Republican
Brown, Paul C.
2437 Rayburn HOB
Washington, DC 20515-1010
Phone: 202-225-4101

Georgia-11th, Republican
Gingrey, Phil
442 Cannon HOB
Washington, DC 20515-1011
Phone: 202-225-2931

Georgia-12th, Democrat
Barron, John
2202 Rayburn HOB
Washington, DC 20515-1012
Phone: 202-225-2823

Georgia-13th, Democrat
Scott, David
225 Cannon HOB
Washington, DC 20515-1013
Phone: 202-225-2939

Guam-Delegate, Democrat
Bordallo, Madeleine Z.
2441 Rayburn HOB
Washington, DC 20515-5301
Phone: 202-225-1188

Hawaii-1st, Democrat
Hanabusa, Colleen W.
238 Cannon HOB
Washington, DC 20515-1101
Phone: 202-225-2726

Hawaii-2nd, Democrat
Gabbard, Tulsi
502 Cannon HOB
Washington, DC 20515-1102
Phone: 202-225-4906

Idaho-1st, Republican
Labrador, Raul, R.
1523 Longworth HOB
Washington, DC 20515-1201
Phone: 202-225-6611

Idaho-2nd, Republican
Simpson, Michael K.
2312 Rayburn HOB
Washington, DC 20515-1202
Phone: 202-225-5531

Illinois-1st, Democrat
Rush, Bobby L.
2268 Rayburn HOB
Washington, DC 20515-1301
Phone: 202-225-4372

Illinois-2nd, Democrat
Jackson, Jesse L., Jr. Vacancy
2419 Rayburn HOB
Washington, DC 20515-1302
Phone: 202-225-0773

Illinois-3rd, Democrat
Lipinski, Daniel
1717 Longworth HOB
Washington, DC 20515-1303
Phone: 202-225-5701

Illinois-4th, Democrat
Gutierrez, Luis K.
2408 Rayburn HOB
Washington, DC 20515-1304
Phone: 202-225-8203

Illinois-5th, Democrat
Quigley, Mike
1124 Longworth HOB
Washington, DC 20515-1305
Phone: 202-225-4061

Illinois-6th, Republican
Roskam, Peter J.
227 Cannon HOB
Washington, DC 20515-1306
Phone: 202-225-4561

Illinois-7th, Democrat
Davis, Danny K.
2159 Rayburn HOB
Washington, DC 20515-1307
Phone: 202-225-5006

Illinois-8th, Democrat
Duckworth, Tammy
104 Cannon HOB
Washington, DC 20515-1308
Phone: 202-225-3711

Illinois-9th, Democrat
Schakousky, Janice D.
2367 Rayburn HOB
Washington, DC 20515-1309
Phone: 202-225-2111

Illinois-10th, Democrat
Schneider, Brad
317 Cannon HOB
Washington, DC 20515-1310
Phone: 202-225-4835

Illinois-11th, Democrat
Foster, Bill
1224 Longworth HOB
Washington, DC 20515-1311
Phone: 202-225-3515

Illinois-12th, Democrat
Enyart, William
1722 Longworth HOB
Washington, DC 20515-1312
Phone: 202-225-5661

Illinois-13th, Republican
Davis, Rodney
1740 Longworth HOB
Washington, DC 20515-1313
Phone: 202-225-2371

Illinois-14th, Republican
Hultgren, Randy
332 Cannon HOB
Washington, DC 20515-1314
Phone: 202-225-2976

Illinois-15th, Republican
Shimkas, John
2452 Rayburn HOB
Washington, DC 20515-1315
Phone: 202-225-5271

Illinois-16th, Republican
Kinzinger, Adam
1221 Longworth HOB
Washington, DC 20515-1316
Phone: 202-225-3635

Illinois-17th, Democrat
Bustos, Cheri
507 Cannon HOB
Washington, DC 20515-5905
Phone: 202-225-5905

Illinois-18th, Republican
Schock, Aaron
328 Cannon HOB
Washington, DC 20515-1318
Phone: 202-225-6201

Indiana-1st, Democrat
Visclosky, Peter J.
2256 Rayburn HOB
Washington, DC 20515-1401
Phone: 202-225-2461

Indiana-2nd, Republican
Walorski, Jackie
419 Cannon HOB
Washington, DC 20515-1402
Phone: 202-225-3915

Indiana-3rd, Republican
Stutzman, Marlin A.
1728 Longworth HOB
Washington, DC 20515-1403
Phone: 202-225-4436

Indiana-4th, Republican
Rokita, Todd
236 Cannon HOB
Washington, DC 20515-1404
Phone: 202-225-5037

Indiana-5th, Republican
Brooks, Susan W.
1505 Longworth HOB
Washington, DC 20515-1405
Phone: 202-225-2276

Indiana-6th, Republican
Messer, Luke
508 Cannon HOB
Washington, DC 20515-1406
Phone: 202-225-3021

Indiana-7th, Democrat
Carson, André
2453 Rayburn HOB
Washington, DC 20515-1407
Phone: 202-225-4011

Indiana-8th, Republican
Bucshon, Larry
1005 Longworth HOB
Washington, DC 20515-1408
Phone: 202-225-4636

Indiana-9th, Republican
Young, Todd C.
1007 Longworth HOB
Washington, DC 20515-1409
Phone: 202-225-5315

Iowa-1st, Democrat
Braley, Bruce L.
2263 Rayburn HOB
Washington, DC 20515-1501
Phone: 202-225-2911

Iowa-2nd, Democrat
Loebsack, David
1527 Longworth HOB
Washington, DC 20515-1502
Phone: 202-225-5576

Iowa-3rd, Democrat
Latham, Tom
2217 Rayburn HOB
Washington, DC 20515-1503
Phone: 202-225-5476

Iowa-4th, Republican
King, Steve
2210 Rayburn HOB
Washington, DC 20515-1504
Phone: 202-225-4426

Kansas-1st, Republican
Huelskamp, Tim
129 Cannon HOB
Washington, DC 20515-1601
Phone: 202-225-2715

Kansas-2nd, Republican
Jenkins, Lynn
1007 Longworth HOB
Washington, DC 20515-1602
Phone: 202-225-6601

Kansas-3rd, Republican
Yoder, Kevin
215 Cannon HOB
Washington, DC 20515-1603
Phone: 202-225-2865

Kansas-4th, Republican
Pompeo, Mike
107 Cannon HOB
Washington, DC 20515-1604
Phone: 202-225-6216

Kentucky-1st, Republican
Whitfield, Ed
2184 Rayburn HOB
Washington, DC 20515-1701
Phone: 202-225-3115

Kentucky-2nd, Republican
Guthrie, Brett, R.
308 Cannon HOB
Washington, DC 20515-1702
Phone: 202-225-3501

Kentucky-3rd, Democrat
Yarmuth, John A.
403 Cannon HOB
Washington, DC 20515-1703
Phone: 202-225-5401

Kentucky-4th, Republican
Massie, Thomas
314 Cannon HOB
Washington, DC 20515-1704
Phone: 202-225-5401

Kentucky-5th, Republican
Rogers, Harold
2406 Rayburn HOB
Washington, DC 20515-1705
Phone: 202-225-4601

Kentucky-6th, Republican
Barr, Garland "Andy"
1432 Longworth HOB
Washington, DC 20515-1706
Phone: 202-225-4706

Louisiana-1st, Republican
Scalise, Steve R.
2338 Rayburn HOB
Washington, DC 20515-1801
Phone: 202-225-3015

Louisiana-2nd, Democrat
Richmond, Cedrick
240 Cannon HOB
Washington, DC 20515-1802
Phone: 202-225-6636

Louisiana-3rd, Republican
Boustany Jr., Charles W.
1431 Longworth HOB
Washington, DC 20515-1803
Phone: 202-225-2031

Louisiana-4th, Republican
Fleming, John
416 Cannon HOB
Washington, DC 20515-1804
Phone: 202-225-2777

Louisiana-5th, Republican
Alexander, Rodney
316 Cannon HOB
Washington, DC 20515-1805
Phone: 202-225-8490

Louisiana-6th, Republican
Cassidy, Bill
1131 Longworth HOB
Washington, DC 20515-1806
Phone: 202-225-3901

Maine-1st, Democrat
Pingree, Chellie
1318 Longworth HOB
Washington, DC 20515-1901
Phone: 202-225-6116

Maine-2nd, Democrat
Michaud, Michael H.
1724 Longworth HOB
Washington, DC 20515-1902
Phone: 202-225-6306

Maryland-1st, Republican
Harris, Andy
1533 Longworth HOB
Washington, DC 20515-2001
Phone: 202-225-5311

Maryland-2nd, Democrat
Ruppersberger, C. A. Dutch
2416 Rayburn HOB
Washington, DC 20515-2002
Phone: 202-225-3061

Maryland-3rd, Democrat
Sarbanes, John P.
2444 Rayburn HOB
Washington, DC 20515-2003
Phone: 202-225-4016

Maryland-4th, Democrat
Edwards, Donna F.
2445 Rayburn HOB
Washington, DC 20515-2004
Phone: 202-225-8699

Maryland-5th, Democrat
Hoyer, Steny H.
1705 Longworth HOB
Washington, DC 20515-2005
Phone: 202-225-4131

Maryland-6th, Democrat
Delaney, John
1632 Longworth HOB
Washington, DC 20515-2006
Phone: 202-225-2721

Maryland-7th, Democrat
Cummings, Elijah E.
2235 Rayburn HOB
Washington, DC 20515-2007
Phone: 202-225-4741

Maryland-8th, Democrat
Hollen, Chris Van
1707 Longworth HOB
Washington, DC 20515-2008
Phone: 202-225-5341

Massachusetts-1st, Democrat
Neal, Richard
2208 Rayburn HOB
Washington, DC 20515-2101
Phone: 202-225-5601

Massachusetts-2nd, Democrat
McGovern, James
438 Cannon HOB
Washington, DC 20515-2101
Phone: 202-225-6101

Massachusetts-3rd, Democrat
Tsongas, Niki
1607 Longworth HOB
Washington, DC 20515-2103
Phone: 202-225-3411

Massachusetts-4th, Democrat
Kennedy III, Joseph C.
1218 Longworth HOB
Washington, DC 20515-2104
Phone: 202-225-5931

Massachusetts-5th, Democrat
Mackey, Ed
2108 Rayburn HOB
Washington, DC 20515-2105
Phone: 202-225-2836

Massachusetts-6th, Democrat
Tierney, John F.
2238 Rayburn HOB
Washington, DC 20515-2106
Phone: 202-225-8020

Massachusetts-7th, Democrat
Capuano, Michael F.
1414 Longworth HOB
Washington, DC 20515-2107
Phone: 202-225-5111

Massachusetts-8th, Democrat
Lynch, Stephen F.
2133 Rayburn HOB
Washington, DC 20515-2108
Phone: 202-225-8273

Massachusetts-9th, Democrat
Keating, William
315 Cannon HOB
Washington, DC 20515-2109
Phone: 202-225-3111

Michigan-1st, Republican
Benishek, Dan
514 Cannon HOB
Washington, DC 20515-2201
Phone: 202-225-4735

Michigan-2nd, Republican
Huizenga, Bill
1217 Longworth HOB
Washington, DC 20515-2202
Phone: 202-225-4401

Michigan-3rd , Republican
Amash, Justin
114 Cannon HOB
Washington, DC 20515-2203
Phone: 202-225-3831

Michigan-4th, Republican
Camp, Dave
341 Cannon HOB
Washington, DC 20515-2204
Phone: 202-225-3561

Michigan-5th, Democrat
Kildee, Dale E.
327 Cannon HOB
Washington, DC 20515-2205
Phone: 202-225-3611

Michigan-6th, Republican
Upton, Fred
2183 Rayburn HOB
Washington, DC 20515-2206
Phone: 202-225-3761

Michigan-7th, Republican
Walberg, Tim
2436 Rayburn HOB
Washington, DC 20515-2207
Phone: 202-225-6276

Michigan-8th, Republican
Rogers, Mike
2112 Rayburn HOB
Washington, DC 20515-2208
Phone: 202-225-4872

Michigan-9th, Democrat
Levin, Sander
1236 Longworth HOB
Washington, DC 20515-2209
Phone: 202-225-4961

Michigan-10th, Republican
Miller, Candice S.
320 Cannon HOB
Washington, DC 20515-2210
Phone: 202-225-2106

Michigan-11th, Republican
Bentivolio, Kathy
226 Cannon HOB
Washington, DC 20515-2211
Phone: 202-225-8171

Michigan-12th, Democrat
Dingell, John
2426 Rayburn HOB
Washington, DC 20515-2212
Phone: 202-225-5120

Michigan-13th, Democrat
Conyers, Jr., John
2426 Rayburn HOB
Washington, DC 20515-2213
Phone: 202-225-5126

Michigan-14th, Democrat
Peters, Gary
1609 Longworth HOB
Washington, DC 20515-2214
Phone: 202-225-5802

Minnesota-1st, Democrat
Walz, Timothy J.
1034 Longworth HOB
Washington, DC 20515-2301
Phone: 202-225-2472

Minnesota-2nd, Republican
Kline, John
2439 Rayburn HOB
Washington, DC 20515-2302
Phone: 202-225-2271

Minnesota-3rd, Republican
Paulsen, Erik
127 Cannon HOB
Washington, DC 20515-2303
Phone: 202-225-2871

Minnesota-4th, Democrat
McCollum, Betty
1714 Longworth HOB
Washington, DC 20515-2304
Phone: 202-225-6631

Minnesota-5th, Democrat
Ellison, Keith
2244 Rayburn HOB
Washington, DC 20515-2305
Phone: 202-225-4755

Minnesota-6th, Republican
Bachmann, Michele
2417 Rayburn HOB
Washington, DC 20515-2306
Phone: 202-225-2331

Minnesota-7th, Democrat
Peterson, Collin C.
2109 Rayburn HOB
Washington, DC 20515-2307
Phone: 202-225-2165

Minnesota-8th, Democrat
Nolan, Rick
2447 Rayburn HOB
Washington, DC 20515-2308
Phone: 202-225-6211

Mississippi-1st, Republican
Nunnelle, Alan
1427 Longworth HOB
Washington, DC 20515-2401
Phone: 202-225-5031

Mississippi-2nd, Democrat
Thompson, Bennie G.
2466 Rayburn HOB
Washington, DC 20515-2402
Phone: 202-225-5876

Mississippi-3rd, Republican
Harper, Gregg
307 Cannon HOB
Washington, DC 20515-2403
Phone: 202-225-5031

Mississippi-4th, Republican
Palazzo, Steven M.
331 Cannon HOB
Washington, DC 20515-2404
Phone: 202-225-5772

Missouri-1st, Democrat
Clay, William Lacy
2418 Rayburn HOB
Washington, DC 20515-2501
Phone: 202-225-2406

Missouri-2nd, Republican
Wagner, Ann
435 Cannon HOB
Washington, DC 20515-2502
Phone: 202-225-1621

Missouri-3rd, Republican
Luetkemeyer, Blaine
2440 Rayburn HOB
Washington, DC 20515-2503
Phone: 202-225-2956

Missouri-4th, Republican
Hartzler, Vicky
1023 Longworth HOB
Washington, DC 20515-2504
Phone: 202-225-2876

Missouri-5th, Democrat
Cleaver, Emanuel
2335 Longworth HOB
Washington, DC 20515-2505
Phone: 202-225-4535

Missouri-6th, Republican
Graves, Sam
1415 Longworth HOB
Washington, DC 20515-2506
Phone: 202-225-2506

Missouri-7th, Republican
Long, Billy
1541 Longworth HOB
Washington, DC 20515-2507
Phone: 202-225-6536

Missouri-8th, Republican
Emerson, Jo Ann – Vacancy
2230 Rayburn HOB
Washington, DC 20515-2508
Phone: 202-225-4404

Montana-At Large, Republican
Daines, Steve
206 Cannon HOB
Washington, DC 20515-2601
Phone: 202-225-3211

Nebraska-1st, Republican
Fortenberry, Jeff
1514 Longworth HOB
Washington, DC 20515-2701
Phone: 202-225-4806

Nebraska-2nd, Republican
Terry, Lee
2331 Rayburn HOB
Washington, DC 20515-2702
Phone: 202-225-4155

Nebraska-3rd, Republican
Smith, Adrian
2241 Rayburn HOB
Washington, DC 20515-2703
Phone: 202-225-6435

Nevada-1st, Democrat
Titus, Dina
401 Cannon HOB
Washington, DC 20515-2801
Phone: 202-225-5965

Nevada-2nd, Republican
Amodei, Mark
222 Cannon HOB
Washington, DC 20515-2802
Phone: 202-225-6155

Nevada-3rd, Republican
Heck, Joseph
132 Cannon HOB
Washington, DC 20515-2803
Phone: 202-225-3252

Nevada-4th, Democrat
Horsford, Steven
1330 Longworth HOB
Washington, DC 20515-2804
Phone: 202-225-9894

New Hampshire-1st, Republican
Shea-Porter, Carol
1530 Longworth HOB
Washington, DC 20515-2901
Phone: 202-225-5456

New Hampshire-2nd, Democrat
Kuster, Ann
137 Cannon HOB
Washington, DC 20515-2902
Phone: 202-225-5206

New Jersey-1st, Democrat
Andrews, Robert E.
2265 Rayburn HOB
Washington, DC 20515-3001
Phone: 202-225-6501

New Jersey-2nd, Republican
LoBiondo, Frank A.
2427 Rayburn HOB
Washington, DC 20515-3002
Phone: 202-225-6572

New Jersey-3rd, Republican
Runyan, Jon
1239 Longworth HOB
Washington, DC 20515-3003
Phone: 202-225-4765

New Jersey-4th, Republican
Smith, Christopher H.
2373 Rayburn HOB
Washington, DC 20515-3004
Phone: 202-225-3765

New Jersey-5th, Republican
Garrett, Scott
2232 Rayburn HOB
Washington, DC 20515-3005
Phone: 202-225-4465

New Jersey-6th, Democrat
Pallone, Frank, Jr.
237 Cannon HOB
Washington, DC 20515-3006
Phone: 202-225-4671

New Jersey-7th, Democrat
Lance, Leonard
133 Cannon HOB
Washington, DC 20515-3007
Phone: 202-225-5361

New Jersey-8th, Democrat
Sires, Abio
2302 Rayburn HOB
Washington, DC 20515-3008
Phone: 202-225-7919

New Jersey-9th, Democrat
Pascrell, Bill
2342 Rayburn HOB
Washington, DC 20515-3009
Phone: 202-225-5751

New Jersey-10th, Democrat
Payne, Donald M.
103 Cannon HOB
Washington, DC 20515-3010
Phone: 202-225-3436

New Jersey-11th, Republican
Frelinghuysen, Rodney P.
2306 Rayburn HOB
Washington, DC 20515-3012
Phone: 202-225-5034

New Jersey-12th, Democrat
Holt, Rush
1214 Longworth HOB
Washington, DC 20515-5801
Phone: 202-225-5801

New Mexico-1st, Democrat
Lujan Grisham, Michelle
214 Cannon HOB
Washington, DC 20515-3101
Phone: 202-225-6190

New Mexico-2nd, Republican
Pearce, Steven
2432 Rayburn HOB
Washington, DC 20515-3102
Phone: 202-225-2365

New Mexico-3rd, Democrat
Luján, Ben Ray
2446 Rayburn HOB
Washington, DC 20515-3103
Phone: 202-225-6190

New York-1st, Democrat
Bishop, Timothy H.
306 Cannon HOB
Washington, DC 20515-3201
Phone: 202-225-3826

New York-2nd, Republican
King, Peter T.
339 Cannon HOB
Washington, DC 20515-3202
Phone: 202-225-7896

New York-3rd, Democrat
Israel, Steve
2457 Rayburn HOB
Washington, DC 20515-3203
Phone: 202-225-3335

New York-4th, Democrat
McCarthy, Carolyn
2346 Rayburn HOB
Washington, DC 20515-3204
Phone: 202-225-5516

New York-5th, Democrat
Meeks, Gregory W.
2234 Rayburn HOB
Washington, DC 20515-3205
Phone: 202-225-3461

New York-6th, Democrat
Meng, Grace
1317 Longworth HOB
Washington, DC 20515-3206
Phone: 202-225-2601

New York-7th, Democrat
Velázquez, Nydia M.
2302 Rayburn HOB
Washington, DC 20515-3207
Phone: 202-225-2361

New York-8th, Democrat
Jeffries, Hakeem
1339 Longworth HOB
Washington, DC 20515-3208
Phone: 202-225-5936

New York-9th, Democrat
Clarke, Yvette D.
2351 Rayburn HOB
Washington, DC 20515-3209
Phone: 202-225-6231

New York-10th, Democrat
Nadler, Jerrold
2110 Rayburn HOB
Washington, DC 20515-3210
Phone: 202-225-5635

New York 11th, Republican
Grimm, Michael G.
512 Cannon HOB
Washington, DC 20515-3211
Phone: 202-225-3371

New York-12th, Democrat
Maloney, Carolyn
2308 Rayburn HOB
Washington, DC 20515-3212
Phone: 202-225-7944

New York-13th, Democrat
Rangel, Charles B.
2354 Rayburn HOB
Washington, DC 20515-3213
Phone: 202-225-4365

New York-14th, Democrat
Crowley, Joseph
1436 Longworth HOB
Washington, DC 20515-3214
Phone: 202-225-3965

New York-15th, Democrat
José E. Serrano
2227 Rayburn HOB
Washington, DC 20515-3215
Phone: 202-225-4361

New York-16th, Democrat
Engel, Eliot
2161 Rayburn HOB
Washington, DC 20515-3216
Phone: 202-225-2464

New York-17th, Democrat
Lowey, Nita M.
2365 Rayburn HOB
Washington, DC 20515-3217
Phone: 202-225-6506

New York-18th, Democrat
Maloney, Sean Patrick
1529 Longworth HOB
Washington, DC 20515-3218
Phone: 202-225-5441

New York-19th, Republican
Gibson, Chris
1708 Longworth HOB
Washington, DC 20515-3219
Phone: 202-225-5614

New York-20th, Democrat
Tonko, Paul D.
2463 Rayburn HOB
Washington, DC 20515-3220
Phone: 202-225-5076

New York-21st, Democrat
Owens, Bill
405 Cannon HOB
Washington, DC 20515-3221
Phone: 202-225-4611

New York-22nd, Republican
Hanna, Richard
405 Cannon HOB
Washington, DC 20515-3222
Phone: 202-225-4611

New York-23rd, Republican
Reed, Tom
1504 Longworth HOB
Washington, DC 20515-3223
Phone: 202-225-3161

New York-24th, Republican
Maffei, Daniel
422 Cannon HOB
Washington, DC 20515-3224
Phone: 202-225-3701

New York-25th, Democrat
Slaughter, Louise
2469 Rayburn HOB
Washington, DC 20515-3225
Phone: 202-225-3615

New York-26th, Democrat
Higgins, Brian
2459 Rayburn HOB
Washington, DC 20515-3226
Phone: 202-225-3306

New York-27th, Republican
Collins, Chris
1117 Longworth HOB
Washington, DC 20515-3227
Phone: 202-225-5265

North Carolina-1st, Democrat
Butterfield, G. K.
2305 Rayburn HOB
Washington, DC 20515-3301
Phone: 202-225-3101

North Carolina-2nd, Republican
Ellmers, Renee L.
426 Cannon HOB
Washington, DC 20515-3302
Phone: 202-225-4531

North Carolina-3rd, Republican
Jones, Walter B.
2333 Rayburn HOB
Washington, DC 20515-3303
Phone: 202-225-3415

North Carolina-4th, Democrat
Price, David E.
2162 Rayburn HOB
Washington, DC 20515-3304
Phone: 202-225-1784

North Carolina-5th, Republican
Foxx, Virginia
2350 Rayburn HOB
Washington, DC 20515-3305
Phone: 202-225-2071

North Carolina-6th, Republican
Coble, Howard
2188 Rayburn HOB
Washington, DC 20515-3306
Phone: 202-225-3065

North Carolina-7th, Democrat
McIntyre, Michael
2428 Rayburn HOB
Washington, DC 20515-3307
Phone: 202-225-2731

North Carolina-8th, Republican
Hudson, Richard
429 Cannon HOB
Washington, DC 20515-3308
Phone: 202-225-3032

North Carolina-9th, Republican
Pittenger, Robert
224 Cannon HOB
Washington, DC 20515-3309
Phone: 202-225-1976

North Carolina-10th, Republican
McHenry, Patrick T.
2334 Rayburn HOB
Washington, DC 20515-3310
Phone: 202-225-2576

North Carolina-11th, Republican
Meadows, Mark
1516 Longworth HOB
Washington, DC 20515-3311
Phone: 202-225-6401

North Carolina-12th, Democrat
Watt, Melvin L.
2304 Rayburn HOB
Washington, DC 20515-3312
Phone: 202-225-1510

North Carolina-13th, Republican
Holding, George
507 Cannon HOB
Washington, DC 20515-3313
Phone: 202-225-3032

North Dakota-At Large, Rep.
Cramer, Kevin
1032 Longworth HOB
Washington, DC 20515-3401
Phone: 202-225-2611

Northern Mariana Islands-Delegate, Democrat
Sablan, Grejorio Kilili Camacho
423 Cannon HOB
Washington, DC 20515-5201
Phone: 202-225-2646

Ohio-1st, Republican
Chabot, Steve
2371 Rayburn HOB
Washington, DC 20515-3501
Phone: 202-225-2216

Ohio-2nd, Republican
Wenstrap, Brad
1223 Longworth HOB
Washington, DC 20515-3502
Phone: 202-225-3164

Ohio-3rd, Republican
Beatty, Joyce
417 Cannon HOB
Washington, DC 20515-3503
Phone: 202-225-4324

Ohio-4th, Republican
Jordan, Jim
1524 Longworth HOB
Washington, DC 20515-3504
Phone: 202-225-2676

Ohio-5th, Republican
Latta, Rober E.
2448 Rayburn HOB
Washington, DC 20515-3505
Phone: 202-225-6405

Ohio-6th, Republican
Johnson, Bill
1710 Longworth HOB
Washington, DC 20515-3506
Phone: 202-225-5705

Ohio-7th, Republican
Gibbs, Bob
329 Cannon HOB
Washington, DC 20515-3507
Phone: 202-225-6265

Ohio-8th, Republican
Boehner, John A.
1011 Longworth HOB
Washington, DC 20515-3508
Phone: 202-225-6205

Ohio-9th, Democrat
Kaptur, Marcy
2186 Rayburn HOB
Washington, DC 20515-3509
Phone: 202-225-4146

Ohio-10th, Republican
Turner, Michael
2239 Rayburn HOB
Washington, DC 20515-3510
Phone: 202-225-6465

Ohio-11th, Republican
Fudge, Marcia L.
2344 Rayburn HOB
Washington, DC 20515-3511
Phone: 202-225-6465

Ohio-12th, Republican
Tiberi, Patrick J.
106 Cannon HOB
Washington, DC 20515-3512
Phone: 202-225-5355

Ohio-13th, Democrat
Ryan, Tim
1535 Longworth HOB
Washington, DC 20515-3513
Phone: 202-225-2015

Ohio-14th, Republican
Joyce, David
1535 Longworth HOB
Washington, DC 20515-3514
Phone: 202-225-5731

Ohio-15th, Republican
Stivers, Steve
1022 Longworth HOB
Washington, DC 20515-3515
Phone: 202-225-2015

Ohio-16th, Republican
Renacci, James B.
130 Cannon HOB
Washington, DC 20515-3516
Phone: 202-225-3876

Oklahoma-1st, Republican
Bridenstine, Jim
434 Cannon HOB
Washington, DC 20515-3601
Phone: 202-225-2211

Oklahoma-2nd, Republican
Mullin, Mark Wayne
1113 Longworth HOB
Washington, DC 20515-3602
Phone: 202-225-2701

Oklahoma-3rd, Republican
Lucas, Frank
2311 Rayburn HOB
Washington, DC 20515-3603
Phone: 202-225-5565

Oklahoma-4th, Republican
Cole, Tom
2458 Rayburn HOB
Washington, DC 20515-3604
Phone: 202-225-6165

Oklahoma-5th, Republican
Lankford, James
228 Cannon HOB
Washington, DC 20515-3605
Phone: 202-225-2132

Oregon-1st, Democrat
Bonamici, Suzanne
439 Cannon HOB
Washington, DC 20515-3701
Phone: 202-225-0855

Oregon-2nd, Republican
Walden, Greg
2182 Rayburn HOB
Washington, DC 20515-3702
Phone: 202-225-6730

Oregon-3rd, Democrat
Blumenauer, Earl
1111 Longworth HOB
Washington, DC 20515-3703
Phone: 202-225-4811

Oregon-4th, Democrat
DeFazio, Peter A.
2134 Rayburn HOB
Washington, DC 20515-3704
Phone: 202-225-6416

Oregon-5th, Democrat
Schrader, Kurt
108 Cannon HOB
Washington, DC 20515-3705
Phone: 202-225-5711

Pennsylvania-1st, Democrat
Brady, Robert A.
102 Cannon HOB
Washington, DC 20515-3801
Phone: 202-225-4731

Pennsylvania-2nd, Democrat
Fattah, Chaka
2301 Rayburn HOB
Washington, DC 20515-3802
Phone: 202-225-4001

Pennsylvania-3rd, Republican
Kelly, Mike
1519 Longworth HOB
Washington, DC 20515-3803
Phone: 202-225-5406

Pennsylvania-4th, Republican
Perry, Scott
126 Cannon HOB
Washington, DC 20515-3804
Phone: 202-225-5836

Pennsylvania-5th, Republican
Thompson, Glen
124 Cannon HOB
Washington, DC 20515-3805
Phone: 202-225-5121

Pennsylvania-6th, Republican
Gerlach, Jim
2442 Rayburn HOB
Washington, DC 20515-3806
Phone: 202-225-4315

Pennsylvania-7th, Republican
Meehan, Patrick
204 Cannon HOB
Washington, DC 20515-3807
Phone: 202-225-3011

Pennsylvania-8th, Republican
Fitzpatrick, Michael
2400 Rayburn HOB
Washington, DC 20515-3808
Phone: 202-225-4276

Pennsylvania-9th, Republican
Shuster, Bill
2209 Rayburn HOB
Washington, DC 20515-3809
Phone: 202-225-2431

Pennsylvania-10th, Republican
Marino, Tom
410 Cannon HOB
Washington, DC 20515-3810
Phone: 202-225-3731

Pennsylvania-11th, Republican
Barletta, Lou
115 Cannon HOB
Washington, DC 20515-3811
Phone: 202-225-6511

Pennsylvania-12th, Republican
Rothfus, Keith
503 Cannon HOB
Washington, DC 20515-3812
Phone: 202-225-2065

Pennsylvania-13th, Democrat
Schwartz, Allyson Y.
1227 Longworth HOB
Washington, DC 20515-3813
Phone: 202-225-6111

Pennsylvania-14th, Democrat
Doyle, Michael F.
401 Cannon HOB
Washington, DC 20515-3814
Phone: 202-225-2135

Pennsylvania-15th, Republican
Dent, Charles W.
2455 Rayburn HOB
Washington, DC 20515-3815
Phone: 202-225-6411

Pennsylvania-16th, Republican
Pitts, Joseph R.
420 Cannon HOB
Washington, DC 20515-3816
Phone: 202-225-2411

Pennsylvania-17th, Democrat
Cartwright, Matthew
1419 Longworth HOB
Washington, DC 20515-3817
Phone: 202-225-5546

Pennsylvania-18th, Republican
Murphy, Tim
2332 Rayburn HOB
Washington, DC 20515-3818
Phone: 202-225-2301

Puerto Rico-At Large, Democrat
Pierluisi, Pedro R.
1213 Longworth HOB
Washington, DC 20515-5401
Phone: 202-225-2615

Rhode Island-1st, Democrat
Cicilline, David
128 Cannon HOB
Washington, DC 20515-3901
Phone: 202-225-4911

Rhode Island-2nd, Democrat
Langevin, James R.
109 Cannon HOB
Washington, DC 20515-3902
Phone: 202-225-2735

South Carolina-1st, Republican
Scott, Tim-Vacancy
322 Cannon HOB
Washington, DC 20515-4001
Phone: 202-225-3176

South Carolina-2nd, Republican
Wilson, Joe
2229 Rayburn HOB
Washington, DC 20515-4002
Phone: 202-225-2452

South Carolina-3rd, Republican
Duncan, Jeff
116 Cannon HOB
Washington, DC 20515-4003
Phone: 202-225-5301

South Carolina-4th, Republican
Gowdy, Trey
1404 Longworth HOB
Washington, DC 20515-4004
Phone: 202-225-6030

South Carolina-5th, Republican
Mulvaney, Mick
1207 Longworth HOB
Washington, DC 20515-4005
Phone: 202-225-5501

South Carolina-6th, Democrat
Clyburn, James E.
242 Cannon HOB
Washington, DC 20515-4006
Phone: 202-225-3315

South Carolina-7th, Republican
Rice, Tom
325 Cannon HOB
Washington, DC 20515-4007
Phone: 202-225-9895

South Dakota At-Large, Rep.
Noem, Kristi, L.
1323 Longworth HOB
Washington, DC 20515-4101
Phone: 202-225-2801

Tennessee-1st, Republican
Roe, Phil
407 Cannon HOB
Washington, DC 20515-4201
Phone: 202-225-6356

Tennessee-2nd, Republican
Duncan Jr., John J.
2207 Rayburn HOB
Washington, DC 20515-4202
Phone: 202-225-5435

Tennessee-3rd, Republican
Fleischmann, Charles, J. "Chuck"
230 Cannon HOB
Washington, DC 20515-4203
Phone: 202-225-3271

Tennessee-4th, Republican
Des Jarlais, Scott
413 Cannon HOB
Washington, DC 20515-4204
Phone: 202-225-6831

Tennessee-5th, Democrat
Cooper, Jim
1536 Longworth, HOB
Washington, DC 20515-4205

Phone: 202-225-4311

Tennessee-6th, Republican
Black, Diane
1531 Longworth, HOB
Washington, DC 20515-4206
Phone: 202-225-4231

Tennessee-7th, Republican
Blackburn, Marsha
217 Cannon HOB
Washington, DC 20515-4207
Phone: 202-225-2811

Tennessee-8th, Republican
Fincher, Stephen Le
1118 Longworth HOB
Washington, DC 20515-4208
Phone: 202-225-4714

Tennessee-9th, Democrat
Cohen, Steve
2404 Rayburn HOB
Washington, DC 20515-4209
Phone: 202-225-3265

Texas-1st, Republican
Gohmert, Louie
2440 Rayburn HOB
Washington, DC 20515-4301
Phone: 202-225-3035

Texas-2nd, Republican
Poe, Ted
2412 Rayburn HOB
Washington, DC 20515-4302
Phone: 202-225-6565

Texas-3rd, Republican
Johnson, Sam
1211 Longworth HOB
Washington, DC 20515-4303
Phone: 202-225-4201

Texas-4th, Republican
Hall, Ralph M.
2405 Rayburn HOB
Washington, DC 20515-4304
Phone: 202-225-6673

Texas-5th, Republican
Hensarling, Jeb
2228 Rayburn HOB
Washington, DC 20515-4305
Phone: 202-225-3484

Texas-6th, Republican
Barton, Joe
2107 Rayburn HOB
Washington, DC 20515-4306
Phone: 202-225-2002

Texas-7th, Republican
Culberson, John Abney
2352 Rayburn HOB
Washington, DC 20515-4307
Phone: 202-225-2571

Texas-8th, Republican
Brady, Kevin
301 Cannon HOB
Washington, DC 20515-4308
Phone: 202-225-4901

Texas-9th, Democrat
Green, Al
2201 Rayburn HOB
Washington, DC 20515-4309
Phone: 202-225-7508

Texas-10th, Republican
McCaul, Michael T.
131 Cannon HOB
Washington, DC 20515-4310
Phone: 202-225-2401

Texas-11th, Republican
Conaway, K. Michael
2430 Rayburn HOB
Washington, DC 20515-4311
Phone: 202-225-3605

Texas-12th, Republican
Granger, Kay
1026 Longworth HOB
Washington, DC 20515-4312
Phone: 202-225-5071

Texas-13th, Republican
Thornberry, Mac
2329 Rayburn HOB
Washington, DC 20515-4313
Phone: 202-225-3706

Texas-14th, Republican
Weber, Randy
510 Cannon HOB
Washington, DC 20515-4314
Phone: 202-225-2831

Texas-15th, Democrat
Hinojosa, Rubén
2262 Rayburn HOB
Washington, DC 20515-4315
Phone: 202-225-2531

Texas-16th, Democrat
O'Rourke, Beto
1721 Longworth HOB
Washington, DC 20515-4316
Phone: 202-225-4831

Texas-17th, Republican
Flores, Bill
1030 Longworth HOB
Washington, DC 20515-4317
Phone: 202-225-6105

Texas-18th, Democrat
Jackson Lee, Sheila
2160 Rayburn HOB
Washington, DC 20515-4318
Phone: 202-225-3816

Texas-19th, Republican
Neugebauer, Randy
1424 Longworth HOB
Washington, DC 20515-4319
Phone: 202-225-4005

Texas-20th, Democrat
Castro, Joaquin
212 Cannon HOB
Washington, DC 20515-4320
Phone: 202-225-3236

Texas-21st, Republican
Smith, Lamar
2409 Rayburn HOB
Washington, DC 20515-4321
Phone: 202-225-4236

Texas-22nd, Republican
Olson, Pete
312 Cannon HOB
Washington, DC 20515-4322
Phone: 202-225-5951

Texas-23rd, Republican
Gallego, Pete
1339 Longworth HOB
Washington, DC 20515-4323
Phone: 202-225-4511

Texas-24th, Republican
Marchant, Kenny
1110 Longworth, HOB
Washington, DC 20515-4324
Phone: 202-225-6605

Texas-25th, Republican
Williams, Roger
1122 Longworth, HOB
Washington, DC 20515-4325
Phone: 202-225-9896

Texas-26th, Republican
Burgess, Michael C.
2336 Rayburn, HOB
Washington, DC 20515-4326
Phone: 202-225-7772

Texas-27th, Republican
Farenthold, Blake
117 Cannon HOB
Washington, DC 20515-4327
Phone: 202-225-7742

Texas-28th, Democrat
Cuellar, Henry
2431 Rayburn, HOB
Washington, DC 20515-4328
Phone: 202-225-1640

Texas-29th, Democrat
Green, Gene
2470 Rayburn HOB
Washington, DC 20515-4329
Phone: 202-225-1688

Texas-30th, Democrat
Johnson, Eddie Bernice
2468 Rayburn HOB
Washington, DC 20515-4330
Phone: 202-225-8885

Texas-31st, Republican
Carter, John
409 Cannon HOB
Washington, DC 20515-4331
Phone: 202-225-3864

Texas-32nd, Republican
Sessions, Pete
2233 Rayburn HOB
Washington, DC 20515-4332
Phone: 202-225-2231

Texas-33rd, Democrat
Veasey, Mare
414 Cannon HOB
Washington, DC 20515-4333
Phone: 202-225-9897

Texas-34th, Democrat
Vela, Filemon
437 Cannon HOB
Washington, DC 20515-4334
Phone: 202-225-9901

Texas-35th, Democrat
Doggett, Lloyd
201 Cannon HOB
Washington, DC 20515-4335
Phone: 202-225-4865

Texas-36th, Republican
Stockmen, Steve
326 Cannon HOB
Washington, DC 20515-4336
Phone: 202-225-1555

Utah-1st, Republican
Bishop, Rob
123 Cannon HOB
Washington, DC 20515-4401
Phone: 202-225-0453

Utah-2nd, Republican
Stewart, Chris
323 Cannon HOB
Washington, DC 20515-4402
Phone: 202-225-9730

Utah-3rd, Republican
Chaffetz, Jason
2464 Rayburn HOB

Washington, DC 20515-4403
Phone: 202-225-7751

Utah-4th, Democrat
Matheson, Jim
2211 Rayburn HOB
Washington, DC 20515-4404
Phone: 202-225-3011

Vermont-At-Large, Democrat
Welch, Peter
2303 Rayburn HOB
Washington, DC 20515-4501
Phone: 202-225-4115

Virgin Islands-At Large, Democrat
Christensen, Donna M.
1510 Longworth HOB
Washington, DC 20515-5501
Phone: 202-225-1790

Virginia-1st, Republican
Wittman, Robert J.
2454 Rayburn HOB
Washington, DC 20515-4601
Phone: 202-225-4261

Virginia-2nd, Republican
Rigell, E. Scott
418 Cannon HOB
Washington, DC 20515-4602
Phone: 202-225-4215

Virginia-3rd, Democrat
Scott, Robert C. "Bobby"
1201 Longworth HOB
Washington, DC 20515-4603
Phone: 202-225-8351

Virginia-4th, Republican
Forbes, J. Randy
2135 Rayburn HOB
Washington, DC 20515-4604
Phone: 202-225-6365

Virginia-5th, Republican
Hurt, Robert
125 Cannon HOB
Washington, DC 20515-4605
Phone: 202-225-4711

Virginia-6th, Republican
Goodlatte, Bob
2309 Rayburn HOB
Washington, DC 20515-4606
Phone: 202-225-5431

Virginia-7th, Republican
Cantor, Eric
303 Cannon HOB
Washington, DC 20515-4607
Phone: 202-225-2815

Virginia-8th, Democrat
Moran, James P.
2252 Rayburn HOB
Washington, DC 20515-4608
Phone: 202-225-4376

Virginia-9th, Republican
Griffith, H. Morgan
1108 Longworth HOB
Washington, DC 20515-4609
Phone: 202-225-3861

Virginia-10th, Republican
Wolf, Frank
233 Cannon HOB
Washington, DC 20515-4610
Phone: 202-225-5136

Virginia-11th, Democrat
Connolly, Gerald E.
424 Cannon HOB
Washington, DC 20515-4611
Phone: 202-225-1402

Washington-1st, Democrat
Del Bene, Susa
318 Cannon HOB
Washington, DC 20515-4701
Phone: 202-225-6311

Washington-2nd, Democrat
Larsen, Rick
2113 Rayburn HOB
Washington, DC 20515-4702
Phone: 202-225-2605

Washington-3rd, Republican
Beutler, Jaime Herrera
1130 Longworth HOB
Washington, DC 20515-4703

Phone: 202-225-3536

Washington-4th, Republican
Hastings, Doc
1203 Longworth HOB
Washington, DC 20515-4704
Phone: 202-225-5816

Washington-5th, Republican
McMorris Rodgers, Cathy
203 Cannon HOB
Washington, DC 20515-4705
Phone: 202-225-2006

Washington-6th, Democrat
Kilmer, Derek
1429 Longworth HOB
Washington, DC 20515-4706
Phone: 202-225-5916

Washington-7th, Democrat
McDermott, Jim
1035 Longworth HOB
Washington, DC 20515-4707
Phone: 202-225-3106

Washington-8th, Republican
Reichert, David G.
1127 Longworth HOB
Washington, DC 20515-4708
Phone: 202-225-7761

Washington-9th, Democrat
Smith, Adam
2264 Rayburn HOB
Washington, DC 20515-4709
Phone: 202-225-8901

Washington-10th, Democrat
Heck, Denny
425 Cannon HOB
Washington, DC 20515-4710
Phone: 202-225-9740

West Virginia-1st, Republican
McKinley, David B.
412 Cannon HOB
Washington, DC 20515-4801
Phone: 202-225-4172

West Virginia-2nd, Republican
Capito, Shelley Moore
2366 Rayburn HOB
Washington, DC 20515-4802
Phone: 202-225-2711

West Virginia-3rd, Democrat
Rahall, Nick J., II
2307 Rayburn HOB
Washington, DC 20515-4803
Phone: 202-225-3452

Wisconsin-1st, Republican
Ryan, Paul
1233 Longworth HOB
Washington, DC 20515-4901
Phone: 202-225-3031

Wisconsin-2nd, Democrat
Pocan, Mark
313 Cannon HOB
Washington, DC 20515-4902
Phone: 202-225-2906

Wisconsin-3rd, Democrat
Kind, Ron
1502 Longworth HOB
Washington, DC 20515-4903
Phone: 202-225-5506

Wisconsin-4th, Democrat
Moore, Gwen
2245 Rayburn HOB
Washington, DC 20515-4904
Phone: 202-225-4572

Wisconsin-5th, Republican
Sensenbrenner, F. James, Jr.
2449 Rayburn HOB
Washington, DC 20515-4905
Phone: 202-225-5101

Wisconsin-6th, Republican
Petri, Thomas E.
2462 Rayburn HOG
Washington, DC 20515-4906
Phone: 202-225-2476

Wisconsin-7th, Republican
Duffy, Sean P.
1208 Longworth HOB
Washington, DC 20515-4907
Phone: 202-225-3365

Wisconsin-8th, Republican
Ribble, Reid
1513 Longworth HOB
Washington, DC 20515-4908
Phone: 202-225-5665

Wyoming-At Large, Republican
Lummis, Cynthia M.
113 Cannon HOB
Washington, DC 20515-5001
Phone: 202-225-2311

U. S. Congressmen
U.S. Senate

Alabama-Republican
Sessions, Jeff
335 Russell Senate Office Building
Washington, DC 20510
Phone: 202-224-4124
Web Form: sessions.senate.gov/public/
index.cfm?FuseAction=Constitue...

Alabama-Republican
Shelby, Richard C.
304 Russell Senate Office Building
Washington, DC 20510
Phone: 202-224-5744
Web Form: shelby.senate.gov/public/in-
dex.cfm?p=ContactSenatorShelby

Alaska-Democrat
Begich, Mark
111 Russell Senate Office Building
Washington, DC 20510
Phone: 202-224-3004
Web Form: begich.senate.gov/public/in-
dex.cfm?p=EmailSenator

Alaska-Republican
Murkowski, Lisa
709 Hart Senate Office Building
Washington, DC 20510
Phone: 202-224-6665
Web Form: murkowski.senate.gov/public/
index.cfm?p=Contact

Arizona-Republican
Kyl, Jon
730 Hart Senate Office Building
Washington, DC 20510
Phone: 202-224-4521
Web Form: kyl.senate.gov/contact.cfm

Arizona-Republican
McCain, John
241 Russell Senate Office Building
Washington, DC 20510
Phone: 202-224-2235

Arkansas-Republican
Boozman, John
1 Russell Courtyard
Washington, DC 20510
Phone: 202-224-4843
Web Form: boozman.senate.gov/
contact_form.cfm

Arkansas-Democrat
Pryor, Mark L.
255 Dirksen Senate Office Building
Washington, DC 20510
Phone: 202-224-2353
Web Form: pryor.senate.gov/public/
index.cfm?p=Conta

California-Democrat
Boxer, Barbara
112 Hart Senate Office Building
Washington, DC 20510
Phone: 202-224-3553
Web Form: boxer.senate.gov/en/contact/

California-Democrat
Feinstein, Dianne
331 Hart Senate Office Building
Washington, DC 20510
Phone: 202-224-3841
Web Form: feinstein.senate.gov/public/
index.cfm?FuseAction=ContactU...

Colorado-Democrat
Bennet, Michael F.
458 Russell Senate Office Building
Washington, DC 20510
Phone: 202-224-5852
Web Form: bennet.senate.gov/contact/

Colorado-Democrat
Udall, Mark
328 Hart Senate Office Building
Washington, DC 20510
Phone: 202-224-5941
Web Form: markudall.senate.
gov/?p=contact

Connecticut-Democrat
Blumentahl, Richard
G55 Dirksen Senate Office Building
Washington, DC 20510
Phone: 202-224-2823
Web Form: blumenthal.senate.gov/contact/

Connecticut-Democrat
Liebeman, Joseph I.
706 Hart Senate Office Building
Washington, DC 20510
Phone: 202-224-4041
Web Form: lieberman.senate.gov/index.
cfm/contact/email-me-about-an-...

Delaware-Democrat
Carper, Thomas R.
513 Hart Senate Office Building
Washington, DC 20510
Phone: 202-224-2441
Web Form: carper.senate.gov/contact/

Delaware-Democrat
Coons, Christopher A.
383 Russell Senate Office Building
Washington, DC 20510
Phone: 202-224-5042
Web Form: coons.senate.gov/contact/

Florida-Democrat
Nelson, Bill
716 Hart Senate Office Building
Washington, DC 20510
Phone: 202-224-5274
Web Form: billnelson.senate.gov/contact/
index.cfm
Florida-Republican
Rubio, Marco
B40A Dirksen Senate Office Building
Washington, DC 20510
Phone: 202-224-3041
Web Form: rubio.senate.gov/public/in-
dex.cfm/contact

Georgia-Republican
Chambliss, Saxby
416 Russell Senate Office Building
Washington, DC 20510
Phone: 202-224-3521
Web Form: chambliss.senate.gov/public/
index.cfm?p=Email

Georgia-Republican
Isakson, Johnny
131 Russell Senate Office Building
Washington, DC 20510
Phone: 202-224-3643
Web Form: isakson.senate.gov/contact.cfm

Hawaii-Democrat
Akaka, Daniel K.
141 Hart Senate Office Building
Washington, DC 20510
Phone: 202-224-6361
Web Form: akaka.senate.gov/email-
senator-akaka.cfm

Hawaii-Democrat
Inouye, Daniel K.
722 Hart Senate Office Building
Washington, DC 20510
Phone: 202-224-3934
Web Form: inouye.senate.gov/Contact/
ContactDKI.cfm

Idaho-Republican
Crapo, Mike
239 Dirksen Senate Office Building
Washington, DC 20510
Phone: 202-224-6142
Web Form: crapo.senate.gov/contact/
email.cfm

Idaho-Republican
Risch, Maes E.
483 Russell Senate Office Building
Washington, DC 20510
Phone: 202-224-2752
Web Form: risch.senate.gov/public/index.
cfm?p=Email

Illinois-Democrat
Durbin, Richard J.
711 Hart Senate Office Building
Washington, DC 20510
Phone: 202-224-2152
Web Form: durbin.senate.gov/contact.
cfm

Illinois-Republican
Kirk, Mark
387 Russell Senate Office Building
Washington, DC 20510
Phone: 202-224-2854
Web Form: www.kirk.senate.gov/
contact_form.cfm

Indiana-Republican
Coats, Daniel
B40E Dirksen Senate Office Building
Washington, DC 20510
Phone: 202-224-5623
Web Form: coats.senate.gov/contact/

Indiana-Republican
Lugar, Richard G.
306 Hart Senate Office Building
Washington, DC 20510
Phone: 202-224-4814
Web Form: lugar.senate.gov/contact/

Iowa-Republican
Grassley, Chuck
135 Hart Senate Office Building
Washington, DC 20510
Phone: 202-224-3744
Web Form: grassley.senate.gov/contact.cfm

Iowa-Democrat
Harkin, Tom
731 Hart Senate Office Building
Washington, DC 20510
Phone: 202-224-3254
Web Form: harkin.senate.gov/contact.cfm

Kansas-Republican
Moran, Jerry
4 Russell Courtyard
Washington, DC 20510
Phone: 202-224-6521
Web Form: moran.senate.gov/public/index.cfm?p=e-mail-jerry

Kansas-Republican
Roberts, Pat
109 Hart Senate Office Building
Washington, DC 20510
Phone: 202-224-4774
Web Form: www.roberts.senate.gov/public/index.cfm?p=EmailPat

Kentucky-Republican
McConnell, Mitch
361A Russell Senate Office Building
Washington, DC 20510
Phone: 202-224-2541
Web Form: www.mcconnell.senate.gov/public/index.cfm?p=contact

Kentucky-Republican
Paul, Rand
5 Russell Courtyard
Washington, DC 20510
Phone: 202-224-4343
Web Form: paul.senate.gov/contact_form.cfm

Louisiana-Democrat
Landrieu, Mary L.
431 Dirksen Senate Office Building
Washington, DC 20510
Phone: 202-224-5824
Web Form: landrieu.senate.gov/about/contact.cfm

Louisiana-Republican
Vitter, David
516 Hart Senate Office Building
Washington, DC 20510
Phone: 202-224-4623
Web Form: vitter.senate.gov/public/index.cfm?FuseAction=Contact.Con.

Maine-Republican
Collins, Susan M.
413 Dirksen Senate Office Building
Washington, DC 20510
Phone: 202-224-2523
Web Form: collins.senate.gov/public/continue.cfm?FuseAction=Contact...

Maine-Republican
Snowe, Olympia J.
154 Russell Senate Office Building
Washington, DC 20510
Phone: 202-224-5344
Web Form: snowe.senate.gov/public/index.cfm/contact?p=email

Maryland-Democrat
Cardin, Benjamin L.
509 Hart Senate Office Building
Washington, DC 20510
Phone: 202-224-4524
Web Form: cardin.senate.gov/contact/email.cfm

Maryland-Democrat
Mikulski, Barbara A.
503 Hart Senate Office Building
Washington, DC 20510
Phone: 202-224-4654
Web Form: mikulski.senate.gov/contact/

Massachusetts-Republican
Brown, Scott P.
317 Russell Senate Office Building
Washington, DC 20510
Phone: 202-224-4543
Web Form: scottbrown.senate.gov/public/
    index.cfm/emailscottbrown

Massachusetts-Democrat
Kerry, John F.
218 Russell Senate Office Building
Washington, DC 20510
Phone: 202-224-2742
Web Form: kerry.senate.gov/contact/

Michigan-Democrat
Levin, Carl
269 Russell Senate Office Building
Washington, DC 20510
Phone: 202-224-6221
Web Form: levin.senate.gov/contact/

Michigan-Democrat
Stabenow, Debbie
133 Hart Senate Office Building
Washington, DC 20510
Phone: 202-224-4822
Web Form: stabenow.senate.
    gov/?p=contact

Minnesota-Democrat
Franken, Al
309 Hart Senate Office Building
Washington, DC 20510
Phone: 202-224-5641
Web Form: franken.senate.gov/?p=contact

Minnesota-Democrat
Klobuchar, Amy
302 Hart Senate Office Building
Washington, DC 20510
Phone: 202-224-3244
Web Form: klobuchar.senate.gov/emaila-
    my.cfm

Mississippi-Republican
Cochran, Thad
113 Dirksen Senate Office Building
Washington, DC 20510
Phone: 202-224-5054
Web Form: cochran.senate.gov/email.
    html

Mississippi-Republican
Wicker, Roger F.
555 Dirksen Senate Office Building
Washington, DC 20510
Phone: 202-224-6353
Web Form: wicker.senate.gov/public/
    index.cfm?FuseAction=Contact.
    EMa...

Missouri-Republican
Blunt, Roy
B40C Dirksen Senate Office Building
Washington, DC 20510
Phone: 202-224-5721
Web Form: blunt.senate.gov/public/
    index.cfm/contact

Missouri-Democrat
McCaskill, Claire
506 Hart Senate Office Building
Washington, DC 20510
Phone: 202-224-6154
Web Form: mccaskill.senate.gov/?

Montana-Democrat
Baucus, Max
511 Hart Senate Office Building
Washington, DC 20510
Phone: 202-224-2651
Web Form: baucus.senate.gov/contact/
    emailForm.cfm?subj=issue

Montana-Democrat
Tester, Jon
724 Hart Senate Office Building
Washington, DC 20510
Phone: 202-224-2644
Web Form: tester.senate.gov/Contact/
    index.cfm

Nebraska-Republican
Johanns, Mike
404 Russell Senate Office Building
Washington, DC 20510
Phone: 202-224-4224
Web Form: johanns.senate.gov/
    public/?p=ContactSenatorJohanns

Nebraska-Republican
Nelson, Ben
720 Hart Senate Office Building
Washington, DC 20510
Phone: 202-224-6551
Web Form: bennelson.senate.gov/
    contact-me.cfm

Nevada-Republican
Ensign, John
119 Russell Senate Office Building
Washington, DC 20510
Phone: 202-224-6244
Web Form: ensign.senate.gov/public/
    index.cfm?FuseAction=Contact.
    Con...

Nevada-Democrat
Reid, Harry
522 Hart Senate Office Building
Washington, DC 20510
Phone: 202-224-3542
Web Form: reid.senate.gov/contact/index.
    cfm

New Hampshire-Republican
Ayotte, Kelly
188 Russell Senate Office Building
Washington, DC 20510
Phone: 202-224-3324
Web Form: ayotte.senate.gov/contact_
    form.cfm

New Hampshire-Democrat
Shaheen, Jeanne
520 Hart Senate Office Building
Washington, DC 20510
Phone: 202-224-2841
Web Form: shaheen.senate.gov/contact/

New Jersey-Democrat
Lautenberg, Frank R.
324 Hart Senate Office Building
Washington, DC 20510
Phone: 202-224-3224
Web Form: lautenberg.senate.gov/
    contact/routing.cfm

New Jersey-Democrat
Menendez, Robert
528 Hart Senate Office Building
Washington, DC 20510
Phone: 202-224-4744
Web Form: menendez.senate.gov/contact/

New Mexico-Democrat
Bingaman, Jeff
703 Hart Senate Office Building
Washington, DC 20510
Phone: 202-224-5521
Web Form: bingaman.senate.gov/
    contact/=

New Mexico-Democrat
Udall, Tom
110 Hart Senate Office Building
Washington, DC 20510
Phone: 202-224-6621
Web Form: tomudall.senate.
    gov/?p=contact

New York-Democrat
Gillibrand, Kirsten E.
478 Russell Senate Office Building
Washington, DC 20510
Phone: 202-224-4451
Web Form: gillibrand.senate.gov/contact/

New York-Democrat
Schumer, Charles E.
322 Hart Senate Office Building
Washington, DC 20510
Phone: 202-224-6542
Web Form: schumer.senate.gov/new_
    website/contact.cfm

North Carolina-Republican
Burr, Richard
217 Russell Senate Office Building
Washington, DC 20510
Phone: 202-224-3154
Web Form: burr.senate.gov/public/index.
    cfm?FuseAction=Contact.Conta...

North Carolina-Democrat
Hagan, Kay R.
521 Dirksen Senate Office Building
Washington, DC 20510
Phone: 202-224-6342
Web Form: hagan.senate.gov/?p=contact

North Dakota-Democrat
Conrad, Kent
530 Hart Senate Office Building
Washington, DC 20510
Phone: 202-224-2043
Web Form: conrad.senate.gov/contact/
webform.cfm

North Dakota-Republican
Hoeven, John
G11 Dirksen Senate Office Building
Washington, DC 20510
Phone: 202-224-2551
Web Form: hoeven.senate.gov/public/
index.cfm/email-the-senator

Ohio-Democrat
Brown, Sherrod
713 Hart Senate Office Building
Washington, DC 20510
Phone: 202-224-2315
Web Form: brown.senate.gov/contact/

Ohio-Republican
Portman, Rob
B40D Dirksen Senate Office Building
Washington, DC 20510
Phone: 202-224-3353
Web Form: portman.senate.gov/con-
tact_form.cfm

Oklahoma-Republican
Cobum, Tom
172 Russell Senate Office Building
Washington, DC 20510
Phone: 202-224-5754
Web Form: coburn.senate.gov/public/in-
dex.cfm/contactsenatorcoburn?p...

Oklahoma-Republican
Inhofe, James M.
205 Russell Senate Office Building
Washington, DC 20510
Phone: 202-224-4721
Web Form: inhofe.senate.gov/public/in-
dex.cfm?FuseAction=Contact.Con...

Oregon-Democrat
Merkley, Jeff
313 Hart Senate Office Building
Washington, DC 20510
Phone: 202-224-3753
Web Form: merkley.senate.gov/contact/

Oregon-Democrat
Wyden, Ron
223 Dirksen Senate Office Building
Washington, DC 20510
Phone: 202-224-5244
Web Form: wyden.senate.gov/contact/

Pennsylvania-Democrat
Casey, Robert P., Jr.
393 Russell Senate Office Building
Washington, DC 20510
Phone: 202-224-6324
Web Form: casey.senate.gov/contact/

Pennsylvania-Republican
Toomey, Patrick J.
B40B Dirksen Senate Office Building
Washington, DC 20510
Phone: 202-224-4254
Web Form: toomey.senate.gov/contact_
form.cfm

Rhode Island-Democrat
Reed, Jack
728 Hart Senate Office Building
Washington, DC 20510
Phone: 202-224-4642
Web Form: reed.senate.gov/contact/
contact-share.cfm

Rhode Island-Democrat
Whitehouse, Sheldon
717 Hart Senate Office Building
Washington, DC 20510
Phone: 202-224-2921
Web Form: whitehouse.senate.gov/
contact/

South Carolina-Republican
DeMint, Jim
167 Russell Senate Office Building
Washington, DC 20510
Phone: 202-224-6121
Web Form: demint.senate.gov/public/in-
dex.cfm?p=ContactInformation

South Carolina-Republican
Graham, Lindsey
290 Russell Senate Office Building
Washington, DC 20510
Phone: 202-224-5972
Web Form: lgraham.senate.gov/public/
index.cfm?FuseAction=Contact.Em

South Dakota-Democrat
Johnson, Tim
136 Hart Senate Office Building
Washington, DC 20510
Phone: 202-224-5842
Web Form: johnson.senate.gov/public/
index.cfm?p=Contact

South Dakota-Republican
Thune, John
493 Russell Senate Office Building
Washington, DC 20510
Phone: 202-224-2321
Web Form: thune.senate.gov/public/in-
dex.cfm?FuseAction=Contact.Email

Tennessee-Republican
Alexander, Lamar
455 Dirksen Senate Office Building
Washington, DC 20510
Phone: 202-224-4944
Web Form: alexander.senate.gov/public/
index.cfm?p=Email

Tennessee-Republican
Corker, Bob
185 Dirksen Senate Office Building
Washington, DC 20510
Phone: 202-224-3344
Web Form: corker.senate.gov/public/
index.cfm?p=ContactMe

Texas-Republican
Cornyn, John
517 Hart Senate Office Building
Washington, DC 20510
Phone: 202-224-2934
Web Form: cornyn.senate.gov/public/
index.cfm?p=ContactForm

Texas-Republican
Hutchinson, Kay Bailey
284 Russell Senate Office Building
Washington, DC 20510
Phone: 202-224-5922
Web Form: hutchison.senate.
gov/?p=email_kay

Utah-Republican
Hatch, Orrin G.
104 Hart Senate Office Building
Washington, DC 20510
Phone: 202-224-5251
Web Form: hatch.senate.gov/public/in-
dex.cfm?FuseAction=Offices.Cont...

Utah-Republican
Lee, Mike
825 Hart Senate Office Building
Washington, DC 20510
Phone: 202-224-5444
Web Form: lee.senate.gov/contact_form.
cfm

Vermont-Democrat
Leahy, Patrick J.
433 Russell Senate Office Building
Washington, DC 20510
Phone: 202-224-4242
Web Form: leahy.senate.gov/contact/

Vermont-Independent
Sanders, Bernard
332 Dirksen Senate Office Building
Washington, DC 20510
Phone: 202-224-5141
Web Form: sanders.senate.gov/contact/

Virginia-Democrat
Warmer, Mark R.
459A Russell Senate Office Building
Washington, DC 20510
Phone: 202-224-2023
Web Form: warner.senate.gov/public/
index.cfm?p=Contact

Virginia-Democrat
Webb, Jim
248 Russell Senate Office Building
Washington, DC 20510
Phone: 202-224-4024
Web Form: webb.senate.gov/contact.cfm

Washington-Democrat
Cantwell, Maria
511 Dirksen Senate Office Building
Washington, DC 20510
Phone: 202-224-3441
Web Form: cantwell.senate.gov/contact/

Washington-Democrat
Murray, Patty
448 Russell Senate Office Building
Washington, DC 20510
Phone: 202-224-2621
Web Form: murray.senate.gov/email/
    index.cfm

West Virginia-Democrat
Manchin, Joe, III
311 Hart Senate Office Building
Washington, DC 20510
Phone: 202-224-3954
Web Form: manchin.senate.gov/con-
    tact_form.cfm

West Virginia-Democrat
Rockefeller, John D., IV
531 Hart Senate Office Building
Washington, DC 20510
Phone: 202-224-6472
Web Form: rockefeller.senate.gov/con-
    tact/email.cfm

Wisconsin, Republican
Johnson, Ron
2 Russell Courtyard
Washington, DC 20510
Phone: 202-224-5323
Web Form: ronjohnson.senate.gov/pub-
    lic/index.cfm/contact

Wisconsin, Democrat
Kohl, Herb
330 Hart Senate Office Building
Washington, DC 20510
Phone: 202-224-5653
Web Form: kohl.senate.gov/contact.cfm

Wyoming-Republican
Barrasso, John
307 Dirksen Senate Office Building
Washington, DC 20510
Phone: 202-224-6441
Web Form: barrasso.senate.gov/public/
    index.cfm?FuseAction=ContactUs...

Wyoming-Republican
Enzi, Michael B.
379A Russell Senate Office Building
Washington, DC 20510
Phone: 202-224-3424
Web Form: enzi.senate.gov/public/index.
    cfm?FuseAction=ContactInform...

APPENDIX C

Child Support Agencies Office of State Child Support Enforcement

Alabama
Department of Human Resources
Child Support Enforcement Division
50 Ripley Street
P O Box 304000
Montgomery, AL 36130-1801
Phone: 334-242-9300
Fax: 334-242-0606

Alaska
Child Support Services Division
Department of Revenue
550 West 7th Avenue, Suite 280
Anchorage, AK 99501-6699
Phone: 907-269-6900
Fax: 907-269-6813

Arizona
Division of Child Support Enforcement
Arizona Department of Economic Security
3443 N. Central, 4th Floor
Phoenix, AZ 85012
Phone: 602-771-8190
Fax: 602-771-8191

Arkansas
Office of Child Support Enforcement
Department of Finance and Administration
P O Box 8133
Little Rock, AR 72203-8133
Phone: 501-682-6169
Fax: 501-682-6002

California
Department of Child Services
P O Box 419064
Mail Station – 10
Rancho Cordova, CA 95741-9064
Phone: 866-249-0773
Fax: 916-464-5211

Colorado
Division of Child Support Enforcement
Department of Human Services
1575 Sherman Street, 5th Floor
Denver, CO 80203-1714
Phone: 303-866-4300
Fax: 303-866-4360

Connecticut
Department of Social Services
Bureau of Child Support Enforcement
25 Sigourney Street
Hartford, CT 06106
Phone: 860-424-4989
Fax: 860-951-2996

Delaware
Division of Child Support Enforcement
Delaware Health and Social Services
P O Box 11223
Wilmington, DE 19850
Phone: 302-395-6500
Fax: 302-395-6733
Customer Service: 302-577-7171

District of Columbia
Child Support Services Division
Office of the Attorney General
Judiciary Square 441 Fourth Street NW
    5th Floor
Washington, DC 20001
Phone: 202-724-2131
Fax: 202-724-3710
Customer Service: 202-442-9900

Florida
Child Support Enforcement
Department of Revenue
P O Box 8030
Tallahassee, FL 32399-7016
Phone: 850-922-9590
Fax: 850-921-0792
Customer Service: 1-800-622-5437

Georgia
Child Support Services
Department of Human Resources
2 Peachtree Street, Room 20-460
Atlanta, GA 30303
Phone: 404-657-3851
Fax: 404-657-3326

Guam
Office of the Attorney General
Child Support Enforcement Division
287 West O'Brien Drive
Hagatna, Guam 96910
Phone: 671-475-3360
Fax: 671-475-3203

Hawaii
Child Support Enforcement Agency
Department of the Attorney General
601 Kamokila Boulevard, Suite 207
Kapolei, HI 96707
Phone: 808-692-7000
Fax: 808-692-7134

Idaho
Bureau of Child Support Services
Department of Health and Welfare
P O Box 83720
Boise, ID 83720-0036
Phone: 1-800-356-9868
Fax: 208-334-5571

Illinois
Division of Child Support Enforcement
Illinois Department of Public Aid
509 S. 6th St., 6th Floor
Springfield, IL 62701
Phone: 800-447-4278
Fax: 217-524-6049

Indiana
Child Support Bureau
Department of Child Services
402 West Washington St. Room W360
Indianapolis, IN 46204-2739
Phone: 317-233-5437
Fax: 317-233-4932

Iowa

Bureau of Collections
Department of Human Services
400 S.W. 8th Street, Suite H
Des Moines, IA 50319-4691
Phone: 515-281-5647
Fax: 515-281-8854

Kansas

Child Support Enforcement Program
Dept. of Social & Rehabilitation Services
P O Box 497
Topeka, KS 66601
Phone: 785-296-3237
Fax: 785-296-8395

Kentucky

Child Support Enforcement Program
Department for Income Support
Cabinet for Families and Children
730 Schenkel Lane
P O Box 2150
Frankfort, KY 40602-2150
Phone: 502-564-2285
Fax: 502-564-5988

Louisiana

Office of Family Support
Support Enforcement Services Division
P O Box 94065
627 N. Fourth Street
Baton Rouge, LA 70802
Phone: 225-342-4780
Fax: 225-342-7397

Maine

Department of Human Services
Division of Support Enforcement & Recovery
Office of Integrated Access and Support
State House Station 11, 268 Whitten Road
Augusta, ME 04333
Phone: 207-624-4100
Fax: 207-287-2334

Maryland

Child Support Enforcement Administration
Department of Human Resources
Saratoga State Center
311 West Saratoga Street, Room 301
Baltimore, MD 21201-3521
Phone: 410-767-7065
Fax: 410-333-6264
Customer Service: 800-332-6347

Massachusetts

Child Support Enforcement
Massachusetts Dept. of Revenue
P O Box 9561
Boston, MA 02114-9561
Phone: 800-332-2733
Fax: 617-887-7570

Michigan

Office of Child Support
Department of Human Services
235 South Grand Avenue
P O Box 30478
Lansing, MI 48909-7978
Phone: 517-241-7460
Fax: 517-373-4980

Minnesota

Office of Child Support Enforcement
Department of Human Services
444 Lafayette Road
P O Box 64946
St. Paul, MN 55164-0946
Phone: 651-431-4400
Fax: 651-431-7517

Mississippi

Division of Child Support Enforcement
Department of Human Services
750 North State Street
Jackson, MS 39202
Phone: 601-359-4861
Fax: 601-359-4415

Missouri
Family Support Division
Child Support Enforcement
615 Howerton Court Building
P O Box 2320
Jefferson City, MO 65102-2320
Phone: 573-751-4247
Fax: 573-751-0507

Montana
Child Support
Dept. of Public Health & Human
    Services
3075 N. Montana Avenue, Suite 112
Helena, MT 59620
Phone: 406-444-9855
Fax: 406-444-1370

Nebraska
Department of Health and Human
    Services
P O Box 94728
220 South 17th Street
Lincoln, NE 68509-4728
Phone: 402-471-1400
Fax: 402-471-7311

Nevada
State of Nevada
Division of Welfare and Supportive
    Services
1470 College Parkway
Carson City, NV 89706-7924
Phone: 775-684-0705
Fax: 775-684-0702
Customer Service: 775-684-7200
Customer Service: 702-486-1646
Toll Free: 1-800-992-0900

New Hampshire
Division of Child Support Services
Health & Human Services
129 Pleasant Street
Concord, NH 03301-8711
Phone: 800-852-3345
Fax: 603-271-4787

New Jersey
Office of Child Support
Department of Human Services
P O Box 716
Trenton, NJ 08625-0716
Phone: 609-584-5093
Fax: 609-588-2354

New Mexico
Child Support Enforcement Division
Department of Human Services
P O Box 25110
Santa Fe, NM 87502
Phone: 505-476-7207
Fax: 505-476-7045

New York
Division of Child Support Enforcement
40 North Pearl Street, 13th Floor
Albany, NY 12243-0001
Phone: 518-474-1078
Fax: 518-486-3127

North Carolina
Office of Child Support Services
Division of Social Services
North Carolina Dept. of Health and
    Human Services
2401 Mail Service Center
325 North Salisbury Street
Raleigh, NC 27699-2401
Phone: 919-255-3800
Fax: 919-212-3840

North Dakota
Child Support Enforcement Program
North Dakota Dept. of Human Services
P O Box 7190
Bismarck, ND 58507-7190
Phone: 701-328-3582
Fax: 701-328-5497

Ohio
Office of Child Support Enforcement
Department of Human Services and Job
and Family Services
30 East Broad Street, 31st Floor
Columbus, OH 43215-3414
Phone: 614-752-6561
Fax: 614-752-9760

Oklahoma
Oklahoma Child Support Services
Department of Human Services
P O Box 53552
Oklahoma City, OK 73152
Phone: 405-522-2874
Fax: 405-522-2753

Oregon
Division of Child Support
Oregon Department of Justice
494 State Street, S.E. Suite 300
Salem, OR 97301
Phone: 503-986-6166
Fax: 503-986-6158

Pennsylvania
Bureau of Child Support Enforcement
Department of Public Welfare
P O Box 8018
Harrisburg, PA 17105-8018
Phone: 800-932-0211
Fax: 717-787-9706

Puerto Rico
Administration for Child Support
Enforcement
P O Box 70376
San Juan, PR 00936-8376
Phone: 787-767-1500
Fax: 787-282-8324

Rhode Island
Office of Child Support Services
Department of Human Services
77 Dorrance Street
Providence, RI 02903
Phone: 401-458-4400
Fax: 401-458-4407

South Carolina
Child Support Enforcement Division
Department of Social Services
P O Box 1469
Columbia, SC 29202-1469
Phone: 803-898-9210
Fax: 803-898-9201
Toll Free: 1-800-768-5858

South Dakota
Division of Child Support
Department of Social Services
700 Governor's Drive
Pierre, SD 57501-2291
Phone: 605-773-3641
Fax: 605-773-7295

Tennessee
Child Support Services
Department of Human Services
400 Deadrick Street
Nashville, TN 37243-1403
Phone: 615-313-4880
Fax: 615-532-2791

Texas
Child Support Division
Office of the Attorney General
P O Box 12017
Austin, TX 78711-2017
Phone: 1-800-252-8014
Fax: 512-460-6867

Utah
Child Support Services
Department of Human Services
Office of Recovery Services
P O Box 45033
Salt Lake, UT 84145-0033
Phone: 801-536-8901
Fax: 801-536-8509

Vermont
Office of Child Support
103 South Main Street
Waterbury, VT 05671-1901
Phone: 802-786-3214
Fax: 802-241-2319

Virgin Islands
U.S. Virgin Islands Department of Justice
Paternity and Child Support Division
8000 Nisky Center, 2nd Floor, Suite 500
St. Thomas, VI 00802
Phone: 340-778-5958
Fax: 340-775-3808
Fax: St. Croix: 340-779-3800

Virginia
Division of Child Support Enforcement
7 N. Eighth Street, 1st Floor
Richmond, VA 23219
Phone: 1-800-257-9986
Fax: 804-726-7476

Washington
Division of Child Support
Economic Services Administration
P O Box 9162
Olympia, WA 98507
Phone: 360-664-5000
Fax: 360-664-5444

West Virginia
WV Dept. of Health and Human
   Resources
Bureau for Child Support Enforcement
350 Capitol Street, Room 147
Charleston, WV 25301-3703
Phone: 1-800-249-3778
Fax: 304-558-2445

Wisconsin
Bureau of Child Support
Division of Economic Support
201 E. Washington Avenue E 200
P O Box 7935
Madison, WI 53707-7935
Phone: 608-266-9909
Fax: 608-267-2824

Wyoming
Department of Family Services
Child Support Enforcement
122 W. 25th Herschler Building
1301 1st Floor East
Cheyenne, WY 82002
Phone: 307-777-6948
Fax: 307-777-5588

Region I

Connecticut, Maine, Massachusetts, New Hampshire, Rhode Island, Vermont
OCSE Program Manager
Administration for Children and Families
John F. Kennedy Federal Building, Room 2000
Boston, MA 02203-0003
Phone: 617-565-2478
Web Address: http://www.acf.hhs.gov/programs/region1/index.html

Region II

New York, New Jersey, Puerto Rico, Virgin Islands
OCSE Program Manager
Administration for Children and Families
Federal Building, Room 4048
New York, NY 10278-4199
Phone: 212-264-2890 x 274
Web Address: http://www.acf.hhs.gov/programs/region2/index.html

Region III

Delaware, Maryland, Pennsylvania, Virginia, West Virginia, District of Columbia
OCSE Program Manager
Administration for Children and Families
150 South Independence Mall West, Suite 864
Philadelphia, PA 19106-3499
Phone: 215-861-4790
Web Address: http://www.acf.hhs.gov/programs/region3/index.html

Region IV

Alabama, Florida, Georgia, Kentucky, Mississippi, North Carolina, South Carolina, Tennessee
OCSE Program Manager
Administration for Children and Families
61 Forsyth Street, Suite 4M60
Atlanta, GA 30303-8909
Phone: 404-562-2871
Web Address: http://www.acf.hhs.gov/programs/region4/index.html

Region V

Illinois, Indiana, Michigan, Minnesota, Ohio, Wisconsin
OCSE Program Manager
Administration for Children and Families
233 N. Michigan Avenue, Suite 400
Chicago, Il 60601-5519
Phone: 312-353-4237
Web Address: http://www.acf.hhs.gov/programs/region5/index.html

Region VI

Arkansas, Louisiana, New Mexico, Oklahoma, Texas
OCSE Program Manager
Administration for Children and Families
1301 Young Street, Room 945
Dallas, TX 75202-5433
Phone: 214-767-3749
Web Address: http://www.acf.hhs.gov/programs/region6/index.html

Region VII

Iowa, Kansas, Missouri, Nebraska
OCSE Program Manager
Administration for Children and Families
Federal Office Building, 601 E. 12th Street, Room 276
Kansas City, MO 64106-2858
Phone: 816-426-2256
Web Address: http://www.acf.hhs.gov/programs/region7/index.html

Region VIII

Colorado, Montana, North Dakota, South Dakota, Utah, Wyoming
OCSE Program Manager
Administration for Children and Families
Federal Office Building, 1961 Stout Street, Room 926
Denver, CO 80294-3538
Phone: 303-844-3100
Web Address: http://www.acf.hhs.gov/programs/region8/index.html

Region IX

Arizona, California, Hawaii, Nevada, Guam
OCSE Program Manager
Administration for Children and Families
90 7th Street 9th Floor
San Francisco, CA 94103-6710
Phone: 415-437-8463
Web Address: http://www.acf.hhs.gov/programs/region9/index.html

Region X

Alaska, Idaho, Oregon, Washington
OCSE Program Manager
Administration for Children and Families
2201 Sixth Avenue, Suite 300
Mail Stop 75
Seattle, WA 98121-1827
Phone: 206-615-2547
Web Address: http://www.acf.hhs.gov/programs/region10index.html

U.S. Marshals Service

Northern District of Alabama (N/AL)
U.S. Marshal: Chester Martin Keely
1729 N. 5th Avenue, Room 240
Birmingham, AL 35203
Phone: 205-776-6200

Middle District of Alabama (M/AL)
U.S. Marshal: Arthur D. Baylor
Frank M. Johnson Federal Building
15 Lee Street, Room 224
Montgomery, AL 36104
Phone: 334-223-7401

Southern District of Alabama (S/AL)
U.S. Marshal: Charles Andrews
U.S. Courthouse
113 St. Joseph Street, Room 413
Mobile, AL 36602
Phone: 251-690-2841

District of Alaska (D/AK)
U.S. Marshal: Robert Heun
U.S. Courthouse
222 W. 7th Avenue, Room 189
Anchorage, AK 99513
Phone: 907-271-5154

District of Arizona (D/AZ)
U.S. Marshal: David Gonzales
Sandra Day O'Connor U.S. Courthouse
401 W. Washington St., SPC 64,
    Suite 270
Phoenix, AZ 85003-2159
Phone: 602-382-8767

Eastern District of Arkansas (E/AR)
U.S. Marshal: Clifton T. Massanelli
U.S. Courthouse
600 W. Capitol Avenue, Room A328
Little Rock, AR 72201
Phone: 501-324-6256

Western District of Arkansas (W/AR)
U.S. Marshal: Harold M. Oglesby
Judge Isaac C. Parker Federal Building
30 S. 6th Street, Room 243
Fort Smith, AR 72901
Phone: 479-424-5000

Northern District of California (N/CA)
U.S. Marshal: Donald M. O'Keefe
U.S. Courthouse/Phillip Burton Building
450 Golden Gate Avenue,
    Room 20-6888
San Francisco, CA 94102
Phone: 415-436-7677

Eastern District of California (E/CA)
U.S. Marshal: Albert Nájera
U.S. Courthouse
501 I Street
Sacramento, CA 95814
Phone: 916-930-2030

Central District of California (C/CA)
U.S. Marshal: David M. Singer
U.S. Courthouse
312 N. Spring Street, Room G-23
Los Angeles, CA 90012
Phone: 213-894-6820

Southern District of California (S/CA)
U.S. Marshal: Steven C. Stafford
U.S. Courthouse
940 Front Street, Room LL B-71
San Diego, CA 92189
Phone: 619-557-6620

District of Colorado (D/CO)
U.S. Marshal: John Kammerzell
U.S. Courthouse
901 19th St., 3rd Floor
Denver, CO 80294
Phone: 303-335-3400

District of Connecticut (D/CT)
U.S. Marshal: Joseph P. Faughnan
U.S. Courthouse
141 Church Street, Room 323
New Haven, CT 06510
Phone: 203-773-2107

District of Columbia (DC/DC)
U.S. Marshal: Edwin D. Sloane
U.S. Courthouse
3rd & Constitution Avenue, N.W.
 Room 1103
Washington, DC 20001
Phone: 202-353-0600

District of Columbia (Superior Court)
U.S. Marshal: Thomas Hedgepeth
 (Acting)
H. Carl Moultrie Courthouse
500 Indiana Avenue, N.W., Room C-250
Washington, DC 20001
Phone: 202-616-8600

District of Delaware (D/DE)
U.S. Marshal: Joseph A. Papilli
U.S. Courthouse
844 King Street, Room 4311
Wilmington, DE 19801
Phone: 302-573-6176

Northern District of Florida (N/FL)
U.S. Marshal: Dennis A. Williamson
U.S. Courthouse
111 N. Adams Street, Room 277
Tallahassee, FL 32301
Phone: 850-942-8400

Middle District of Florida (M/FL)
U.S. Marshal: Thomas D. Hurburt, Jr.
U.S. Courthouse
801 N. Florida Avenue, 4th Floor
Tampa, FL 33602-4519
Phone: 813-274-6401

Southern District of Florida (S/FL)
U.S. Marshal: Neil DeSousa (Acting)
Federal Courthouse Square
400 N. Miami Avenue, 6th Floor
Miami, FL 33128
Phone: 786-433-6340

Northern District of Georgia (N/GA)
U.S. Marshal: Beverly J. Harvard
Federal Building
75 Spring Street, S.W., Room 1669
Atlanta, GA 30303
Phone: 404-331-6833

Middle District of Georgia (M/GA)
U.S. Marshal: Willie Lee Richardson Jr.
U.S. Courthouse
3rd & Mulberry Street, Room 101
Macon, GA 31201
Phone: 912-752-8280

Southern District of Georgia (S/GA)
U.S. Marshal: Stephen J. Smith
U.S. Courthouse
125 Bull Street, Room 333
Savannah, GA 31401
Phone: 912-652-4212

District of Guam (D/GU)
U.S. Marshal: Frank Leon Guerrero
344 U.S. Courthouse
520 West Soledad Avenue
Hagatna, Guam 96910
Phone: 011-671-477-7827

District of Hawaii (D/HI)
U.S. Marshal: Gervin Miyamoto
U.S. Courthouse
300 Ala Moana Boulevard, Room C-103
Honolulu, HI 96850
Phone: 808-541-3000

District of Idaho (D/ID)
U.S. Marshal: Brian T. Underwood
U.S. Courthouse
550 W. Fort Street, MSC-10, Room 777
Boise, ID 83724
Phone: 208-334-1298

Northern District of Illinois (N/IL)
U.S. Marshal: Darryl K. McPherson
219 S. Dearborn Street, Room 2444
Chicago, IL 60604
Phone: 312-353-5290

Central District of Illinois (C/IL)
U.S. Marshal: Kenneth F. Bohac
600 E. Monroe Street, Room 333
Springfield, IL 62701
Phone: 217-492-4430

Southern District of Illinois (S/IL)
U. S. Marshal: Don Slazinik
U.S. Courthouse
750 Missouri Avenue, Room 127
East St. Louis, IL 62201
Phone: 618-482-9336

Northern District of Indiana (N/IN)
U.S. Marshal: Myron M. Sutton
Federal Building
204 S. Main Street, Room 233
South Bend, IN 46601
Phone: 574-236-8291

Southern District of Indiana (S/IN)
U.S. Marshal: Kerry J. Forestal
U.S. Courthouse
46 E. Ohio Street, Room 179
Indianapolis, IN 46204
Phone: 317-226-6566

Northern District of Iowa (N/IA)
U.S. Marshal: Kenneth Runde
4200 C Street, SW, Bldg. B
Cedar Rapids, IA 52404
Phone: 319-362-4411

Southern District of Iowa (S/IA)
U.S. Marshal: Michael R. Bladel
U.S. Courthouse
123 E. Walnut Street, Room 208
Des Moines, IA 50309
Phone: 515-284-6240

District of Kansas (D/KS)
U.S. Marshal: Walter Bradley
Robert Dole Federal Courthouse
500 State Avenue, Suite G-22
Kansas City, KS 66101
Phone: 913-551-6727

Eastern District of Kentucky (E/KY)
U.S. Marshal: Loren Carl
Federal Building
Barr & Limestone Streets, Room 162
Lexington, KY 40507
Phone: 859-233-2513

Western District of Kentucky (W/KY)
U.S. Marshal: James E. Clark
U.S. Courthouse
601 W. Broadway, Room 162
Louisville, KY 40202
Phone: 502-588-8000

Eastern District of Louisiana (E/LA)
U.S. Marshal: Genny May
U.S. Courthouse
500 Camp Street, Room C-600
New Orleans, LA 70130
Phone: 504-589-6079

Middle District of Louisiana (M/LA)
U.S. Marshal: Kevin Harrison
U.S. Courthouse
777 Florida Street, Room G-48
Baton Rouge, LA 70801
Phone: 225-389-0364

Western District of Louisiana (W/LA)
U.S. Marshal: Henry L. Whitehorn Sr.
U.S. Courthouse
300 Fannin Street, Suite 1202
Shreveport, LA 71101
Phone: 318-676-4200

District of Maine (D/ME)
U.S. Marshal: Noel C. March
156 Federal Street, 1ˢᵗ Floor
Portland, ME 04101
Phone: 207-780-3355

District of Maryland (D/MD)
U.S. Marshal: Johnny L. Hughes
U.S. Courthouse
101 W. Lombard Street, Room 605
Baltimore, MD 21201
Phone: 410-962-2220

District of Massachusetts (D/MA)
U.S. Marshal: John Gibbons
John Joseph Moakley Courthouse
1 Courthouse Way, Suite 1-500
Boston, MA 02210
Phone: 617-748-2500

Eastern District of Michigan (E/MI)
U.S. Marshal: Robert M. Grubbs
U.S. Courthouse
231 W. Lafayette Street, Suite 300
Detroit, MI 48226
Phone: 313-234-5600

Western District of Michigan (W/MI)
U.S. Marshal: Peter Munoz
Federal Building
110 Michigan Avenue, N.W., Room 544
Grand Rapids, MI 49503
Phone: 616-456-2438

District of Minnesota (D/MN)
U.S. Marshal: Sharon Lubinski
U.S. Courthouse
300 South Fourth Street
Minneapolis, MN 55415
Phone: 612-664-5900

Northern District of Mississippi (N/MS)
U.S. Marshal: Jeff Woodfin (Acting)
Federal Building
911 Jackson Avenue, Room 348
Oxford, MS 38655
Phone: 662-234-6661

Southern District of Mississippi (S/MS)
U.S. Marshal: George White
James O. Eastland Courthouse Building
245 E Capitol Streets, Suite 305
Jackson, MS 39201
Phone: 601-965-4444

Eastern District of Missouri (E/MO)
U.S. Marshal: William C. Sibert
Thomas Eagleton Courthouse
111 S. 10ᵗʰ Street, Room 2.319
St. Louis, MO 63102-1116
Phone: 314-539-2212

Western District of Missouri (W/MO)
U.S. Marshal: C. Mauri Sheer
U.S. Courthouse
400 E. 9ᵗʰ St., Room 3740
Kansas City, MO 64106
Phone: 816-512-2000

District of Montana (D/MT)
U.S. Marshal: Darrell Bell
U.S. Courthouse
5405 Federal Building
316 N. 26ᵗʰ Street
Billings, MT 59101
Phone: 406-247-7030

District of Nebraska (D/NE)
U.S. Marshal: Mark Martinez
Roman L. Hruska – United States
    Courthouse
111 South 18ᵗʰ Plaza – Suite B06
Omaha, NE 68102
Phone: 402-221-4781

District of Nevada (D/NV)
U.S. Marshal: Christopher Hoye
U.S. Courthouse
300 Las Vegas Boulevard S., Room 448
Las Vega, NV 89101
Phone: 702-388-6355

District of New Hampshire (D/NH)
U.S. Marshal: David L. Cargill, Jr.
Federal Building
55 Pleasant Street, Room 409
Concord, NH 03301
Phone: 603-225-1632

District of New Jersey (D/NJ)
U.S. Marshal: James T. Plousis
U.S. Courthouse
50 Walnut Street
Newark, NJ 07102
Phone: 973-645-2404

District of New Mexico (D/NM)
U.S. Marshal: Conrad E. Candelaria
U.S. Courthouse
333 Lomas Boulevard, N.W., Suite 180
Albuquerque, NM 87101
Phone: 505-346-6400

Northern District of New York (N/NY)
U.S. Marshal: James Parmley
100 S. Clinton Street
Syracuse, NY 13261
Phone: 315-473-7601

Eastern District of New York (E/NY)
U.S. Marshal: Charles Dunne
U.S. Courthouse
225 Cadman Plaza
Brooklyn, NY 11201
Phone: 718-260-0400

Southern District of New York (S/NY
U.S. Marshal: Joseph R. Guccione
500 Pearl Street
Suite 400
New York, NY 10007
Phone: 212-331-7200

Western District of New York (W/NY)
U.S. Marshal: Bryan Matthews (Acting)
U.S. Courthouse
68 Court Street, Room 129
Buffalo, NY 14202
Phone: 716-551-4851

Eastern District of North Carolina (E/NC)
U.S. Marshal: Scott Parker
Federal Building
310 New Bern Avenue, Room 744
Raleigh, NC 27611
Phone: 919-856-4153

Middle District of North Carolina (M/NC)
U.S. Marshal: Willie R. Stafford
U.S. Courthouse
324 W. Market Street, Room 234
Greensboro, NC 27401
Phone: 336-332-8700

Western District of North Carolina (W/NC)
U. S. Marshal: Kelly M. Nesbit
401 West Trade Street
P O Box 34247
Charlotte, NC 28234
Phone: 704-334-6234

District of North Dakota (D/ND)
U. S. Marshal: Paul Ward
Old Federal Building
655 1st Avenue N., Room 317
Fargo, ND 58108
Phone: 701-297-7300

District of the Northern Mariana Islands (D/NMI)
U.S. Marshal: Frank Leon Guerrero
(Located on Guam)
U. S. Courthouse – Horiguchi Federal Bld.
P O Box 500570, Garapan Village Beach Rd.
Salpan, MP 96950
Phone: 670-236-2954

Northern District of Ohio (N/OH)
U.S. Marshal: Peter Elliott
U.S. Courthouse
801 West Superior Avenue, Suite 1200
Cleveland, OH 44113
Phone: 216-522-2150

Southern District of Ohio (S/OH)
U.S. Marshal: Cathy Jones
U.S. Courthouse
85 Marconi Boulevard, Room 460
Columbus, OH 43215
Phone: 614-469-5540

Northern District of Oklahoma (N/OK)
U.S. Marshal: Vacant
U.S. Courthouse
333 W. 4th Street, Room 4557
Tulsa, OK 74103
Phone: 918-581-7738

Eastern District of Oklahoma (E/OK)
U.S. Marshal: John W. Lloyd
U.S. Courthouse
111 N. 5th Street, Room 136
Muskogee, OK 74401
Phone: 918-687-2523

Western District of Oklahoma (W/OK)
U.S. Marshal: Charles Thomas Weeks II
U.S. Courthouse
200 N.W. 4th Street, Room 2418
Oklahoma City, OK 73102
Phone: 405-231-4206

District of Oregon (D/OR
U.S. Marshal: Russel Burger
Mark O. Hatfield U.S. Courthouse
1000 S.W. 3rd Avenue, Room 401
Portland, OR 97204
Phone: 503-326-2209

Eastern District of Pennsylvania (E/PA)
U.S. Marshal: John Patrignani (Acting)
U.S. Courthouse
601 Market Street, Room 2110
Philadelphia, PA 19106
Phone: 215-597-7273

Middle District of Pennsylvania (M/PA)
U.S. Marshal: Martin J. Pane (Acting)
Federal Building
Washington Avenue & Linden Street,
    Room 231
Scranton, PA 18501
Phone: 570-346-7277

Western District of Pennsylvania (W/PA)
U.S. Marshal: Thomas Fitzgerald
U.S. Courthouse
700 Grant Street, Suite 2360
Pittsburgh, PA 15219
Phone: 412-644-3351

District of Puerto Rico (D/PR)
U.S. Marshal: Eric Timberman (Acting)
Federal Building
150 Carlos Chardon Avenue, Room 200
Hato Rey, PR 00918
Phone: 787-766-6000

District of Rhode Island (D/RI)
U.S. Marshal: Steven G. O'Donnell
Kennedy Plaza
Fleet Center, Suite 300
Providence, RI 02901
Phone: 401-528-5300

District of South Carolina (D/SC)
U.S. Marshal: Kelvin Washington
U.S. Courthouse
901 Richland Street, Suite 1300
Columbia, SC 29201
Phone: 803-765-5821

District of South Dakota (D/SD)
U.S. Marshal: Paul C. Thielen
Federal Building
400 S. Phillips Avenue, Room 216
Sioux Falls, SD 57104
Phone: 605-330-4351

Eastern District of Tennessee (E/TN)
U.S. Marshal: James T. Fowler
Eastern District of Tennessee
Federal Building
800 Market Street, Suite 2-3107
Knoxville, TN 37902
Phone: 865-545-4182

Middle District of Tennessee (M/TN)
U.S. Marshal: Denny W. King
Estes Kefauver Federal Building
110 9th Avenue S., Room A750
Nashville, TN 37203
Phone: 615-736-5417

Western District of Tennessee (W/TN)
U.S. Marshal: Jeffrey T. Holt
Federal Building
167 N. Main Street, Room 1029
Memphis, TN 38103
Phone: 901-544-3304

Northern District of Texas (N/TX
U.S. Marshal: Randy Paul Ely
Federal Building
1100 Commerce Street, Room 16F47
Dallas, TX 75242
Phone: 214-767-0836

Eastern District of Texas (E/TX)
U.S. Marshal: Gary Brown (Acting)
Federal Building
300 Willow Street, Room 329
Beaumont, TX 75702
Phone: 409-839-2581

Southern District of Texas (S/TX
U.S. Marshal: Elizabeth Saenz (Acting)
U.S. Courthouse
515 Rusk Avenue, Room 10130
Houston, TX 77002
Phone: 713-718-4800

Western District of Texas (W/TX)
U.S. Marshal: Robert R. Almonte
U.S. Courthouse
655 E. Durango Boulevard, Room 235
San Antonio, TX 78206
Phone: 210-472-6540

District of Utah (D/UT)
U.S. Marshal: James A. Thompson
U.S. Post Office & Courthouse
350 S. Main Street, Room B-20
Salt Lake City, UT 84101
Phone: 801-524-5693

District of Vermont (D/VT)
U.S. Marshal: David E. Demag
11 Elmwood Avenue
Suite 601
Burlington, VT 05401
Phone: 802-951-6271

District of the Virgin Islands (D/VI)
U.S. Marshal: Vacant
U.S. Courthouse
Veteran's Drive, Room 371
St. Thomas, VI 00801
Phone: 340-774-2743

Eastern District of Virginia (E/VA)
U.S. Marshal: John R. Hackman
401 Courthouse Square
Alexandria, VA 22314
Phone: 703-837-5500

Western District of Virginia (W/VA)
U.S. Marshal: Gerald S. Holt
247 Federal Building
210 Franklin Road SW
Roanoke, VA 24009
Phone: 540-857-2230

Eastern District of Washington (E/WA)
U.S. Marshal: Craig Thayer
U.S. Courthouse
920 W. Riverside Avenue, Room 888
Spokane, WA 99201
Phone: 509-353-2781

Western District of Washington (W/WA)
U.S. Marshal: Mark L. Ericks
700 Stewart Street, Suite 9000
Seattle, WA 98101-1271
Phone: 206-370-8600

Northern District of West Virginia (N/WV)
U.S. Marshal: Gary M. Gaskins
U.S. Courthouse
500 W. Pike Street
P O Box 2807
Clarksburg, WV 26302
Phone: 304-623-0486

Southern District of West Virginia (S/WV)
U.S. Marshal: John D. Foster
300 Virginia Street East, Suite 3602
Charleston, WV 25301
Phone: 304-347-5136

Eastern District of Wisconsin (E/WI)
U.S. Marshal: Kevin Carr
U.S. Courthouse
517 E. Wisconsin Avenue, Suite 38
Milwaukee, WI 53202
Phone: 414-297-3707

Western District of Wisconsin (W/WI)
U.S. Marshal: Dallas S. Neville
U.S. Courthouse
120 N. Henry Street, Room 440
Madison, WI 53703
Phone: 608-661-8300

District of Wyoming (D/WY)
U.S. Marshal: Vacant
Joseph C. O'Mahoney Federal Center
2120 Capitol Avenue, Room 2124
Cheyenne, WY 82001
Phone: 307-772-2196

APPENDIX E

State Prison Commissions

Alabama Department of Corrections
Kim T. Thomas, Director
301 S. Ripley Street
P O Box 301501
Montgomery, AL 36130-1501
Phone: 334-353-3883

Alaska Department of Corrections
Joe Schmidt, Commissioner
550 West 7th Avenue, Suite 601
Anchorage, AK 99501
Phone: 907-761-5616
Fax: 907-761-5605

American Samoa Department of Corrections
Leonard Seumanutafa, Acting Director
A. P. Lutali Executive Office Building
Pago Pago, American Samoa 96799
Phone: 684-633-4116
Fax: 684-633-2269

Arizona Department of Corrections
Charles L. Ryan, Director
1601 W. Jefferson
Phoenix, AZ 85007
Phone: 602-542-5497
E-Mail: media@azcorrections.gov

Arkansas Department of Corrections
Ray Hobbs, Director
P O Box 8707
Pine Bluff, AR 71611-8707
Phone: 870-267-6999
Fax: 870-267-6258

California Department of Corrections
Kamala D. Harris, Attorney General
P O Box 944255
Sacramento, CA 94244-2550
Phone: 800-952-5225
Fax: 916-323-5341

Colorado Department of Corrections
Tom Clements, Director
2862 South Circle Drive
Colorado Springs, CO 80906
Phone: 719-226-4701

Connecticut Department of Corrections
Leo Arnone, Commissioner
24 Wolcott Hill Road
Wethersfield, CT 06109
Phone: 860-692-7780
Fax: 860-692-7783
E-mail: DOC.PIO@po.state.ct.us

Delaware Department of Corrections
Carl C. Danberg Commissioner
Administration Building
245 McKee Road
Dover, DE 19904
Phone: 302-857-5221

District of Columbia Department of Corrections
Vincent C. Gray, Mayor
1923 Vermont Ave. NW, Room 203 N
Washington, DC 20001
Phone: 202-673-7316
Fax: 202-323-1470

Florida Department of Corrections
Daniel G. Ronay, Chief Deputy
2601 Blair Stone Road
Tallahassee, FL 32399
Phone: 850-487-2165
Fax: 850-487-4427

Georgia Department of Corrections
Brian Owens, Commissioner
P O Box 1529
Forsyth, GA 31029
Phone: 478-992-5358

Guam Department of Corrections
J B Palacios, Director
P O Box 3236
Hagatna, GU 96932
Phone: 671-734-2459
Fax: 671-734-4490

Hawaii Department of Corrections
Joe W. Booker, Jr., Director
919 Ala Moana Blvd., Room 400
Honolulu, HI 96814
Phone: 808-587-1288
Fax: 808-587-1282
E-mail: psd.office.of.thedirector@hawaii.
    gov

Idaho Department of Corrections
Brent Reinke, Director
381 W. Hospital Drive
Orofino, ID 83544
Phone: 208-476-3655

Illinois Department of Corrections
Gladyse Taylor, Acting Director
1301 Concordia Court
P O Box 19277
Springfield, IL 62794-9277
Phone: 217-558-2200
E-mail: info@doc.iliinois.gov

Indiana Department of Corrections
Bruce Lemmon, Commissioner
302 W. Washington Street, Room E-334
Indianapolis, IN 46204
Phone: 317-232-5727

Iowa Department of Corrections
Terry Bransford, Commissioner
510 East 12th
Des Moines, IA 50319
Phone: 515-725-5701

Kansas Department of Corrections
Ray Roberts, Secretary of Corrections
Landon State Office Building
900 SW Jackson - 4th Floor
Topeka, KS 66612-1284
Phone: 785-296-3317
E-mail: kdocpub@doc.ks.gov

Kentucky Department of Corrections
LaDonna H. Thompson, Director
Health Services Building
275 East Main Street
P O Box 2400
Frankfort, KY 40602-2400
Phone: 502-564-4726
Fax: 502-564-5037

Louisiana Department of Corrections
James M. LeBlanc, Secretary
504 Mayflower Street
Baton Rouge, LA 70802-9304
Phone: 225-342-6740
Fax: 225-342-3095

Maine Department of Corrections
Joseph Ponte, Commissioner
25 Tyson Drive, 3rd Floor
State House Station 111
Augusta, ME 04333-0111
Phone: 207-287-2711
Fax: 207-287-4370

Maryland Division of Corrections
Gary D. Maynard, Secretary
6776 Reisterstown Road, Suite 310
Baltimore, MD 21215
Phone: 410-585-3300

Massachusetts Division of Corrections
Curtis M. Wood, Commissioner
50 Maple Street, Suite 3
Milford, MA 01757-3698
Phone: 508-422-3300
Fax: 508-422-3386

Michigan Department of Corrections
John S. Rubitschun, Deputy Director
P O Box 30003
Lansing, MI 48909
Phone: 517-373-3184
Fax: 517-373-0508

Minnesota Department of Corrections
Tom Roy, Commissioner
1450 Energy Park Drive, Suite 200
St. Paul, MN 55108-5219
Phone: 651-361-7226
Fax: 651-642-0414
E-mail: Tom.Roy@state.mn.us

Mississippi Department of Corrections
Christopher B. Epps, Commissioner
723 N. President Street
Jackson, MS 39202
Phone: 681-359-5600

Missouri Department of Corrections
George Lombardi, Director
2729 Plaza Drive
P O Box 236
Jefferson City, MO 65102
Phone: 573-751-2389
Fax: 573-751-4099

Montana Department of Corrections
Mike Ferriter, Director
2273 Boot Hill Court #130
Bozeman, MT 59715-7249
Phone: 406-444-3930
Fax: 406-444-4920

Nebraska Department of Corrections
Robert P. Houston, Director
P O Box 94661
Lincoln, NE 68509-4661
Phone: 402-471-2654

Nevada Department of Corrections
James "Greg" Cox, Acting Director
P O Box 7011
Carson City, NV 89702
Phone: 775-887-3285
Fax: 775-887-6715

New Hampshire Department of Corrections
William L. Wrenn, Commissioner
P O Box 1806
Concord, NH 03302-1806
Phone: 603-271-5600
Fax: 603-271-5643
E-mail: info@nhdoc.state.nh.us

New Jersey Department of Corrections
Gary M. Lanigan, Commissioner
Whittlesey Road
P O Box 863
Trenton, NJ 08625
Phone: 609-292-4036
Fax: 609-292-9083

New Mexico Department of Corrections
Lupe Martinez, Corrections Secretary
P O Box 27116
Santa Fe, NM 87502-0116
Phone: 505-827-8709
Fax: 505-827-8220

New York Department of Corrections
Brian Fischer, Commissioner
Dept. of Correction Services
Building 2
1220 Washington Avenue
Albany, NY 12226-2050
Phone: 518-457-8126

North Carolina Department of Corrections
Alvin W. Keller, Secretary of Correction
2020 Yonkers Road, MSC-4250
Raleigh, NC 27699-4250
Phone: 919-716-3100
Fax: 919-716-3996

North Dakota Department of Corrections
Sandy Tudela, Commissioner
3100 Railroad Avenue
P O Box 1898
Bismarck, ND 58502-1898
Phone: 701-328-6362
Fax: 701-328-6651

Northern Mariana Islands Department of Corrections
Benigno R. Fitial, Governor
Juan A. Sablan Memorial Bldg.
Capitol Hill Caller Box 10007
Saipan, MP 96950

Ohio Department of Corrections
Gary C. Mohr, Director
770 West Broad Street
Columbus, OH 43222
Phone: 614-752-1164

Oklahoma Department of Corrections
Justin Jones, Director
3400 N Martin Luther King Avenue
Oklahoma City, OK 73111-4298
Phone: 405-425-2500

Oregon Department of Corrections
Max Williams, Director
2575 Center St. NE
Salem, OR 97301-4667
Phone: 503-945-9090
Fax: 503-373-1173

Pennsylvania Department of Corrections
Harry P. Jones, Acting Director
2520 Lisburn Road
P O Box 598
Camp Hill, PA 17001-0598
Phone: 717-975-4859
E-mail: ra-contactdoc@state.pa.us

Puerto Rico Department of Corrections
Luis G. Fortuno, Governor
P O Box 9020082
San Juan, PR 00902-0082
Phone: 787-721-7000
Fax: 787-721-5072

Rhode Island Department of Corrections
Ashbel T. Wall, II, Director
40 Howard Avenue
Cranston, RI 02920
Phone: 401-462-1000

South Carolina Department of Corrections
William R. Byars, Jr., Director
502 Beckman Road
Columbia, SC 29203-3173
Phone: 803-896-8555

South Dakota Department of Corrections
Tim Riesch, Director
3200 East Highway 34
c/o 500 East Capitol Avenue
Pierre, SD 57501
Phone: 605-773-3478
Fax: 605-773-3194

Tennessee Department of Corrections
Derrick D. Schofield, Commissioner
Rachel Jackson Building, Sixth Floor
320 Sixth Avenue North
Nashville, TN 37243-0465
Phone: 615-741-1000

Texas Department of Corrections
Brad Livingston, Executive Director

TDCJ
13084-Capitol Station
Austin, TX 78711-3084
Phone: 512-463-9988

TDCJ
P O Box 99
Huntsville, TX 77342-0099
Phone: 936-295-6371

Utah Department of Corrections
Thomas Patterson, Commissioner
14717 S Minuteman Drive
Draper, UT 84020
Phone: 801-545-5500
Fax: 801-545-5670

Vermont Department of Corrections
Andrew Palliot, Commissioner
103 South Main Street
Waterbury, VT 05671-1001
Phone: 802-241-2276
Fax: 802-241-2565

Virgin Islands Department of Corrections
Vincent F. Frazer, Esq., Attorney General
34-38 Kronprindsens Gade
GERS Bldg., 2nd Floor
St. Thomas, Virgin Islands 00802
Phone: 340-774-5666, Ext. 107
Fax: 304-774-9710

Virginia Department of Corrections
Harold Clarke, Director
P O Box 26963
Richmond, VA 23261-6963
Phone: 804-674-3000

Washington Department of Corrections
Eldon Vail, Secretary of Corrections
P O Box 41100, Mail Stop 41100
Olympia, WA 98504-1100
Phone: 360-725-8213

West Virginia Department of Corrections
Jim Rubenstein, Commissioner
1409 Greenbrier Street
Charleston, WV 25311
Phone: 304-558-2036
Fax: 304-558-5367

Wisconsin Department of Corrections
Gary Hamblin, Secretary of Corrections
P O Box 7969
Madison, WE 53707-7969
Phone: 608-240-5055
Fax: 608-240-3305

Wyoming Department of Corrections
Bob Lampert, Director
1934 Wyott Drive, Suite 100
Cheyenne, WY 82002
Phone: 307-777-7208
Fax: 307-777-7846

APPENDIX F

Federal Prisons and Federal Bureau of Prisons Offices

Central Office

320 First St., NW
Washington, DC 20534
Phone: 202-307-3198
Fax: 202-514-6620

Regional Offices

Mid-Atlantic Regional Office
10010 Junction Drive, Suite 100-N
Annapolis Junction, MD 20701
Phone: 301-317-3100
Fax: 301-317-3115

South Central Regional Office
4211 Cedar Springs Road, Suite 300
Dallas, TX 75219
Phone: 214-224-3389
Fax: 214-224-3420

North Central Regional Office
Gateway Complex Tower II, 8th Floor,
    400 State Avenue
Kansas City, KS 66101-2492
Phone: 913-621-3939
Fax: 913-551-1175

Southeast Regional Office
3800 Campo Creek Pky., S.W., Bldg.
    2000
Atlanta, GA 30331-6226
Phone: 678-686-1200
Fax: 678-686-1229

Northeast Regional Office
U.S. Custom House, 7th Floor, 2nd and
    Chestnut Streets
Philadelphia, PA 19106
Phone: 215-521-7300
Fax: 215-521-7476

Western Regional Office
7950 Dublin Boulevard, 3rd Floor
Dublin, CA 94568
Phone: 925-803-4700
Fax: 925-803-4802

Minimum–Security Work Camps for Men

Alabama
FPC Montgomery
FCI Talladega (Camp)

Arkansas
FCI Forrest City Low (Camp)

California
FCI Herlong (Camp)
USP Lompoc (Camp)

Colorado
FCI Englewood (Camp)
FCI Florence (Camp)

Florida
FPC Elgin
FCI Miami (Camp)
FPC Pensacola

Georgia
USP Atlanta (Camp)
FCI Jesup (Camp)

Illinois
USP Marion (Camp)

Indiana
FCI Terre Haute (Camp)

Kansas
USP Leavenworth (Camp)

Kentucky
FCI Ashland (Camp)
USP Big Sandy (Camp)
FCI Manchester (Camp)
USP McCreary (Camp)

Louisiana
FDC Oakdale (Camp)
USP Pollock (Camp)

Maine
FPC Duluth

Maryland
FCI Cumberland (Camp)

Massachusetts
FMC Devens (Camp)

Mississippi
FCI Yazoo City Baja (Camp)

Nevada
FPC Nellis

New Jersey
FCI Fairton (Camp)
FCI Fort Dix (Camp)

New York
FCI Otisville (Camp)

North Carolina
FCI Butner Medium I (Camp)
FPC Seymour Johnson

Oregon
FCI Sheridan (Camp)

Pennsylvania
USP Canaan (Camp)
USP Lewisburg (Camp)
FCI Loretto (Camp)
FCI Mckean (Camp)
FCI Schuylkill (Camp)

South Carolina
FCI Bennettsville (Camp)
FCI Estill (Camp)
FCI Williamsburg (Camp)

South Dakota
FPC Yankton

Tennessee
FCI Memphis (Camp)

Texas
FCI Bastrop (Camp)
FCI Beaumont Low (Camp)
FCI La Tuna (Camp)
FCI Seagoville (Camp)
FCI Texarkana (Camp)
FCI Three Rivers (Camp)

Virginia
USP Lee (Camp)
FCI Petersburg Low (Camp)

West Virginia
FCI Beckley (Camp)
FCI Gilmer (Camp)
USP Hazelton (Camp)
FCI Morgantown

Wisconsin
FCI Oxford (Camp)

Low-Security Prisons for Men

Arizona
FCI Safford

Arkansas
FCI Forrest City (Low)

California
FCI Lompoc

Florida
FCI Coleman (Low)
FCI Miami

Georgia
FCI (FSL) Jesup Satellite (Low)

Kentucky
FCI Ashland

Maine
FCI Sandstone
FCI Waseca

Michigan
FCI Milan

Mississippi
FCI Yazoo City Baja

New Jersey
FCI Fort Dix

North Carolina
FCI Butner (Low)

Ohio
FCI Elkton

Pennsylvania
FCI Allenwood
FCI Loretto

Texas
FCI Bastrop
FCI Beaumont (Low)
FCI Big Spring
FCI La Tuna
FCI (FSL) La Tuna at Ft. Bliss, El Paso
FCI Seagoville
FCI Texarkana

Virginia
FCI Petersburg

Medium-Security Prisons for Men

Alabama
FCI Talladega

Arizona
FCI Phoenix
FCI Tucson

Arkansas
FCI Forrest City Medium

California
FCI Herlong
FCI Terminal Island
FCI Victorville Medium I
FCI Victorville Medium II

Colorado
FCI Englewood

Florida
FCI Coleman Medium
FCI Marianna

Georgia
FCI Jesup

Illinois
FCI Greenville
FCI Pekin

Indiana
FCI Terre Haute

Kentucky
FCI Manchester

Louisiana
FCI Oakdale

Maryland
FCI Cumberland

Mississippi
FCI Yazoo City Medium

New Jersey
FCI Fairton

New York
FCI Otisville
FCI Ray Brook

North Carolina
FCI Butner Medium I

Oklahoma
FCI El Reno

Oregon
FCI Sheridan

Pennsylvania
FCI Allenwood Medium
FCI Mckean
FCI Schuylkill

South Carolina
FCI Bennettsville
FCI Edgefield
FCI Estill
FCI Williamsburg

Tennessee
FCI Memphis

Texas
FCI Beaumont Medium
FCI Three Rivers

Virginia
FCI Petersburg Medium

West Virginia
FCI Beckley
FCI Gilmer

Wisconsin
FCI Oxford

High-Security Prisons for Men

California
USP Atwater
USP Lompoc
USP Victorville

Florida
USP Coleman I
USP Coleman II

Colorado
USP Florence-Alta

Georgia
USP Atlanta

Illinois
USP Marion

Indiana
USP Terre Haute

Kansas
USP Leavenworth

Kentucky
USP Big Sandy
USP McCreary

Louisiana
USP Pollock

Pennsylvania
USP Allenwood
USP Lewisburg
USP Canaan

Texas
USP Beaumont

Virginia
USP Lee

West Virginia
USP Hazelton

Minimum-Security Prisons for Women

Arizona
FCI Phoenix Camp

California
FCI Dublin (Camp)
FCI Victorville Medium I (Camp)

Florida
FCI Coleman Medium (Camp)

Illinois
FCI Greenville (Camp)
FCI Pekin Camp

Kentucky
FMC Lexington Camp

Texas
FPC Bryan
FMC Carswell Camp, Ft. Worth

West Virginia
FPC Alderson

Low-Security Prisons for Women

Arizona
FCI Tucson

California
FCI Dublin

Connecticut
FCI Danbury

Florida
FCI Tallahassee

Community Correction Managers

Community Correction Managers (CCM's) supervise halfway houses and community treatment centers (CTC's). If you have an issue with a halfway house, CTC, or a placement issue, start with the CCM in your area.

Annapolis Junction CCM Office
10010 Junction Drive, Suite 100-N
Annapolis Junct, MD 20701
Phone: 301-317-3142
Fax: 301-317-3138

Atlanta CCM Office (Districts: Savannah, Georgia, South Carolina)
715 McDonough Blvd., SE
Atlanta GA 30315
Phone: 404-635-5673
Fax: 404-730-9785

Chicago CCM Office (Districts: Central/Northern Illinois, Eastern/Western Wisconsin)
200 West Adams, Suite 2915
Chicago, IL 60606
Phone: 312-886-2114
Fax: 312-886-2118

Cincinnati CCM Office (Districts: Northern/Southern Ohio)
36 East 7th Street, Suite 2107-A
Cincinnati, OH 45202
Phone: 513-684-2603
Fax: 513-684-2603

Dallas CCM Office (Districts: Oklahoma, Northern Texas)
4211 Cedar Springs Road, Suite 100
Dallas, TX 75219
Phone: 214-224-3522
Fax: 214-224-3367

Denver CCM Office (District: Colorado)
9595 W. Quincy Avenue
Littleton, CO 80123
Phone: 303-980-2373
Fax: 303-980-2374

Detroit CCM Office (Districts: Eastern/Western Michigan, Northern Indiana)
211 West Fort Street, Suite 620, 6th Floor
Detroit, MI 48226
Phone: 313-226-6186
Fax: 313-226-7327

El Paso CCM Office (Districts: New Mexico, Western Texas (Midland, Pecos, Del Rio, and El Paso Division))
4849 North Mesa Street
Suite 208
El Paso, TX 79912
Phone: 915-534-6326
Fax: 915-534-6432

Houston CCM Office (Districts: Southern/Eastern Texas)
515 Rusk Avenue, Room 12102
Houston, TX 77002
Phone: 713-718-4781
Fax: 713-718-4780

Glossary

5K1.1 Letter of Cooperation: A letter of recommendation from a defendant's prosecutor to a defendant's judge. The letter recommends that the judge go leniently on the defendant in sentencing because the defendant has given critical information that helped prosecute other defendants.

Achillee's Heel: A vulnerable point.

Administrative Appeal: A formal process in which an inmate files a written complaint about the facility in which they live.

Affidavit: A written, sworn statement made especially under oath or an affirmation before an authorized magistrate or office.

Allegation: A statement made by a party to a legal action of what the party undertakes to prove.

Allocution: A formal, authoritative speech made to a judge.

Ankle Bracelet: A type of radiofrequency monitor worn by suspects or ex-offenders. It detects if the person is in a specific location, such as his home.

American Correctional Association (ACA): An accreditation organization for prisons.

Anti-Riot Strike Force: A group of specially-trained Correctional Officers (CO's) in a prison that work together to suppress riots.

Arrears: The amount of money one owes due to delinquent payments.

Arrest: To take or keep in custody by authority of law.

Arrest Warrant: A legal document in which a judge directs law enforcement personnel to arrest someone for violating the law.

Assistant U.S. Attorney (AUSA): A federal prosecuting attorney that works for a head U.S. Attorney (USA) in a specific federal district.

Attorney-Client Privilege: A legal rule that allows attorneys and their clients to keep their communication and records private, shielded from prosecutors, the judge, and the jury.

Bail and Bond: A sum of money a suspect gives in trust to the government which allows a suspect to get out of jail while the case is investigated. This occurs before a trial or plea bargain takes place. The judge is trusting the suspect to attend all of his court appearances while he is trusting the government to return his money if he follows all the rules.

Bailiffs: A minor officer of some U.S. courts usually serving as a messenger or usher.

Banking Power of Attorney: A legal document that allows someone to manage the bank account of another person.

Bench: The desk the judge sits behind.

Body Mass Index: A person's mass in kilograms divided by the square of their height in meters.

BP-8, BP-9, BP-10, BP-11: A series of forms used by federal inmates to appeal decisions made by the staff of federal prisons.

Brady Motion: A legal tool in which the judge orders the prosecutor to turn over any and all evidence – good or bad – to the defense lawyers.

Brief: A legal document in which a lawyer argues why his or her point of view should be adopted by the judge.

Buddy System: A strategy in which two or more inmates operate in a unit in federal prison for security purposes.

Case Law: A type of law in which an appeals court clarifies an ambiguity in traditional law.

Certified Public Accountant: An accountant who has met the requirements of a state law and has been granted a certificate.

Change of Venue: A change in the location of a trial from one location to another location.

Character Letter: A letter of support written by a friend or family member of a defendant.

Child Support: Money paid by a parent to the custodian of a child until the child becomes an adult.

Circumstantial Evidence: Evidence that always contains an element of inference.

Closed Compound: The state of a prison in which all of the various doors and gates are closed and inmates cannot travel across the compound.

Closing Statements/Closing Arguments: A series of remarks made by an attorney to the jury at the end of a trial.

Cluster: An aggregation of objects or people.

Commissary: A store inside a jail or prison where inmates shop.

Community Corrections Center (CCC): A Halfway House (HH) run by prison officials. Also known as a Residential Re-entry Center (RRC).

Community Safety Zone: A specific region in which a suspect in a crime or a convicted person on supervised release, parole, or probation is not allowed to travel. The zone is established to protect the public.

ConAir: An airline operated by the U.S. Marshals to transport federal inmates.

Concurrent Prison Sentence: Concurrent prison sentences allow inmates to serve several prison sentences at one time.

Confidential BP-10: A form used by federal inmates to file a private complaint directly to the Regional Office of the Federal Bureau of Prisons (BOP).

Consecutive Prison Sentence: Inmates must finish serving time in prison on one sentence before beginning serving time on the next sentence.

Contact Restriction: An order made by a judge or law enforcement officer in which a person is ordered not to associate with, touch, or communicate with a specific person or group of persons.

Contraband: Objects a person is not supposed to legally possess, such as illegal narcotics.

Control Center Officer (CCO): A Correctional Officer (CO) that generates all lists that are used during each head count in a prison.

Cop-Out (Inmate Request to Staff form S148.055 in the BOP): A form federal inmates can fill out to request something from a Correctional Officer (CO).

Correctional Officer (CO): A type of police officer that works in a jail, detention center, or prison.

Court Report: Transcriptionist.

Courtroom: A room in which a court of law is held.

Courtroom Melodrama: The series of pronounced and often exaggerated methods used by attorneys to present evidence to build their side of the case. The melodramatic methods are used to create an emotional response from the judge and jury.

Credit Bureau File: A financial file created by a credit bureau that keeps track of individual financial credit scores.

Credit Score: A measurement of a person's financial or commercial trustworthiness.

Criminal Conduct History: A record of all of the crimes of which a person has been convicted of.

Criminal Complaint: A legal document written by law enforcement personnel alleging a specific crime was committed.

Criminal Defense Attorney: A lawyer who represents defendants in criminal cases.

Criminal Elements: The specific details of an alleged activity that are defined in the law and make the activity illegal.

Criminal History: The prior history of significant crimes committed in a person's lifetime.

Criminal History Category: The Criminal History Category is the level of prior significant crimes committed in a person's lifetime. The more significant the crimes, the higher the Criminal History Category.

Criminal Indictment: A legal document formally accusing a person committing a crime.

Criminal Information: A legal instrument prepared by the prosecuting authority (i.e. U.S. Attorney (USA) or District Attorney (DA)) which formally charges a person with a crime. In federal criminal procedures, it is called a criminal complaint, but it is prepared by the USA, not the "police."

Criminal Statutes: The specific laws that define what constitutes a crime and how it is to be punished.

Debriefing: A snitching session between a defendant, prosecutor, and investigators.

Defendant: A person required to make an answer in a legal action or suit.

Designation and Sentence Computation Center (DSCC): A government center operated by the Federal Bureau of Prisons (BOP) that decides an initial prison location for an inmate.

Detainer: A formal request from some prosecuting authority (city, county, state, or United States)asking the jail or detention center where a person is confined not to release that person.

Diesel Treatment: A type of unofficial punishment given by officers to an inmate. The inmate is shipped across the country away from their family. The trip is convoluted with the inmate getting little time to rest, eat, or catch up on mail.

Direct Evidence: Evidence based upon the personal knowledge of a witness.

Disciplinary Hearing: A meeting in front of a group of Correctional Officers (CO's) in which an inmate accused of a prison rule violation is tried and punished, if found guilty.

Disciplinary Hearing Officer (DHO): A Correctional Officer (CO) that is in charge of a disciplinary hearing.

Disciplinary Segregation: Also known as "seg" or "the hole." An area of the prison where dangerous or delinquent inmates are brought to live.

Discovery: The pretrial disclosure of pertinent facts or documents by one or both parties to a legal action or proceeding.

Docket: The court's appointment calendar.

Double Jeopardy: A situation in which a prosecutor charges a defendant with two different counts involving the same crime on the same date. A defendant can only be convicted of one count.

Downward Departure: A sentence that is below the statutory sentencing guidelines.

Electronic Harassment: The use of electronic equipment to annoy persistently.

Electronic Law Library (ELL): A collection of legal books, laws, and legal cases that are stored on computers and are available to inmates in prison.

Electronic Radiofrequency Monitoring: A type of monitoring that consists of a pager-size ankle bracelet that detects if a person is home or not. The ankle bracelet emits a radiofrequency signal to the base unit, which is connected to a phone line. The base unit sends a signal to a monitoring company, which contacts law enforcement personnel if the person's curfew is broken.

Enhancement: Additional time added to a defendant's sentence because of certain features of alleged criminal activity. For instance, there were five people committing a crime but one of them gets an enhancement for being a leader.

Evidence: Something such as an object or statement, which is presented in a legal proceeding.

Evidentiary Hearing: A type of hearing conducted so that evidence may be preserved.

Expert Witness: A person that is testifying in a legal proceeding who has or displays special skills derived from training or experience.

Federal Bureau of Prisons (BOP): A national government agency in charge of locking up federal inmates in prisons.

Federal Correctional Institution (FCI): A federal prison other than a Federal Work Camp (FWC), Federal Satellite Camp (FSC), Federal Medical Center (FMC), or United States Penitentiary (USP).

Federal Custody Classification Table: A form used by the staff of the Federal Bureau of Prisons (BOP) to assess the security risks each inmate poses to a prison. The risk assessment is then used to assign each inmate to a prison with an appropriate level of security.

Federal Detention Center (FDC): The federal equivalent of a jail.

Federal District: A federal legal designation for a specific jurisdiction. There are several hundred federal districts in the U.S. Each district encompasses a few hundred to a few thousand square miles.

Federal Home Confinement: The state of being restricted at home while on pretrial release, supervised release, parole, or probation.

Federal Magistrate Judge: A local federal judiciary official having limited original jurisdiction especially in criminal cases.

Federal Medical Center (FMC): A type of federal prison which houses a formal hospital.

Federal Parole: A conditional release of a federal prisoner serving an indeterminate or unexpired sentence.

Federal Probation: The action of suspending the sentence of a convicted federal offender and giving the offender freedom during good behavior under the supervision of a Probation Officer (PO).

Federal Prison Camp (FPC): Also known as a Federal Work Camp (FWC). A minimum-security federal prison where inmates work while serving their sentences.

Federal Register Number/U.M. Number: A unique 8-digit number assigned to each federal inmate.

Federal Supervised Release: See "Supervised Release."

Federal Transfer Center (FTC): A Federal Detention Center (FDC) operated by the Federal Bureau of Prisons (BOP). Federal inmates are temporarily housed in FTC's when moving between prisons.

Federal Work Camp (FWC): Also known as a Federal Prison Camp (FPC). These are minimum-security federal prisons where inmates work while serving their sentences.

Fine: A sum of money imposed by a judge as a punishment for an offense.

Freedom of Information Act (FOIA): A law that forbids the release of information from agency records without a written request or by a prior written consent of the individual except for specific instances.

Freezer Treatment: A type of unofficial punishment given by Correctional Officers (CO's) to an inmate. The inmate is placed in a freezing cell.

Gang: A group of persons working to unlawful or antisocial ends.

General Population (GP): The majority of inmates that are of average risk in a prison and therefore live amongst each other.

Global Positioning Satellite System (GPS System): The GPS system uses a series of satellites to triangulate the location of the GPS device, allowing the government to track the location of a suspect.

Good Behavior Time/Good Conduct Time (GCT): Time off from a prison sentence because the individual is following the rules.

Grand Jury: A group of law abiding citizens randomly selected to participate in grand jury hearings.

Grand Jury Hearing: A private meeting held with a grand jury, prosecutors, and federal magistrate judges several times each month to determine if there is evidence to warrant criminal indictments against suspects.
Grievance: The formal expression of a complaint.

Head Count: A census of the inmates in a jail or prison.

Health Service Unit (HSU): The name given to a medical/dental clinic in the Federal Bureau of Prisons (BOP).

Hearing: A meeting with the judge, prosecutor, defense attorneys, and the defendant.

Hearsay: A rumor. Direct evidence is superior to hearsay.

Hole: In the Federal Bureau of Prisons (BOP), the "hole" refers to the Special Housing Unit (SHU), which are segregated living quarters. The "hole" is sometimes referred to as "seg" or "solitary confinement".

Home Confinement: A condition in which a person is confined to live in their home. One may leave with authorization from specific law enforcement personnel. Home confinement is more strict than home detention.

Home Detention: A condition in which one is confined to live in their home part of the time while they are authorized to leave with permission from specific law enforcement personnel. Home detention is less strict than home confinement.

Hung Jury: A jury that is split on its decision. Some jurors vote guilty while one or more jurors vote not guilty. A person cannot be convicted of a crime with a hung jury.

Immigration and Customs Enforcement (ICE): A federal agency in charge of immigration and the transfer of goods into and out of the U.S.

Incriminating Evidence: Evidence which shows proof of involvement in a crime.

Indictment: A formal written statement framed by a prosecuting authority and found by a jury charging a person with an offense.

Ineffective Assistance of Counsel: A type of argument used during an appeal in which a person argues that he had a bad attorney to represent him through a criminal legal proceeding.

Inmate Financial Responsibility Program (IFRP): A payment plan established by the Federal Bureau of Prisons (BOP) to compel inmates to pay any special assessments, fines, or restitution.

Inmate Locator: A tool from www.BOP.gov that locates all federal inmates except for those in witness protection.

Inmate Trust Fund (Commissary Fund): A fund established in federal prison where inmates can use their money to purchase items at the prison's commissary, make phone calls, use e-mail, purchase music, pay court-ordered fines, pay some routine bills, and for other purposes.

Innocence by Reputation Defense: A type of defense used when the jury's decision of guilt versus innocence is a very close debatable call. The jury can essentially rely upon the defendant's good reputation to vote in favor of the defendant's innocence.

Inquiry Form for Incarcerated Parents: A type of form that allows inmates to request information from the Texas Attorney General's Office regarding their children.

Interstate Commerce: A financial transaction that occurs across state lines or a transaction that affects commerce across state lines.

Ion Spectrometer: A device used to search inmates and visitors for narcotics.

Irrelevant Evidence: Evidence which does not have a tendency to prove or disprove an issue in the case.

Joint Commission on Accreditation of Healthcare Organizations: A group that oversees the operation of hospitals and health clinics including those in Federal Detention Centers (FDC's) and prisons.

Judgment and Commitment (J&C) Orders: A set of orders issued by a judge which states how long an inmate will serve in prison, fines, special assessments, and restitution. It states how long an inmate will be on supervised release and which rules he will be expected to follow.

Jurisdiction: The limits or territory within which authority may be exercised.

Jury: A group of people sworn to give a decision on some matter submitted to them.

Jury Poll: A jury poll is conducted by the judge after the jury issues its verdict. The judge reads each count out loud one by one and asks each member of the jury if they voted guilty or not guilty, if they are certain of their vote, and if they were threatened to make their vote.

Jury Selection Form: A form created by an attorney that is filled out by potential jurors to help attorneys learn about any conflicts of interest or any strong predispositions they may have.

Jury Selection Specialist: An attorney or psychologist that assists criminal attorneys in choosing a jury.

Law Library: A library that is dedicated to legal issues.

Legal Fees: Money paid to an attorney for their services.

Legal Motion: An application made to a court or judge to obtain an order, ruling, or direction.

Living Will: A document in which the signer makes specific medical requests to their doctor. For example, the signer requests to be allowed to die rather than be kept alive by artificial means if disabled beyond a reasonable expectation of recovery.

Lockdown: A time during which inmates are locked in their cells or Housing Units.

Management Variables (MGTV's): A factor assigned to an inmate by the BOP to help decide which type of prison in which the inmate should live.

Managing Conservators: Adults that have custody of children after a divorce and full rights to make all decisions regarding those children.

MAX-ADX: The highest security level federal prison. Also known as a "Super Max."

Medical Power of Attorney (MPOA): A legal instrument authorizing one to act as another's attorney or agents for healthcare decisions.

Minimum Mandatory Sentence: Most federal crimes carry a minimum mandatory sentence established by federal statutory guidelines. Inmates must serve that minimum amount of time unless they get a downward departure.

Miranda Rights: Basic rights of all U.S. citizens when they are under investigation by law enforcement. The rights were defined in a U.S. Supreme Court case known as U.S. versus Miranda.

Mock Jury: A group of people hired by an attorney to act as a practice jury that hears a miniature version of a trial.

Motion for Continuance: An application to a court for a ruling on a delay in a case.

Motion in limine: A motion an attorney files with the judge arguing that evidence another attorney wishes to use is prejudicial and should not be shown to the jury.

Motion to Suppress Evidence: A federal motion filed by an attorney that attempts to block specific evidence from being presented to a jury during a trial.

Move: In a prison, a "move" refers to a time period during which the Correctional Officers (CO's) allow inmates to travel from one location in the prison to the next location.

"My Bad": Slang for saying "I'm sorry."

Notary Public: A legally-authorized person commissioned by the government to correctly identify people that sign legal documents in their presence.

Objection: When one side of a court case calls "foul" on the other. The judge then has to decide if the objection will be sustained (validated) or denied (invalidated).

Obstruction of Justice: The act of impeding or an attempt to impede the conduct of legal matters, such as an investigation or trial.

Offense Level: There are federal sentencing guidelines for different offense levels of prison sentences. The higher the offense level, the more time one is sentenced to serve in prison.

Office of Medical Designations Transportation (OMDT): A Federal Bureau of Prisons (BOP) office that reviews cases where inmates have medical or mental health issues.

Open Compound: The state of a prison in which some of the various doors and gates are open to allow inmates to cross the compound.

Opening Statements: A series of remarks made by an attorney to the jury at the beginning of a trial.

Own Recognizance Bond (OR Bond): The best type of bail and bond as one pays absolutely nothing for either bail or bond unless he doesn't show up for his court appearances. OR bonds are also known as Personal Recognizance Bonds (PR bonds).

Parole: The conditional release of a prisoner before his or her term of incarceration has expired.

Peremptory Challenges: A series of objections made to the use of potential jury members made during voir dire (jury selection).

Perp Walk: A walk done by a convicted defendant as he leaves the courthouse directly in front of the media.

Personal Recognizance Bond (PR Bond): The best type of bail and bond as one pays absolutely nothing for either bail or bond unless one doesn't show up for court appearances. PR bonds are also known as Own Recognizance Bonds (OR bonds).

Petition for a Writ of Habeas Corpus: An application for a written court order commanding the party to whom it is addressed to perform a specified act, such as releasing an inmate from prison for legal reasons.

Plea Bargain/Plea Agreement: A legal agreement in which a defendant agrees to plead guilty on one or more of the counts against him. Certain details are agreed upon.

Possessory Conservators: Adults who, after a divorce, have the right to make some limited decisions while their children are visiting, such as discipline, religious instruction, some types of medical care, etc.

Power of Attorney (POA): A legal document that allows someone to do something in one's absence, such as operate a business.

Preliminary Hearing: A type of hearing conducted to determine if there is sufficient evidence to prosecute an accused person.

Pre-Plea Pre-Sentence Report: A pre-plea Pre-Sentence Report is a report generated from the information gathered in the Pre-Sentence Interview (PSI). The pre-plea PSR is given to the accused before he signs a plea bargain. The same pre-plea PSR is given to the judge who uses it to sentence the accused.

Pre-Sentence Interview (PSI): A meeting between the defendant, the Probation Officer (PO), and the defendant's attorney. Information from the meeting is used by the PO to generate a Pre-Sentence Report (PSR), which the judge uses during sentencing.

Pre-Sentence Report (PSR): A PSR is a report generated from the information gathered in the Pre-Sentence Interview (PSI). The PSR is used by the judge during sentencing.

Pretrial Motion: An application to the court for a ruling on an issue prior to a trial.

Pretrial Services Officer (PTSO): An officer of the court that supervises suspects of a crime that have not yet been sentenced.

Private Investigator (PI): A confidential detective.

Probable Cause: A term that means there is enough evidence to believe something.

Probation: The action of suspending the sentence of one convicted of a minor offense and granting the offender provisional freedom on the promise of good behavior.

Probation Officer (PO): An officer of the court that monitors people convicted of a crime while they are on probation.

Project Angel Tree: A program that allows inmates to have people donate a Christmas gift for their children.

Prosecutor: One who initiates and carries out a legal action, such as a criminal proceeding.

Protective Custody (PC): A part of the prison where vulnerable inmates live. The vulnerable inmates include former cops, prosecutors, judges, sex offenders, or snitches.

Public Defender: A usually publicly appointed attorney or staff of attorneys having responsibility for the legal defense of those unable to afford or obtain legal assistance.

Public Safety Factors (PSF's): A type of risk that may be assigned to an inmate by the Federal Bureau of Prisons (BOP) when the BOP believes the inmate presents a safety risk to the community.

Recidivism: The habit of repeatedly committing a crime and returning to prison.

Recreation Yard: In a prison, it is a type of playground surrounded by fences, barbed wire, and Correctional Officers (CO's).

Relevant Evidence: Evidence having any tendency to prove or disprove an issue in the case.

Remanding Into Custody: The process during which a defendant is incarcerated.

Request for Withdrawal of Inmate's Personal Funds (BP-199.045): A form that requests the Federal Bureau of Prisons (BOP) to pay a bill using funds from an inmate's trust fund account.

Residential Drug and Abuse Program (RDAP): A formal drug rehabilitation program in which federal inmates live and rehabilitate in a designated Housing Unit.

Residential Re-entry Center (RRC): A Halfway House (HH) run by prison officials. Also known as a Community Corrections Center (CCC).

Restitution: An act of repaying or compensating for loss, damage, or injury.

Review and Adjustment Form: A type of form used by state child support agencies to review one's income to see if one's child support payment can be lowered.

Rule 29 Motion: A legal motion that asks the federal judge to decide if the prosecution produced enough evidence to satisfy each element of each count in the case.

Rule of Sequestration: A federal court policy that forbids witnesses from being in the courtroom while other witnesses are on the witness stand. This keeps witnesses from influencing each other's testimony.

Safety Valve: A legal rule that helps certain defendants receive a smaller sentence.

Search Warrant: A search warrant is a legal document in which a judge authorizes law enforcement personnel to search a person's property without permission for the purpose of looking for specific evidence related to a crime.

Sentencing Guidelines Range: A range in months in which a person can be incarcerated. The range is stipulated from Title 18 U.S. Code § 3553: The Sentencing Guidelines.

Sex Offender: One who is convicted of a sex crime.

Shadow Jury: A group of people that sit in the courtroom during an actual trial. They give their opinion to the defense attorney on each piece of evidence and each witness.

Shakedown: A search of a person's cell, bag, or clothes for contraband.

Shots: Also known as an inmate disciplinary reprimand. A written disciplinary charge brought up by a Correctional Officer (CO) against an inmate for an alleged violation of the prison's policy.

Solitary Confinement: A cell in the Special Housing Unit (SHU also known as "seg" or "the hole") in which bad inmates are locked up as a means of punishment or for security reasons. In some instances, troublesome inmates live alone while in other cases, two inmates live together.

Special Assessments: A fee imposed by a judge for court costs.

Special Housing Unit (SHU): A segregated part of prison ("the hole") in the Federal Bureau of Prisons (BOP) where unique inmates, such as highly dangerous, disruptive, medically ill, or vulnerable inmates live.

Spousal Maintenance: An amount of money one has to pay a divorced spouse because he or she is disabled and single.

Statement of Reasons (SOR): A list of reasons used by a judge to issue a particular sentence.

Statutory Durable Power of Attorney: A legal instrument authorizing one to act as another's attorney or agent for making decisions.

Statutory Guideline Maximum: The longest amount of time a defendant can be punished for a specific crime as it is defined under federal law.

Subpoena: A legal order from a judge that compels a person or business to give the information needed to fight a case.

Super-Controlled Move: The transfer of inmates across a prison compound that is under high security with intense monitoring.

Super Max Security (ADX): Of all the United States Penitentiaries (USP's), Super Max Security is considered the highest level of security in a federal prison.

Supervised Release: A period after the release of an inmate from prison in which monitoring is performed by an officer of the court.

Sustain: To validate a legal decision.

Testify: To submit testimony during a legal proceeding.

Testimony: A solemn declaration usually made orally by a witness under oath in response to interrogation by a lawyer or authorized public official.

The Radar: The state of being highly visible in the public's eye. A person that is "on the radar" is under high public scrutiny while a person that is "under the radar" is operating quietly in the background.

Trial Triad: The three important sets of issues that juries consider: the evidence, the law, and the melodrama.

TRU-Units: A type of electronic currency used by inmates in the Federal Bureau of Prisons (BOP) on the Trust Fund Limited Inmate Computer System (TRULINCS).

Trust Fund Account and Commissary System (TRUFACS): A type of software that tracks Commissary sales, telephone usage, and other financial data on inmates in the Federal Bureau of Prisons (BOP). The data used to be displayed on ATM style machines but it is now displayed via the Trust Fund Limited Inmate Computer System (TRULINCS).

Trust Fund Limited Inmate Computer System (TRULINCS): A secure computer system that is used by inmates in the Federal Bureau of Prisons (BOP) for e-mail, electronic requests, MP3 music downloads, medication refills, etc.

Ultimate Research Method: An extremely thorough investigation technique which seeks to discover every detail that will help one's side of the case.

Unconstitutional: Not in accord with the principles set forth in the constitution of a nation.

Unit Manager: The administrative head of a Housing Unit in the Federal Bureau of Prisons (BOP).

Upward Departures: A sentence above the statutory guidelines.

U.S. Marshal Service: A U.S. federal officer who carries out court orders.

U.S. Parole Commission: A group of federal public officials who review eligible federal inmate prison files to see which inmates have a good prison conduct record and can be released on parole early.

U.S. Patriot Act of 2001: A federal law that was passed after the terrorist attacks of 9/11/01. The law gives enhanced powers to law enforcement and fewer civil liberties protections for U.S. citizens.

U.S. Penitentiary (USP): A maximum security prison in the Federal Bureau of Prisons (BOP).

U.S. Pretrial Services (PTS): A U.S. federal agency that is in charge of monitoring suspects that have been arrested and released while they await final disposition of their criminal cases.

U.S. Probation Officers (PO's): A group of federal law enforcement personnel that work for the federal court in the U.S. Department of Justice (DOJ). PO's monitor defendants on probation, parole, or supervised release.

U.S. Sentencing Commission: A group of people that monitor federal prison sentences and their effectiveness.

U.S. Supreme Court: The highest federal court in the United States, consisting of nine justices and having jurisdiction over all other courts in the nation.

Venue: The place from which a jury is drawn and in which trial is held.

Visitation Points: A series of time units that are periodically given to inmates with good conduct in prison. Each time unit allows the inmate to have visits in the prison. For example, thirty visitation points per month.

Voir Dire: The jury selection process.

Waiver of Notification for a Divorce: Many state laws require one spouse to hire an officer of the court (i.e. a constable or sheriff's deputy) to deliver a Notice for a Divorce. A Waiver of Notification for a Divorce allows the couple to avoid the costs and embarrassment of a Notice for a Divorce.

Witness: One who has seen or heard something. This person may or may not be called upon to testify before a court.

Witness Stand: A stand or an enclosure from which a witness gives evidence in court.

Witness Tampering: Interfering in a harmful way with a person who has seen or heard something involved in a criminal investigation.

Index

Supplemental Materials

This book makes reference to free supplemental materials. If you purchased the book via www.AugustaPublishingCompany.com or www.navigatingthefeds.com, your free materials will be mailed to you shortly. If you purchased this book through a wholesale distributer, please visit www.AugustaPublishingCompany.com to see how to obtain your free supplemental materials.

www.ingramcontent.com/pod-product-compliance
Lightning Source LLC
Chambersburg PA
CBHW072100040426
42334CB00041B/1478